WORLD PENAL SYSTEMS

A Survey

By

NEGLEY K. TEETERS

Temple University

SPONSORED AND DISTRIBUTED BY THE PENNSYLVANIA
PRISON SOCIETY, PHILADELPHIA: 1944

A limited number of copies of this survey is being distributed to a selected list of subscribers of the *Prison Journal* and friends of the *Pennsylvania Prison Society* with the compliments of Temple University and the author. Others wishing copies may order them at cost from the *Pennsylvania Prison Society,* 311 S. Juniper Street, Philadelphia, Pa. Price: $2.00

Dedicated to the Memory of Dr. Enoch C. Wines and Charles Richmond Henderson, American penal reformers and Major Arthur Griffiths, British prison administrator, whose inclusive surveys of earlier years stimulated the author to present his modest venture to the public at this time.

INTRODUCTION

It gives me much pleasure to respond to Professor Teeters' kind invitation to write a few introductory words to his scholarly survey of the world's prison systems. Coming as it does so soon after his and Professor Barnes' monumental *New Horizons in Criminology* it is one more proof of the author's untiring devotion to the cause of penal reform.

The present writer has every reason to be conscious of the great practical significance of international studies on the subject. Through the force of circumstances he has been brought into close contact with the widely differing systems of criminal justice of two big European countries. Moreover, in recent times he has had the good fortune of meeting some of the experts from various parts of the Continent assembled in London which has become their temporary home. The need for international collaboration between penologists could have scarcely been more drastically demonstrated.

Nevertheless, there are obvious limits to what nations can learn from one another in this field. Many methods which seem to work admirably in some countries might completely fail in others where the essential material and ideological prerequisites are not existent. As Professor Teeters reports from one of the countries surveyed: "Turkish penal methods must be based upon the Turkish prisoner and Turkish social conditions, rather than merely copying conditions suitable elsewhere." However, where such a repudiation of foreign methods is regarded as indispensable, it should be based upon the most complete knowledge of actual conditions abroad.

It is, therefore, one of the foremost duties of the penologist to supply that knowledge. It should at least not be his fault if too little use is made of new ideas that have proved their worth in some parts of the globe. A close study of Professor Teeters' book shows that there are indeed very few civilized countries that have nothing to contribute to the general re-making of the various national penal systems which will probably be a common feature of the postwar period. Almost every country surveyed has been a pioneer in developing at least one particular idea worthy of special consideration by an international forum.

i

Reasons of space prevent details and, in addition, it would be unfair to mention at random merely a few of these ideas and to pass over others of equal value. There is, however, in modern penal history one particularly outstanding example of fruitful international collaboration. I refer to the development of the English Borstal system which, established forty years ago on the American model of Elmira, is now generously recognized by American experts as worthy of their attention for the future rebuilding of their reformatories.

The present war has almost completely interrupted the work of the older international organizations such as the International Penal and Penitentiary Commission. Other international bodies, which have come into existence during the war, as, for instance, the Committee set up in London by the Howard League for Penal Reform to make proposals for the future treatment of juvenile delinquents, have not yet had the time to bring the results of their deliberations before a wider public.

Therefore, it is all the more to be welcomed that an individual scholar as Professor Teeters has taken the initiative to collect and present in one handy volume the scattered information at present available. I am sure that his work will fill a real gap.

HERMANN MANNHEIM

The London School of Economic
and Political Science
at the Hostel, Peterhouse
Cambridge, England.
April, 1944

FOREWORD

To sally forth on a worldwide survey of penal treatment is a venturesome undertaking. This is especially true since the author has not had the opportunity of viewing in person any of the penal systems included. However, he has felt free to call upon others who have either visited prisons abroad or written on the penal systems or philosophies of the various countries throughout the world. In this manner it has been possible to paint a reasonably satisfactory picture of the methods used in the past or still in operation.

It may be seen that there is, in general, a similarity about them all, certainly so far as the broad general outlines are concerned. Here may be seen a flash of progressive insight in dealing with the offender: there may be witnessed reaction of the worst sort. It is a fair conclusion to assert that only by the interplay of ideas and methods existing in the various countries of the world can any reform of lasting significance be realized in this dismal sphere of human relations. There is no country so enlightened that it cannot learn from others.

In spite of the fact that in recent months the compelling words of Winston Churchill relative to penal matters have been quoted so often, they are still considered important enough to be set down here. Mr. Churchill has long been a close and assiduous student of penal philosophy since he witnessed John Galsworthy's moving play *Justice*. This play was a condemnation of the separate system of penal treatment, borrowed from Pennsylvania in the middle of the nineteenth century and long practiced in Britain. The Prime Minister said:

> The mood and temper of the public with regard to the treatment of crime and criminals is one of the most unfailing tests of the civilization of any country. A calm, dispassionate recognition of the rights of the accused, and even of the convicted criminal against the State; a constant heart-searching by all charged with the duty of punishment; a desire and eagerness to rehabilitate in the world of industry those who have paid their due in the hard coinage of punishment; tireless efforts toward the discovery of curative and regenerative processes; unfailing faith that there is a treasure, if you can only find it, in the heart of every man— these are the symbols, which, in the treatment of crime and criminals, mark and measure the stored-up strength of a nation and are sign and proof of the living virtue in it.[1]

These words uttered by Mr. Churchill before the House of Commons in 1910 reflect sober, yet optimistic thoughts and should set the pace for penal reformers in all lands. This review of penal treatment proves that if one were to judge the culture of a country only by its treatment of the offender, faith in human nature would be almost dissipated.

One need not go overseas to illustrate this. Here in America are to be found brutality, ignorance, indifference and apathy in penal philosophy. Yet one would not indict American culture primarily by these criteria. It is, however, one of the inexplicable enigmas of American life that those deviating from the normal type of behavior are so wantonly condemned and chastised. There is no doubt some truth in the statement that this country "has not grown up" emotionally since, obviously, there is

(1) Quoted on the front cover of *The Penal Reformer*, January, 1941, published at Lucknow, India; also quoted by Sir Evelyn Ruggles-Brise, *The English Prison System*, 1921, p. 4..

intelligence enough. Part of the explanation also probably lies in the mass hypocricy which is a characteristic of our social, religious and economic life.

The author has found many difficulties in gathering adequate material for this survey. It was obvious from the outset that he could not hope to use original sources written in the diverse languages of the world. He was obliged to restrict himself, in most instances, to sources written in English. Consequently that is the main weakness of the survey. There are no doubt many gaps and errors scattered throughout its entirety but a serious effort has been made to reduce these to a minimum. Footnotes show the sources of the materials used.

In recent years there has been no attempt made to present a birdseye picture of world penology comparable to those compiled by Enoch C. Wines in 1879 or by Charles Richmond Henderson in 1903, both Americans, or by Major Arthur Griffiths, the noted British penologist and administrator, who wrote his series of fascinating volumes in 1906.

In 1931 the American Academy of Political and Social Science published one issue of its *Annals* entitled "Prisons of Tomorrow" and edited by Professors E. H. Sutherland and Thorsten Sellin. But many countries were omitted although the articles presented were excellent and authoritative. Some of this material is incorporated in this survey for which the author makes grateful acknowledgement. In the same year, Professor John L. Gillin published his *Taming the Criminal,* an excellent firsthand description of several penal systems of the world. He had actually seen these system in operation. Professor Gillin has very kindly permitted the author of this survey to lean heavily on his interesting work. To him, therefore, a word of thanks is herewith tendered.

The material on general Latin American penology was written for the author by Señora Clara González de Behringer, Director and Señor Guillermo Zurita, Deputy Director of Child Welfare (*el Instituto de Vigilancia y Protección del Niño*) for the Republic of Panama. The material on the penal system of Ecuador was graciously furnished by Dr. Emilio Uzcátegui, Professor of Jurisprudence and Social Science at the Central University of Quito. The author is deeply indebted to these distinguished scholars for their kind cooperation.

There is a serious lack of material on Latin American penology written in English. It is difficult to understand just why this is so since there are so many distinguished scholars in the fields of criminal law and penology, many of whom have written brilliant works on these subjects. Unfortunately there has been little, if any, reciprocal activity in making such contributions available through translations. This demonstrates forcefully the need for nourishing the continental ties that have flourished so tenuously for so many years. It is, therefore, gratifying to witness the encouraging effects of the Good Neighbor policy which aims at developing a high degree of cultural cooperation between the United States and Latin America.

Mention should be made of the fine help rendered the author by several of his former students in Criminology at Temple University who checked references and assisted in gathering source material. To them, wherever they may now be, he extends his thanks. To Misses Virginia

Becker, only recently graduated from Temple, and Evelia Velarde, a native of Panama and now studying at Temple, he wishes to extend his thanks for their fine assistance in translating the Spanish material dealing with some Latin American countries. Obviously, they are not responsible for mistakes or misinterpretations of fact which may appear in the material. The author assumes all blame for these. A word of appreciation is also extended Mr. Paul Gay of the Biddle Law Library of the University of Pennsylvania for valuable aid in translation.

The staff of the Sullivan Memorial Library of Temple University were also quite helpful in locating material and checking references and the author is grateful to them. Especially does he wish to thank Mr. Elliot Morse of the Reference Department of the library for his many courtesies in assisting the writer in running down clues.

A more than usual word of appreciation is also extended to Dr. Harry Elmer Barnes who collaborated with the author in an earlier work on criminology and penology and who encouraged him from time to time to carry through this study to completion. It is certain that without his sustained interest in the subject matter of this volume and his friendly relationships with the writer, this survey would not have appeared.

To Dr. Hermann Mannheim, of the London School of Economics, author of several books in the field of criminology, the writer wishes to extend appreciation. Dr. Mannheim has read the proofs and made valuable suggestions. In addition he has graciously furnished the survey with its most valuable feature, an Introduction.

The footnotes show the sources of the material used throughout. In addition, however, it is a pleasant duty to record here a statement of acknowledgement to the various publishers of the books and magazines referred to and quoted from; to the professional journals and their editors for the quotations and citations used; and to the many persons who were consulted in gathering the information.

Last, but certainly not least, the author wishes to thank particularly President Robert L. Johnson and the committee on Research and Publications of Temple University for granting the funds to publish this work, and the *Pennsylvania Prison Society* for sponsoring it and assuming responsibility for its distribution.

N. K. T.

Melrose Park,
Montgomery County,
Pennsylvania.
May 8, 1944.

CONTENTS

vii

ix

Page

CHAPTER I

THE DEVELOPMENT OF THE BRITISH PENAL SYSTEM

BRITAIN'S CONTRIBUTION TO THE PHILOSOPHY OF IMPRISONMENT

In any world survey of penal treatment, however incomplete, it is but natural that Americans should, at the outset, turn to an examination of England's methods. This is due to two reasons: first, because we are more closely allied to England's philosophies and institutions through our colonial heritage and common language, and second, because there shuttled back and forth across the Atlantic from the days of John Howard many ideas that were seriously pondered by penal reformers in both countries. In truth it would be difficult to determine which of the two countries is more indebted to the other insofar as penal philosophy is concerned.

The roots of imprisonment as we know it today are to be found in the workhouses of England and on the Continent. Prior to that era criminals were executed, deported, pressed into service to man the medieval galleys or subjected to various forms of brutal and degrading punishments.

It is not necessary to trace here the development of penal treatment throughout the ages nor to describe the historical phases of any one of the methods listed above. The reader is referred to a good source book in penology for this material.[1] However, a word regarding the workhouse, or House of Correction movement, beginning in the last half of the sixteenth century and gaining momentum throughout the seventeenth and eighteenth, is of some moment.

With the eclipse of the feudal system of the Middle Ages, pauperism and petty thievery were rampant all over Europe. The suppression of the monasteries and the decline of the guilds carried misery in their wake. Thousands of ablebodied beggars overran the countryside, refusing to work, and using force to secure food from the free and selfsupporting inhabitants.

In London steps were taken in 1557 to call a halt to the pillaging of this menacing group of riffraff. The royal castle in which Charles V had lived was turned over to the city by Edward VI for a workhouse. It was the site of an ancient well famous for its medicinal waters and known as St. Bridget's Well. After the workhouse was opened it got its name of Bridewell from the corruption of the name of this well by the common people of the city. To this day, workhouses are frequently referred to as Bridewells.

Unruly apprentices, sturdy beggars, strumpets, vagrants and rogues were sent to these establishments for discipline. They were received with manacles and a severe flogging and then were put to work. It was assumed that such treatment would have a deterring effect upon them as well as

(1) See F. H. Wines, *Punishment and Reformation*, Crowell, 1895; H. E. Barnes, *The Story of Punishment*, Stratford, 1930; J. L. Gillin, *Criminology and Penology*, Century, 1926; and H. E. Barnes and Negley K. Teeters, *New Horizons in Criminology*, Prentice-Hall, 1943.

1

upon others who might be thinking of carrying on a life of wantonness, debauchery and idleness.

In 1576 Parliament ordained that there should be such a House in every county throughout England. In due time the movement for this type of imprisonment spread throughout the realm. The new movement also spread to the Continent so that by 1775 Houses of Correction were to be found in practically every city of importance in England and throughout all of Europe.[2]

There was a strong economic motive in establishing the workhouses of Europe. There can be no doubt that the desire to make even vagrant labor productive to the state was of prime importance.[3] Many of these workhouses paid their way by the production and sale of commodities. Many of them were fitted up with spinning rooms, nail factories, carpenters' shops, and a host of other small factories. Men were often taken out of the shops to work at dredging sand and burning lime. The manufacture of pins, laces, gloves, tennis balls and felts was common. Female inmates were employed at washing and ironing of the clothing worn by the inmates. Discipline was usually strict and the whip was a constant threat for insubordination and malingering.

The workhouse proved a great success wherever it was established. But it must be remembered that it was used merely as a place of custody for what we usually refer to as minor offenders. As stated above, convicted felons were rarely sent to such places. The chief contribution of the workhouse was that it ushered in the new concept of imprisonment. It proved to be the model, for instance, upon which William Penn established his farreaching and humane penal code in the colony of Pennsylvania following the establishment of his Great Law in 1682.

It was to the Houses of Correction on the Continent, as well as to the medieval prisons in those countries, that John Howard made his significant visits prior to 1775. He was greatly pleased with many of the former, especially those he found in Holland and Belgium. He was struck with the cleanliness, the industry and classification of the inmates in such places as the prison at Ghent under the able management of that "father of penitentiary science," Hippolyte Vilain.[4] Howard was also impressed with the type of treatment he found in the Hospice of St. Michele at Rome which had been set up by Pope Clement XI in 1704 for wayward boys. Upon his return home and with the publication of his work, *State of Prisons,* in 1777, Howard was resolved to see that the system of imprisonment with productive work and penitence should be created in England.

THE PENITENTIARY ACT OF 1779

Stimulated by Howard's injunction that "penitentiary houses" be created to care for convicted criminals, Sir William Blackstone and Sir William Eden drafted a comprehensive bill calling for the establish-

---

(2)   For an interesting discussion of the workhouse movement, see Austin Van der Slice, "Elizabethan Houses of Correction," *Journal of Criminal Law and Criminology,* vol. 27, June, 1936, pp. 45-67.

(3)   See Georg Rusche and Otto Kirchheimer, *Punishment and Social Structure,* Columbia University Press, 1939, especially Chapter III, "Mercantilism and Imprisonment," for documentary evidence of this motive.

(4)   John Howard, *State of Prisons,* Everyman's Edition, Dutton, 1929, pp. 114-118.

ment of such places in which criminals might be secured in solitary confinement at night and supplied with labor during the day under strict
supervision. Religious instruction was also to be provided. Nothing very
tangible came from this Penitentiary Act of 1779 except the establishment of some of its features in a few local jails, namely at Horsham, Pet-
worth, Gloucester and Norfolk.[5]

A veritable building boom of local county jails followed the passage
of this Act so that Howard could say that no fewer than forty-two new
establishments were built by 1789. Many of these structures were just bare
brick walls with no imagination employed as to architecture or administration, but a few of them did measure up to the ideals set by Howard.
The novel principles of cellular construction, separate confinement and
productive employment were inaugurated at Gloucestershire under the
zealous Sir George O. Paul and at Wymondham in Norfolk under Sir
Thomas Beevor.[6]

It was during this transitional period that Jeremy Bentham conceived
his monstrosity prison which he labeled the *Panopticon* or "inspection-
house." There is no need to discuss this abortive attempt to draw up plans
for a penitentiary since it is too well known in penal circles to more than
mention it.[7]

While no penitentiaries were actually erected as a result of the Penitentiary Act of 1779, its passage at least marks an interesting landmark
in Britain's penal history. It should be remarked here that that country's
sterile experiment with penal transportation to Australia and Gibraltar
delayed any real penal progress for many years, especially in penal administration.

REFORM OF THE CRIMINAL LAW

The next significant step in British penal reform embraces the eloquent
appeal of Sir Samuel Romilly to the House of Commons in 1810 for a
reform of the entire criminal law, including the administration of the local
jails and prisons. A wave of penal reform swept through England during
the decades of 1810 to 1830, witnessed, not only by the writings of Bentham and the appeals of Romilly, Sir James Mackintosh and Sir Robert
Peel, but by the efforts of Elizabeth Fry and her brothers-in-law, Samuel
Hoare and Sir Thomas Fowell Buxton. Nor should the good work of
Stephen Grellet and the brother of Elizabeth Fry, Joseph John Gurney,
be overlooked. Many of these distinguished citizens formed the *Society
for the improvement of Prison Discipline* which, in 1822, with the aid of
the crusading Peel, succeeded in forcing through Parliament an act which
was quite significant in English penal history.

This act represented a great advance in prison administration, since
it applied strict measures to some one hundred thirty local jails and
prisons throughout the realm. However, it was only a beginning since

(5) Cf. Sidney and Beatrice Webb, *English Prisons Under Local Government*, Longmans, 1922.
(6) For an account of Sir George O. Paul's reforms, see the Webbs, *op. cit.*, p. 58 ; for
Beevor's reforms, see Barnes & Teeters, *op. cit.*, pp. 501-502.
(7) For an excellent account of Bentham's *Panopticon*, see *The Works of Jeremy
Bentham*, edited by John Bowring, Edinburgh, 1843, vol. IV, pp. 37-248 ; see also Fred
E. Haynes, *The American Prison System*, McGraw-Hill, 1939, pp. 22-26.

many of the local jails were not touched by the measure nor were the debtors' prisons affected.

For many years, however, penal reform continued. As the result of the efforts of those reformers mentioned above, the British penal code was completely transformed from that time, although legislation bringing this about was forced through Parliament in piecemeal installments. At the beginning of the period some two hundred twenty-two offenses were punishable by the death penalty. In 1820 the law was repealed which made it a capital offense to steal five shillings' worth of goods from a shop; in 1822 the death penalty was removed on some hundred offenses. By 1861 the death penalty was removed 'on all offenses except murder, treason and piracy.

Aside from the erection of the famous Millbank Prison, started in 1812 through the efforts of Romilly and finished nine years later, no centralized effort to develop a prison system took place until 1842 when Pentonville Prison was created.

A word concerning Millbank Prison should be incorporated here although it had little effect on Britain's penal policies. This pile of stone and mortar cost some two million dollars which was no mean sum in those days. The Webbs likened its cost to that of the Taj at Agra, the Cloth Hall at Ypres or the Cathedral at Chartres.[8] The prison was built on a swampland bought at a fancy price from one of the noblemen of the day, Lord Salisbury. It was designed for criminals from London and Middlesex counties only. It contained provisions for both separate confinement and association of inmates and served the metropolitan area until 1891 when it was torn down.[9]

Pentonville Prison was created in 1842 for the purpose of serving as a model of the separate plan which was being studied by British reformers and students of penal treatment following the experiments made in America after 1829. The establishment of the Pennsylvania and Auburn Systems of prison discipline in the first quarter of the nineteenth century had been attracting worldwide interest so it was to be expected that Britain would consider sending commissioners here to study the American penitentiaries.[10]

The grim Pentonville fortress prison had been the result of the recommendations made by William Crawford who had made a detailed study of the two rival systems operating in America. He was a member of the *London Society for the Improvement of Prison Discipline* and if George Ives, English writer on penal methods is to be believed, a "commonplace man of little imagination."[11] He returned with considerable

(8) *op. cit.*, pp. 48-49.

(9) For the architectural plan of Millbank, see F. H. Wines, *op. cit.*, p. 182. For an interesting history of Millbank, see Major Arthur Griffiths, *The World's Famous Prisons, privately printed*, The Grolier Press, London undated, (*circa* 1908) vol 3.

(10) The details of these two systems need not be presented here since they are well known to all penal administrators. If the reader wishes to review the conflict that raged between the advocates 'of the Pennsylvania and Auburn Systems, he is referred to H. E. Barnes, *The Evolution of Penology in Pennsylvania*, Bobbs-Merrill, 1927; Negley K. Teeters, *They Were in Prison*, Winston, 1937, Chapter VI, and Barnes and Teeters, *New Horizons in Criminology*, Prentice-Hall, 1943, Chapters XXII and XXIII.

(11) *A History of Penal Methods*, Stanley Paul, London, 1914, p. 183; see especially Chapters V - IX for a critical account of Crawford's mission and its effects.

partiality to the Pennsylvania System of separate confinement which, with certain modifications, was adopted throughout Great Britain.

Pentonville became famous in penal history because it was used in conjunction with the Australian system of deportation. Convicted criminals were first sent to this institution, where they served in most instances eighteen months of servitude before they were shipped to the Antipodes.[12]

THE AUSTRALIAN EXPERIMENT AND ITS AFTERMATH

Reference has been made above to the system of transporting criminals to faroff lands to which England resorted from the days of Queen Elizabeth to the middle of the nineteenth century. First to the American colonies and later to Australia and to Gibraltar, convicts were sent by the thousands. Transportation, or deportation of convicts as well as debtors, represents the most sordid chapter in the modern history of penal treatment. There is no need to review this era of penal sterility but the reader unfamiliar with its significance should turn to one or more of the clinical accounts for enlightenment.[13]

The Australian episode represents almost a century of cruelty and administrative ignorance. The only ray of enlightenment to break through the unbroken night of dismal and unrelenting brutality was the experiment of Alexander Maconochie on Norfolk Island, one of the penal colonies established in that inaccessible land. His system, known as the Mark System, represented an heroic attempt to bring about reformation of convicts through a positive series of stages. The prisoner was given the opportunity to move from one step to another by his own efforts. If he succeeded he eventually reached the stage of conditional release, or ticket-of-leave, which was similar to what is known in America today as parole.

Maconochie's system, inaugurated on Norfolk Island in 1840, was eventually introduced in Britain and became the basis of penal treatment in both England and America following 1850. Upon his return to England, Maconochie was made governor of the jail at Birmingham in 1849 where he installed his system. But it was short lived. His critics contended that he spent too much of his time promulgating his theories and too little to the detailed administration of the prison.[14]

Nevertheless, Alexander Maconochie's concepts of penal treatment were practically sound. His name is blazoned high in the annals of penology, ranking favorably with John Howard and Elizabeth Fry. While, as the Webbs point out, his name is not even mentioned in the *Dictionary of National Biography*,[15] his contributions to penology are inevitably reviewed in any treatment of the reformation of criminals.

With the passage of the first half of the nineteenth century, a series of acts dealing with penal discipline were those passed in 1853 and 1857

(12) A good description of the early Pentonville prison is that by the institution's assistant chaplain, John T. Burt, *Results of the System of Separate Confinement as Administered at the Pentonville Prison*, London, 1852 ; see also, Henry Mayhew and John Binney, *The Criminal Prisons of London*, Griffin, Bohn, and Co., London, 1862, pp. 112-172.

(13) Cf. H. E. Barnes, *The Story of Punishment*, Chapter VI, for an account of transportation.

(14) See Mary Carpenter, *Our Convicts*, London, 1864, vol. I, p.. 103. See also Maconochie, *The Mark System of Penal Discipline*, London, 1855, and W. L. Clay, *The Prison Chaplain*, London, 1861, p. 254.

(15) *op. cit.*, p. 165.

and known as the Penal Servitude Acts. Briefly, these acts, which were later amended on at least three occasions as the years passed, called for the following steps in the experience of the convicted prisoner: (1) rigorous cellular confinement in isolation, day and night, accompanied by the plank bed, a restricted diet, a prescribed task of isolated labor, and deprivation of all "humanizing privileges"; (2) a period of associated labor under the Silent or Separate System, originally upon public works outdoors; and (3) conditional release, or ticket-of-leave, in the early days to some oversea colony, and later, at home under police supervision. Many of these earlier offenders were sent to Van Diemen's Land (Tasmania), or to one of the Australian colonies.

Due to the confusion of thought during these years, made inevitable by the strong prejudice in favor of transportation by some statesmen and by violent objections to it by many humanitarians, several measures were taken by Parliament to work out some compromise plan. The Progressive Stages System was the result.

The author of this novel plan was Sir Joshua Jebb who tried it out first in England and later in Ireland. In this latter country the plan was adapted to Irish conditions by Sir Walter Crofton in the famous Irish System.[16] In general practice, the Progressive Stages System called for a period of nine months in separate confinement, the remaining term of incarceration to be divided into three stages of discipline. The prisoner passed from the first to the second stage and was awarded extra privileges, and was given a special badge to wear. On arriving at the third stage, further increases in privileges were given with a different type of dress worn from that of the ordinary convict.

This system of Progressive Stages is especially significant since all penal reform in England owes its origin to it. Sir Joshua Jebb deserves more credit for developing this system than has been awarded him in most books on penology.[17] The system was incorporated in the American Reformatory System following 1870 and became known as the Irish System, credit being almost universally given to Sir Walter Crofton rather than to Sir Joshua Jebb.

This unique system was certainly enriched by the incorporation of Maconochie's Mark System. The prisoner was obliged to earn a prescribed number of marks by his labor. His progress through the various stages depended solely upon his willingness and ability to redeem himself through this system of marks. Thus this feature became an integral part of the Penal Servitude System.

THE BEGINNINGS OF CLASSIFICATION OF PRISONERS

In 1877 an inquiry into the condition of the local prisons of England brought about the complete control by the Home Office of all local prisons (jails) as well as penitentiaries. This date is significant in English penal history since, it might be stated, a real system of classification began to be realized.

(16)   For an account of this system, see Barnes & Teeters, op. cit., pp. 549-551.
(17)   Cf. Hugh Evelyn Ruggles-Brise, The English Prison System, Macmillan, London, 1921, pp. 29-30.

One of the most interesting results of the consolidation of all penal institutions throughout the realm by the Home Office was the creation, in 1879, of the "Star Class" of convicts. These are the offenders who have been convicted for the first time. According to Sir Evelyn Ruggles-Brise, the creation of this class represented the first and most practical attempt to introduce the principle of segregation of the better prisoner from the worst. Crude though it was, it marks the beginning of modern classification of prisoners which has had such a remarkable growth during the past quarter century.

But in spite of the many isolated measures designed to improve the English penal system, the deeply imbedded philosophy of hard labor and separate confinement persisted for many years. In fact, during its operation everything was done to make separation real and complete. Exercise was given in separate yards, or in association with masks over the faces of the prisoners. Coffin-like stalls were resorted to in prison chapels with prisoners marching in with masks drawn over their faces. After entering their little stalls they were permitted to remove them. In this way, the chaplain could look into the countenances of the men but none was able to see the others. The mask was not abandoned until the late years of the nineteenth century. The Quaker horror of contamination of prisoners, which motivated the introduction of the separate system in Pennsylvania in 1829, persisted in England down to the beginning of the present century.

THE REGIME OF SIR EDMUND DU CANE

The prisons at this time were placed in the hands of a group of Prison Commissioners, of which Sir Edmund Du Cane was first chairman. His régime was efficient, methodical and totally unimaginative. The watchword of this period was "uniformity."[18]

Uniformity was secured by the adoption of a uniform and scientific dietary, a uniform system of education, a uniform system of hard labor by means of the treadwheel and the crank. Overcrowding in prisons and the persistent fear of coddling convicts as well as protests of trade unions against productive work by prisoners were largely responsible for the impasse reached in British prisons shortly after the introduction of cellular confinement. The heyday of the Houses of Correction with their resort to the manufacture of commodities on a productive basis was long since past. The commonsense penologists were violently opposed to any constructive policy of prison labor.

Hence the efforts of the reformers to use prison employment as a reformative device came to naught. In the jails and penitentiaries were to be found the treadwheel, oakum sheds and the vicious and useless crank. The wheel did, in some cases, actually produce power for use. It might be used to pump water or grind corn, even though at great physical labor to the victims. Contemporary pictures show prisoners employed on the wheel, sometimes referred to as "damnation mills," alternating between this monotonous toil and the equally laborious task of picking oakum. After some thirty revolutions of the wheel, the men em-

(18) *ibid.*, p. 72; see also Du Cane, *The Punishment and Prevention of Crime*, Macmillan, London, 1885.

ployed would step off and sit in little stalls where they cleaned the dirty hemp, one strand at a time. They would be relieved by another batch of prisoners who alternated with them. All of this deadening labor was in strict silence.

But even more widespread and diabolical was the crank. Invented by one Gibbs of Pentonville, probably about 1846, it accomplished nothing useful. It was merely a metal drum on legs to which was attached a crank. The prisoner in his cell war ordered to crank for his meals each day; 1,800 revolutions for breakfast, 4,500 for dinner. Often men turned the handle of this stupid machine for hours in their lonely cells after others, more fortunate, had reached their quotas.

RUGGLES-BRISE AND THE NEW ORDER

In spite of Du Cane's efficient administration there was great criticism of his fetish for uniformity and economy. In 1894 the storm of protest reached such a crescendo that an inquiry was made and he was retired. By that time, however, Du Cane was an old man.

In the year 1894 the Home Secretary, Mr. Asquith, appointed a committee under the chairmanship of Mr. Herbert Gladstone to inquire into the methods of the Prison Commissioners. It had been charged that they had produced a serious state of mental deterioration of convicts in the various jails and prisons by means of "deterrent punishments." It was shown by this commission that recidivism was much greater than would normally be expected in a penal system that attempted to reform or rehabilitate the convict, and it was also suggested that an investigation should be made of the cherished separate system itself. The result was that a recommendation called for a general relaxation of discipline.

The committee went further. They recommended a number of simple privileges such as the right to converse, the wider use of prison libraries and much more exercise. They advocated the abolition of the treadwheel and the crank and, as a substitute, the installation of productive labor. They made special suggestions relative to the efforts of prison aid societies and invited their representatives to visit the men inside the prison rather than, as was the case under Du Cane, to wait for the prisoners' release.

Two years prior to the investigation of prisons by the Gladstone committee, a young man named Hugh Evelyn Ruggles-Brise had been appointed to a vacancy on the Board of Prison Commissioners, much against Du Cane's wish. This young man had been trained at Eton and Oxford, had taken Civil Service and had served as secretary to several of the Home Secretaries. At the age of thirty-five, he had received this important post on the Prison Board where, he records, he was none too welcome.[19]

In 1898, this young college man, at the age of thirty-seven, was made Chairman of the Prison Commission to succeed the old stalwart exponent of the separate system and penal servitude with its deadliness and sterility. Many old acts were repealed or modified.[20] Many innovations were introduced into the new régime. The Prison Act of 1898 was far reaching in effect since it laid the basis for one of the most interesting penal systems

(19)　Ruggles-Brise, *op. cit.*, p. 59.
(20)　For an interesting account of Ruggles-Brise, see Shane Leslie, *Sir Evelyn Ruggles-Brise*, Murray, London, 1938.

in the world. The treadwheel and crank gave way to such productive forms of labor as book binding, printing, carpentry, shoemaking and tailoring—the goods finding their way into governmental departments. This form of prison labor is known as the state-use system in America. Aside from the cases of prisoners sentenced to "hard labor," who were still subjected to stone crushing or oakum picking, all productive labor was carried on in association. The new chairman looked upon his new régime as reformative. But so did also Du Cane and the earlier advocates of separation for in that outmoded system they saw deterrence and hence, reformation.

However, as in the case of every similar housecleaning, reforms as well as reformation came slowly. Progressive measures were introduced but many stumbling blocks were evidenced in translating them into practice. Probably the most difficult was the old prison architecture. Pentonville Prison, erected in 1842, was the oldest institution. It had been planned on principles adaptable to the separate system and also served as a model for the later prisons at Parkhurst, Dartmoor and others. Confusion in the wording of the laws also made it difficult to work out a really constructive penal program. While hard labor, as such, had been abolished, problems of profitable employment became almost insurmountable.

THE BRITISH SYSTEM OF CLASSIFICATION

Perhaps the most interesting reform was that which made a distinction between "convicts" and "prisoners." The former are those sentenced to "penal servitude" in the convict prisons, whereas, offenders sentenced to the local prisons,[21] are known as "prisoners." These are divided into three divisions which are described below.

Preventive detention is another interesting innovation. This form of special treatment was provided for in the Prevention of Crime Act in 1908. It serves as a detainer on those "professional" criminals who, after serving their regular sentence, are forced to serve another term from five to ten years in the Portsmouth Prison, especially set aside for this class of convicts who persist in leading a life of crime.

As stated above, England's "prisoners" are divided into three categories and are, by and large, incarcerated in the various local prisons. The first division prisoners are few in number. They are individuals who have been sentenced for such offenses as contempt of court or for noncompliance of the elementary education act.[22] They are accorded special privileges such as permission to keep and wear their own clothing, buy newspapers and books with their own money, receive visits from friends, and follow their own trade in prison, if practicable. They may even be supplied with beer and wine, if they purchase it with their own funds. Some even have their own furniture which gives rise to the expression that they represent "the aristocrats of the prison world." One irksome drawback is that they may have no contact with their own kind and must remain almost exclusively in their own cell.

(21)   See below for an enumeration of these local prisons.
(22)   Much of this material is taken from John Watson, *Meet the Prisoner,* Jonathan Cape, London, 1939 and John L. Gillin, *Taming the Criminal,* Macmillan, 1939. Acknowledgement is hereby extended these two writers.

The second division is for those who, in the opinion of the court, are likely to suffer from contamination with more depraved inmates, yet who show by their previous record and the nature of their offense, that they need some restraint and treatment. The third division includes all persons who have received a court sentence without any special regard as to the type of treatment they are expected to undergo. Today there is practically no distinction between second and third division prisoners as regards to work, general treatment, or medical observation. The separation is to avoid contamination only.

One additional classification remains, long familiar in English prisons. We allude to the "Star" class. This class has existed in the convict prisons since 1879 but was not introduced into the local prisons until 1896. Owing to the tendency of the courts sometimes to commit depraved and habitual offenders to the second division, due to age or infirmity, it was found necessary to separate prisoners from the second or third divisions, who were not habitual nor depraved, from those who find their way into such categories. Star prisoners are known by the red stars worn on their sleeves. They have not previously been convicted and generally have been sentenced for trivial offenses. Then there are "special class" prisoners, young men between twenty-one and twenty-six, who are ineligible to become "Stars." They are mainly confined in Wandsworth, Wakefield and Lewes local prisons.

In the convict prisons there are also "stars" and "specials." Star convicts are, in general, confined at Maidstone; specials are sent to Chelmsford. However, in recent years, it has become the practice to send a certain number of convict "stars" and "specials" to local prisons where they may mix with prisoners of equal grade. All convicts, that is, those sent to convict, rather than local, prisons are subject to the English system of "progressive stages" introduced, as we mentioned earlier, by Sir Joshua Jebb, as a result of Alexander Maconochie's experiments on Norfolk Island. By the system of accumulation of marks, the convict may pass from one stage to another. In 1920-21 this system was revised so that four distinct stages were developed.

The first stage usually lasts for three months. The prisoner sentenced to a period of less than four months naturally does not enter the second stage. During his incarceration the inmate spends his evenings in his cell occupied with some type of work, usually sewing mailbags. He has certain privileges such as the right to a visit from the outside at specific intervals and to draw books from the library. The second stage is for six months and carries with it additional privileges such as more frequent visits and more library books. After he has qualified by his labor he passes on to the third stage where he enjoys maximum privileges. These include smoking, daily newspapers and recreational advantages. He may also eat his meals in association rather than in his cell.

The fourth stage is designated for those capable of becoming leaders— known as "redbands." Such inmates are trusted and may move about the prison unescorted. However, they have no jurisdiction over other inmates.

The four convict prisons for men are: Maidstone, Parkhurst, Chelmsford and Dartmoor. Old Pentonville is to be discontinued. It is now a local prison. Women convicts are sent to Holloway "local" prison in London. All of the twenty-five local prisons, with the exception of Wormwood Scrubs and Wakefield, contain a certain number of adult recidivists. Brixton local prison is for debtors and remands only. Remand is the English term for detention. Five local prisons are collecting centers for young offenders and four are for "weakminded" prisoners.

Following is the list of English prisons and the types of offenders sent to each:

LIST OF ESTABLISHMENTS IN COMMISSION
LOCAL PRISONS

Name	Sex	Description of Population
Bedford	Male	A mixed population. Centre for young prisoners: i. e. persons under 21 serving sentences of one month and upwards.
Birmingham	Male and Female	A mixed adult population. Centre for weakminded prisoners.
Bristol	Male	A mixed adult population. Centre for young prisoners.
Brixton	Male	London area "trials" and "debtors." High court cases, etc. A few convicted prisoners for the domestic work of the establishment.
Cardiff	Male and Female	A mixed adult population.
Dorchester	Male	A mixed adult population.
Durham	Male and Female	A mixed adult population. Centre for young prisoners.
Exeter	Male and Female	A mixed adult population.
Gloucester	Male	A mixed adult population.
Holloway	Female	All classes of women and girls, including convicts and preventive detention.
Hull	Male	A mixed adult population, with a few special class prisoners from Leeds Prison.
Leeds	Male	A mixed adult population.
Leicester	Male	A mixed adult population.
Lewes	Male	A mixed adult population. A certain number of special class prisoners are transferred to this establishment from Wandsworth Prison.
Lincoln	Male	A mixed adult population. Centre for weakminded prisoners.
Liverpool	Male	A mixed adult population. Centre for young prisoners. Centre for weakminded prisoners.

Manchester	Male and Female	A mixed adult population.
Norwich	Male	A mixed adult population.
Oxford	Male	A mixed adult population.
Pentonville	Male	Adult recidivists.
Shrewsbury	Male	A mixed adult population.
Swansea	Male	A mixed adult population.
Wandsworth	Male	London area "specials." Centre for weakminded prisoners. Adult recidivists.
Winchester	Male	A mixed adult population. Centre for young prisoners.
Wormwood Scrubs	Male	For prisoners in the Greater London area who have not been in prison before. Formerly the London boys' prison. All lads sentenced to Borstal detention formerly passed through this establishment for allocation to Borstal institutions. Prisoners from other establishments are transferred here for surgical and psychological treatment. Feltham Borstal is now the Allocation Centre.
Wakefield	Male	Selected long term locals of sentences of six months and over from Northern and Midland Counties. Selected "Star" convicts. Some of the prisoners are housed at New Hall Camp, seven miles from the prison.

CONVICT PRISONS

Chelmsford	Male	"Special Class" convicts.
Dartmoor	Male	Recidivist convicts.
Maidstone	Male	The main convict prison for "Stars." Young convicts.
Parkhurst	Male	Recidivists and convicts requiring special medical care, either because of their physical health or because they are mentally unstable. Also preventive detention convicts (invalids).

PREVENTIVE DETENTION PRISON

Portsmouth	Male	Preventive detention only.

MODERN PRISON ROUTINE

In many respects, the reception and treatment of the prisoner in England are similar to the American method. Upon entering the prison, he takes a bath and is given an ill fitting suit of cheap prison clothing, is examined by the various dignitaries and taken to his cell. On the lapel of his coat he wears a sort of badge with his name and number clearly showing. The cells in the local prisons are somewhat larger than those in the convict institutions. In the former they average 13 feet by 7 feet, and 9 feet high. The walls are lime whitened brick with the floor of wood or stone. The cell windows are too high to see out without the aid of a stool, the use of which for that purpose is forbidden.

Most English prisons are copied after old Pentonville. They resemble a giant starfish in architecture, the several cellblocks (halls) radiating from the common center. Each hall contains several tiers of cells built against the outer walls. Not many prisons, even today, are equipped with electricity. The old gas jet is in use in many of the cells, covered by a pane of glass. The beds are made of planks covered with coarse bedding and mattress. The same old type of exercise is still employed at Pentonville—walking around in circles.[23] The prisons are too old to be equipped with modern plumbing so the inmates must of necessity resort to the infamous "bucket" which has been abandoned in most American prisons.

Punishments for breaking prison rules are uniform in all prisons. There is some effort in England to clothe the infliction of punishments with official supervision. Minor offenses are punished by demotion to a lower stage, charges and rebuttals by the prisoners being heard before the prison governor (warden). Remission of "marks" may accompany such punishment. If the offense is too serious to be punished by the loss of "marks," the offender may be placed on a restricted diet for a maximum period of three days. However, no dietary punishment may be inflicted without the approval of the prison medical officer. Other penalties are cellular confinement, deprivation of associated labor and the deprivation of a mattress. Corporal punishment may be inflicted only for mutiny, incitement to mutiny or gross personal violence to an officer. The maximum sentence for a prisoner over eighteen years is thirty-six lashes with a cat or birch. The governor of the prison must be present as must also the medical officer. The latter has the authority to stop the flogging at his discretion. During recent years there has been little resort to flogging of adult prisoners for prison offenses.

Employment in English prisons is somewhat of a problem although they have the advantage of what we call the state-use system. In the early days, in the changeover from "hard labor" at the treadwheel and crank to "productive labor," the administration was beset with the same problems found in America. Protests from labor unions were articulate and the public itself objected to convict-made goods. Domestic or maintenance labor makes up the bulk of the employment in most prisons, aside from the present war work. However, prisoners' boots and clothing are also manufactured and, at Maidstone, a printing establishment produces most of the forms that are used in government offices. Reclaiming and cultivating land is also a large part of the employment project in the British system. The convicts at Dartmoor and Parkhurst are employed in the forests and on the moors, and at Wakefield there is a very progressive prison camp. In this latter establishment, opened in 1936 and known as New Hall Camp, exemplary prisoners live in huts and work on farmland at strenuous activities. In the eight years prisoners have been sent there, not one escape has been recorded and this in spite of the fact that there are no guards or weapons to prevent it.

(23)   See Leo Page, *Crime and the Community,* London, 1938.

AFTERCARE OF PRISONERS

British students frankly admit that the weakest element in their system of penal treatment is the aftercare of the offender. Much of what good work is done during incarceration is dissipated after the men come back to an unsympathetic society. This is the case in America, too. The ex-convict is a marked man, hounded by police officers, ignored by private industry, the Civil Service, the army and navy, and at best, given very superficial supervision by societies engaged in aiding the discharged prisoner. Bad as it is in this country, it appears even worse in England. There, most work with this class of person is attempted by private societies with only little state subsidy. Progressive penologists insist that all persons who have had jail or prison experience should be given some sympathetic and understanding aftercare treatment.

The aftercare of convicts who, together with the Preventive Detention prisoners, are released from the convict prisons on license, is in the hands of the Central Association for the Assistance of Discharged Convicts, a semiofficial body under the presidency of the Home Secretary. This organization has trained paid workers who make contacts with convicts while in prison, especially about four months prior to release. They examine data relative to the convict, such as his previous record, the offense, the sentence, residence, aptitudes as to education and work—in short, any information which may be utilized to assist him after release. A representative discusses with him his prospects and his plans, if any. Then members of a voluntary association in the community where the discharged convict is likely to locate are notified to receive and assist him in any way possible.

The National Association of Discharged Prisoners' Aid Societies is a central organization to which all prisoner aid societies must be affiliated. There are many of these organizations and they tend to overlap. An attempt has been made to coordinate these groups but so far it has been unsuccessful. In a typical prisoners' aid society may be found sympathetic persons who attempt to assist the discharged prisoner in obtaining work and in ironing out his personal problems. These local societies handle those prisoners who have been released from the local prisons unconditionally and who are under no obligations to report to the police or to keep in touch with any society.

There seems to be no concept of social case work in the English system, such as has been experimented with in America. While the English system has an excellent personnel within the prison, there is no evidence that it measures up to the serious responsibility of aftercare of the offender. While this phase of penal treatment has a long way to go in the United States, it is somewhat more adequate than in Britain.

PRISON PERSONNEL

Disquieting news regarding personnel is emanating from official sources dealing with this important problem. The war has brought about many problems insofar as personnel is concerned. On the positive side, it is learned that prison officers have organized a union which has recently been recognized by the authorities. As *Correction,* publication of the New York

Department of Correction (discontinued for the duration) remarked a few years ago:

> For the first time in all these years the right of a prison officer to be a human being is recognized . . .The number of working hours has been reduced from 96 to 88, with a very live restriction that no officer should be compelled to work more than a certain number in any one working week.[24]

Aside from the long working week, the problems of the prison officers are serious insofar as discipline is concerned. For example, it is considered disadvantageous to serve at Parkhurst or Dartmoor where "discipline is bad and the environment surrounding these places caused officers to deteriorate mentally." One writer stated that the discipline was "shocking and the whole place a nightmare." Another stated that in the prison where he served, "deputations and 'sitdown' strikes were becoming a daily feature of the routine. Anything which the convicts demanded was conceded." We find the following remarks concerning the prisons at Parkhurst and Dartmoor:

> The Executive had come to the conclusion that the only way in which this situation (lack of discipline) could be tackled was by closing down these places and thus breaking the cliques which had been formed over a period of years. He declared that most of the men in these places had been sent there time and again and eventually they came to regard themselves the "owners" of the place. There was also the danger of familiarity arising as a result of the day-by-day contact of officer and prisoner extending, as it did, over a considerable period of years.[25]

Reference was also made in the journal referred to that the system was losing its best officers "owing to the attitude of the authorities on trivial matters, which were not really worth while." It is evident that the morale among the personnel in certain British prisons is not very high. The same complaints come from the women officers as well. Many of them are forced to live in the prisoners' cells and there is little privacy and rest available.

Handicapped as it is by outmoded prison architecture, one redeeming feature of the British system is its highly trained personnel. Prison work is a career in England, especially in the Borstal System which will be described below. Prison governors are selected by the Prison Commissioners for their interest in social service and for the "sterling worth" of their characters.[26] Political pull no longer determines appointment. The same is true of all subordinate officers. They are all under civil service and are advanced on merit. There is a training school for all prison workers maintained at Wakefield Prison. The course compares favorably with that furnished police officers.[27]

In spite of the splendid efforts attempted to keep prison personnel on a high professional plane, there can be no doubt that some workers scarcely justify the high terms of merit accorded them. Prison work is stultifying to such a degree that many, if not most, of the personnel become institutionalized. They tend to lose interest in their work, goad the prisoners, and, at best, become coldly professional.[28]

(24)   October, 1941, pp. 8-9.
(25)   *ibid.*, p. 8.
(26)   The present Commission is composed of Mr. L. W. Fox, chairman, Alexander Paterson and Dr. J. C. W. Methven and several assistant Commissioners.
(27)   See Watson, *op. cit.*, p. 75, for remarks concerning this training.
(28)   The reader should read James P. Phelan's *Museum*, Morrow & Company, 1937, a fictional account of life in a British prison. It presents evidence that the personnel is none too tolerant or sympathetic. See also a short account of a prison experience by a woman writing in *Spectator*, October 16, 1942, p. 357.

Other significant advantages to be found in the English system are its unification and its complete separation from politics. While it is true that it is under the Home Secretary, which office changes with the Cabinet, the Commissioners who have the real responsibility of operating the prisons are appointed for life. This makes for a continuity of program and policy which is a distinct advantage.

England's excellent system of classification is its most shining example of progressive penal treatment. As Professor J. L. Gillin has stated: "[England] has set the pace for the whole world."[29] The older system of classification within the institution had very decided drawbacks. But since the Home Office took over the local prisons and set up the Borstal System, thus bringing into the entire system some 35 prisons and 9 Borstal units, together with certain centers for the youthful offender, classification between institutions has brought about a most interesting and highly effective program of treatment. Thus unification has been of inestimable value—a situation which is impossible in the United States with its many local and state systems of penal treatment.

PRISON VISITING

The extensive use of prison visiting is another unusual and highly useful feature of Britain's system. Over six hundred laymen call upon the prisoners in the institutions of England. They are organized into an association known as the National Association of Prison Visitors. Only those prisoners who are certified by the governors of the prisons may be visited by these volunteer outsiders. These are generally long termers since it is thought that short termers do not need this service. This idea is not generally shared in America in the few places where lay visiting is in operation.[30] The short termer has problems of a personal nature just as the long termer. He also has the right to expect some understanding visitor to discuss his problems.

The Prison Commissioners are thoroughly in sympathy with prison visiting, which is generally not the case in America. Mr. Alexander Paterson, Commissioner of the English system, says: "Today we have some 600 men and 100 women visiting weekly in English prisons, and we have come to regard their cooperation as an integral part of our English prison system."[31] In proportion to the number of prisoners in English prisons—some 5,000 adults—this is a significant number of volunteer laymen who take time out from their professional lives to visit men in prison.[32]

(29) *Taming the Criminal*, Macmillan, p. 253.

(30) Lay visiting is not encouraged in America. However, the state of Pennsylvania has carried it on for over 150 years. *The Philadelphia Society for Alleviating the Miseries of Public Prisons* (since 1887 known as the *Pennsylvania Prison Society*) has sponsored lay visiting since its inception in 1787. For a treatment of this practice see Teeters, *They Were In Prison*, Chapter XIII ; also Barnes and Teeters, *New Horizons in Criminology*, Chapter XXX.

(31) "The Prison Visitor in England," *Jail Association Journal*, January-February, 1940, pp. 10 f. See also, Watson, *op. cit.* and Gordon Gardiner, *Notes of a Prison Visitor*, Oxford University Press, New York, 1938, for an excellent picture of prison visiting in Britain's prisons.

(32) At the present time there are about 5,000 adults and 1,000 young men and women in prisons and Borstals. According to Mr. Paterson, this represents about half the number prior to the war.. See his article, "The Safest Place Is Prison," *Prison World*, May-June, 1941, pp. 7 ff. (This number has been increased considerably during the past two years.)

One serious problem in Britain's prisons is the labor situation. They are even more hamstrung by the powerful labor unions than are American prisons. However, at present, with the tremendous war effort, there is no idleness in any of the English prisons. As Mr. Paterson remarks:

Idleness is unknown today in English prisons. All work is on defense projects and the inmates manufacture army supplies, clothing, etc. Similarly there is no problem in placing released prisoners. If physically able all ex-prisoners are required to join the armed forces. Their criminal record has no effect upon their eligibility for enlistment or conscription. The latter is binding to all. Sentences, in effect, have been shortened through the expedient of granting additional time off for good behavior. At present one-third of the sentence may be deducted for good behavior instead of the one-fourth allowed prior to the war.[33]

The British system has not availed itself of the services of the psychiatrist or the social case worker, except to a very limited degree. Psychiatrists may be called in for consultation on special mental cases but there is no widespread routine service in sight at this time. There apparently is no social case work, as it is understood in America. What may be learned of the English system leads to the conclusion that the authorities either have not grasped the significance of psychiatric treatment and social case work analysis or have not become convinced of their importance.

THE ENGLISH PRISONS IN WAR TIME

The war has left its imprint on the prisons of England. At the outbreak of hostilities, all prisoners serving sentences of less than three months were released and permitted to "scatter"; all Borstal lads and girls who had served six months or more of their sentences were also permitted their freedom under supervision of their Associates of the Borstal System. Long term prisoners from the more vulnerable prisons, that is, those that were more susceptible to air attack, were moved to safer areas (e. g., Holloway women to Aylesbury, London men to Exeter and Lewes, Birmingham men to Stafford where the old prison was reopened after many years, Leeds recidivists to Wakefield, Wakefield "stars" to Lowdham Grange Borstal, Maidstone convicts to Camp Hill).

In spite of dire predictions, this "scattering" of prisoners produced no serious dislocation of any sort. Crime did not increase among adults but a wave of delinquencies was noted as a result of the war itself. In the first six months of 1940, there was a 50 per cent increase in offenses committed by children under 17 years. These were largely stealing, and breaking into homes and shops. Authorities attributed this wave of lawbreaking among children to a relaxation of parental authority due to war and its impact. Fully half of London's grade schools have been bombed or converted into other uses. Hence, many children were put to work by harassed parents or sent out to beg. Boys' clubs and recreation work were curtailed and leaders of young peoples' activities had gone to war.

Professor Hermann Mannheim, writing in the early days of the war, alludes to the fact that probation officers in London and other cities found many children getting into trouble on account of the freedom and relaxation of parental control following the induction of a large proportion of their parents into the army and war industry.[34] Petty pilfering and looting

(33) loc. cit., p. 9.
(34) "Crime in Wartime England." *The Annals of the American Academy of Political and Social Science,* September, 1941, pp. 128-137.

followed in the wake of the unrestricted bombing of English cities so that
drastic measures were taken to discourage this criminal practice. Much
of it, however, was mere thoughtlessness on the part of otherwise good
citizens. As Mannheim has pointed out in a restricted study of looting, 90
per cent of those arrested had never experienced a conviction.[35] Miss
Margery Fry, touring the United States during the Fall and winter of
1942-43, pointed out that after the serious confusion of the first few months
of the bombings, life for children became more secure, due to evacuation
and also to the development of volunteer war work. Children have more
recently been assigned specific war jobs which has added to their sense of
responsibility.[36]

THE ENGLISH BORSTAL SYSTEM

Perhaps the most hopeful contribution made by Britain to modern penal
science is the Borstal System. There can be no doubt that the philosophy
of this movement furnished the impetus for the Youth Correction Authority plan which was conceived recently by the American Law Institute and
which, except for the war, might well have made favorable progress
throughout the various states.[37]

After Sir Evelyn Ruggles-Brise took over the control of the British
penal system, he came to America to see at first hand, the Reformatory
System which was flourishing with great promise at that time. He was
much impressed with the Elmira, New York, institution and returned
home with a determination to do something for the youth of his native
land.

He immediately set aside a specialized institution at Borstal, near
Rochester, in Kent, for male offenders between the ages of 16 and 21.
According to Mr. John Watson, Ruggles-Brise

. . . having convened an informal meeting for some of his friends—they included
a bishop, an actor, a journalist, a solicitor, a barrister and a stockbroker—he
told them of the objects he had in view. He explained that the system could
not succeed unless he could enlist the services of a few sympathetic people,
who would visit and befriend these young prisoners during their sentence and
try to help them after they were discharged. Out of this group of the Chairman's
friends grew the Borstal Association, today consisting of more than a thousand
associates, who undertake the aftercare of all boys who have undergone Borstal
training in England and Wales.[38]

Thus was born the famous Borstal System which was later consolidated
in the Prevention of Crime Act of 1908 (the Borstal Act), later extended
by the Criminal Justice Administration Act of 1914 and still further improved in 1923.

As far back as 1838, the Parkhurst Act had made possible the incarceration of young men and boys in Parkhurst Prison in lieu of the
ordeal of transportation to Australia, on condition that they agreed to be
placed in charge of a benevolent group called The Philanthropic Institution. Later, the Reformatory Act of 1854 had declared the principle that

(35) See his article in *Fortnightly,* London, January, 1942, "Some Reflections on
Crime in Wartime."

(36) Remarks in *Probation,* December, 1942, p. 57. Also in an interview with the
writer in February, 1943.

(37) For an account of the Youth Correction Authority movement, see the *Prison
Journal,* April-July, 1940, pp. 57-58 ; also Thorsten Sellin, *The Criminality of Youth,*
published by the American Law Institute, Philadelphia, October, 1940.

(38) *op. cit.,* p. 56.

no boy less than sixteen should be regarded as a criminal. Then, in 1894, the Prison Commission stressed the fact that the most dangerous age in the development of criminality is between sixteen and twenty-one.

So by 1897 the time was ripe for Ruggles-Brise to act on his cherished plan for special treatment for boys and young men. Younger men were segregated from the older with a special program of trade, instruction, rewards and routine. Special wings were requisitioned at Dartmoor and Lincoln prisons so, by 1908, this promising experiment was placed on a firm basis by being incorporated into the British penal system.

Later the conviction arose that Borstals must avoid all features of the prison. Gradually they developed into training centers, each with its own unique characteristics for various types of boys needing specific varieties of treatment, with the age limit eventually fixed at twenty-three.

Among the interesting departures were: the installation of the "house plan," patterned after the preparatory schools and colleges from which many of the housemasters were drawn; the gradual substitution by the staff members of civilian clothes for uniforms; and the development of intimate personal relationships between the staff officers and the boys. The unwalled Borstals, developed since 1930, are most progressive in administration and program, employing many of the best techniques known to penal science.

In 1922, the authorities set up (first at Wandsworth and later in a special wing of the prison at Wormwood Scrubs, just outside London) a classification centre where boys sent by the courts for Borstal training could be examined and their problems diagnosed. The boys remained here for one month for observation after which they allocated to one of the nine Borstals which were maintained prior to the war.[39] The present allocation centre for Borstal lads is located at Feltham rather than at Wormwood Scrubs. The list of Borstals is as follows:

Walled or Partially Walled

Rochester, the original Borstal, to which are sent older offenders with good intelligence who need trade training under close supervision. Thirteen trades are here provided.

Feltham, located in a small village thirteen miles from London. Boys characterized by mental dullness or in need of special physical attention are sent to this institution. Aside from a special physical education program, the boys raise hothouse plants, flowers and tomatoes. Most of these occupations are followed after release.

Portland, formerly a prison and taken over by the Borstal Commission for older and tougher young men with an average age of twenty-one. Recidivists and some army deserters are incarcerated here. The program is largely physical with an intensive sports' program featured.

Sherwood, near Nottingham, is used for the oldest of the Borstal inmates. It is interesting to note that in all the units save Sherwood, inmates are known as lads. Here they are designated men. Wood working is the main trade offered. Discipline is more severe than in other units,

(39) Four of the Borstals have been closed down for the duration.

bars and locks being in evidence. Most of the inmates have had a prison experience.

Camp Hill, on the Isle of Wight is not far from the famous Parkhurst Prison. Young but hardened offenders are sent here. The average number of prior offenses is four. Traditional methods of reform are not used here since it is admitted that these boys need a more subtle type of treatment. The objective sought is selfanalysis.

Unwalled Institutions

Lowdham Grange was the first Borstal established apart from prison structures and was planned and erected by the boys themselves. Those sent here have manifested some promise in the skilled trades, especially in the building trade. There are three stone houses used for housing about 160 boys. The boys sleep in dormitories. Creative work is a feature of the institution.

North Sea Camp represents the greatest departure from conventional reformatory methods. It is a camp situated on the border of marsh land near the bay of Boston in Lincolnshire. Buildings, one storied, are built of corrugated iron with finished interiors. Reclamation of marsh land from storms and tides of the North Sea is the main work objective. Boys sent here are rugged and dependable. Hard work for the sheer joy and thrill of living is the slogan of this unique camp.

Hollesley Bay is tame compared to North Sea Camp. It is a colony akin to a small village. Farm, orchard and greenhouse work are the main pursuits. Boys from agricultural regions are sent here. The camp consists of 1,300 acres. Stress is laid on group discussions mainly of social and civic questions.

Usk, in Wales, cares for the boys from the surrounding region. Boys remain here so long as they can adjust to the freedom afforded them. The aim of the camp is to inspire the boys to do things for themselves.[40]

No convicted offender can be committed to a Borstal by the court until he has been approved by the Prison Commission. This board must be guaranteed the suitability of the candidate for treatment in a Borstal institution and be satisfied that his state of health, character and mental condition are likely to profit by the regimen. Those not suited for Borstal training are simply sent off to jail or prison.

Borstal training represents two indeterminate stages within the span of four years, regardless of the boy or the offense. Six to thirty-six months are spent in training at the particular institution, and the remainder of the time on parole or *license* outside the Borstal. Flexibility is the keynote of the system. Interests, aptitudes and personal traits determine the boy's stay in the institution. When it appears the boy is ready to assume the responsibilities of the free community, he is conditionally released to an aftercare department known as the Borstal Association. This organization is unique since it is composed of both volunteer workers and a paid staff.

(40)   This, together with other material on the Borstals is adapted from the recent excellent work, *Criminal Youth and the Borstal System,* by William Healy and Benedict Alper, The Commonwealth Fund, 1941.

Both full time and part time workers are drawn from the ministry, the field of education and business.

Another group, known as the Borstal Volunteer Associates, is also interested in the released Borstal lad. This group is made up of interested persons who give moral support to the boy and assist in securing him employment. Thus we see that the aftercare of each boy is sponsored by at least two persons.

In evaluating the Borstal System we must keep in mind that such a system would be quite difficult to develop in the United States. England is closely compact, so that any form of national service is more easily administered from a central office. In this country we have forty-eight different states, each with its own institutions and separate governments. Distances are great and centralization of authority is resisted.

The Borstal System has many features that are decidedly worth emulating in this country for the young offender. The personal relationship between staff officers and inmates is of particular significance. The absence of the repressive features that are found in practically all our own reformatories is another noteworthy advantage of the Borstals. The practice of recruiting staff officers from preparatory schools and universities is commendable as is also the elimination of uniforms for these officers. Then, too, the aftercare furnished the discharged inmates, with its personal and human relationship, is significant and well worth inaugurating in America.

Two major criticisms might well be noted, however. One, the almost complete lack of psychiatric treatment found in the various units;[41] and two, the specific and definite limit placed at four years' treatment for all offenders. In this country, the exponents of the indeterminate sentence point to the fact that no one knows at the outset just how long it will take to reform or adjust a delinquent to the accepted rules of social living. Definite limits of incarceration pose interesting questions which even now defy adequate answers. Perhaps a four year limit for any boy or young man might well be defended, especially in the light of sympathetic and personal aftercare which is a distinct feature of the Borstal System.

EXPERIMENT AT Q CAMP

Perhaps one of the most interesting and unique forms of democratic living in recent times is the pioneering experiment which was carried on from 1936 to 1940 in a camp near a village in Essex, not far from London, and known officially as Q Camp.

Here was centered a program characterized by "shared responsibility" of a small number of staff officers and a small workable group of "members" of the male sex between the ages of 16½ and 25 who had found it difficult to adjust to conventional society.

The Q camp experiment was, in reality, a therapeutic institution rather than a model community but its most significant feature was the mutual partnership which it emphasized. The members were sent there on their own volition and they remained only on the same basis. While those responsible for the experiment did not claim to have discovered any new principle in treatment they did claim "to have achieved a real syn-

(41) See Healy and Alper, *op. cit.*, pp. 227-228 for their analysis of this weakness.

thesis of sound theory with bold practice, of painstaking study of behavior with personal regard for those whose conduct" was studied.

The function of the camp and its therapeutic program attempted to study and treat antisocial behavior and maladjustment by environmental and educative means with a scientific seriousness comparable to that used for individual methods of psychotherapy.

Each member of the camp participated in what government was finally agreed upon. The attempt to achieve orderliness, without which no group of human beings can possibly live together, was subject to change when enough of the group felt this was necessary. Life had to go on and each was obliged to accept voluntarily the amount of responsibility he felt inclined to accept. Public approval and disapproval were perhaps the most potent forces at work during the life of the experiment. Only on very rare occasions was authority from above invoked. In fact, during one brief period of the experiment pure anarchy was tried but it was obvious even to those advocating it that it could not prove satisfactory if work was to be performed.

Members were accepted at their own evaluation. Each was appraised by his work, or his willingness to work, but he was not punished in the traditional sense if he balked or refused to accept his share of responsibilities. Group sanctions were sufficient to elicit acceptable behavior from anyone not measuring up to the levels of responsibility imposed by the entire membership.

Although engaged in the task of re-education, a technique was evolved at Q Camp in developing human personality through work training, the main points of which were:

1. Faith in the judgment of each member
2. That the minimum of compulsions was used, and that only in the initial stages (and not until after the first month)
3. Work was allocated according to ability and the results judged by the effort and will expended
4. The contribution of each member was valued
5. Work was arranged so that no one was placed on a job beyond his powers (*e. g.,* one group willing to work at anything but for only periods of short duration were known as the General Muck Abouts)
6. Everyone felt personally responsible for the job as a whole and each felt free to criticize and make suggestions

Significant features of Q Camp fall under the following heads, descriptions of which must be omitted for lack of space: the element of pioneering; employment, including hobbies; economics, including work to be done, wages, fines, etc.; affection (perhaps the most potent factor in emotional re-adjustment); absence of traditional punishment; use of the individual approach of therapy; value of the group; informal relations between members and staff; shared responsibility between staff and members; interstaff cooperation; cooperation of nonresident medical psychologists; formal therapy, such as visits to specialists, etc.; physical health; training of student helpers; documentation and keeping of records; examination before admission.

The psychiatric approach was much in evidence at Q Camp. Careful analysis was carried on and much relief was noted in the development of the individual's adjustment to life.

The importance of the experiment at Q Camp can best be summarized by one of those most keenly interested in what was accomplished there from 1936-1940. He writes:

I think the most outstanding lesson of Q centers round the instinctive craving of a gregarious creature to be accepted and valued by his fellows. The men selected for admission were wanted by the Committee of Management; they were welcomed by the Camp Chief and his staff, who looked for and found likeable human qualities in them and looked forward to the pleasure of seeing them increase in sociability as many others had done. They were accepted by their fellow members with a measure of cordiality roughly corresponding with their social attractiveness. Most of them had been unwanted in a previous social environment, and many could not believe that the friendship now offered to them was sincere nor that the camp community had a real use for them. The extent to which a man came to be valued and to know that he was valued in the Camp became the measure of the success of his treatment there.

All members who came to the camp might be labeled "behavior" problems but none of them possessed any deepseated psychotic or psychoneurotic traits nor did any come with a long history of incarceration. They were sent by various social agencies, physicians, probation officers, magistrates, parents or friends, or came on their own initiative. Failures were surprisingly few among those who were expected by the staff to succeed which justified the committee in believing in their forms of therapy.

This camp had to close because of the war but there is little doubt that it will reopen after conditions become normal once again. In fact it has won such approval that there is reason to believe it will be reopened some time during 1944. In fact, present plans call for its expansion to include younger boys also. It is an experiment in re-adaptation of behavior problems that will bear watching by those in America most interested in the field of pre-delinquency especially. The Q Camp bids well to be added to the firstclass contributions made by the British in the field of youth treatment.*

THE CRIMINAL JUSTICE BILL OF 1938

We cannot close this discussion of English penology without paying some attention to the comprehensive Criminal Justice Bill which was sponsored by the Home Secretary at that time, Sir Samuel Hoare, and passed by Commons in November, 1938. Before we present it in outline form, it should be stated that it proved to be one of the first casualties of the war. While its many features met with almost universal approval, the one clause dealing with corporal punishment was much debated. This delay proved unfortunate, since it might well have passed and been put in operation before war struck. We shall comment further on this after we have reviewed the Bill.

This weighty document is thoroughgoing in its five parts, eighty clauses and five schedules. It repeals, wholly or in part, nearly sixty earlier

* The author is indebted to Dr. Hermann Mannheim, lecturer in the London School of Economics, for sending him material on the Q Camp. Dr. Mannheim is a member of the Executive Committee of the Camp. The pamphlet from which the material is drawn, published in 1943, was compiled by the Committee, edited by Marjorie E. Franklin, and entitled "Q Camp, An Epitome of Experiences At Hawkspur Camp." A more thorough treatment of this experiment may be found in *The Hawkspur Experiment*, by W. David Wills. Allen and Unwin, London, 1941,

statutes and clears away the confusion and legal technicalities that have accumulated through the past several decades. We can only summarize its main features here:

The headings of the five parts of the Bill are as follows:

Part I—Establishment of methods and institutions for the treatment of offenders.

Part II—Powers of courts dealing with offenders and persons liable to imprisonment.

Part III—Treatment of offenders after sentence and of persons committed to prisons and remand centres.

Part IV—Provisions as to persons of unsound mind.

Part V—Supplementary.

The Bill covers practically every phase which deals with the treatment of the offender, clarifying each step in language that no one can misinterpret. Its influence and subsequent administration will no doubt have farreaching effects in time; there is little doubt that it will be revived after hostilities cease.

We shall now review some of the main features of the Act:

(a) *Probation*: The Bill consolidates the existing law and introduces certain changes affecting both the organization of the probation service and its workings. A case committee is to be formed in every petty sessional division to review the work of the probation officers in individual cases. In each probaton area there must be at least one male and one female probation officer. A state grant may be given to anyone approved by the Secretary of State for the training of probation officers. At present, the probationer has not been labeled "convicted"; under the Bill the offender will be convicted, but the status will be disregarded in any subsequent conviction. The minimum of probation sentence is fixed at one year, rather than, at present, for six months. The maximum continues at three years.*

(b) *Institutions other than prisons and Borstals created*:

1. *Remand Centres*—These institutions are for persons between the ages of 14 and 23 who have been remanded or committed for trial without bail. Such places will be compulsory as soon as a court is advised that they have been provided.

2. *State Remand Homes*—One or more State Remand Homes may be provided in addition to those already existing under local authorities for children and young persons under 17. Facilities for observation must be provided. Where a person between 14 and 17 is remanded without bail and is certified as being too unruly to be sent to the local remand home, he will be detained in the State Remand Home instead of a prison.

3. *Compulsory Attendance Centres*—These establishments are for the punishment of minor offenses committed by youths and for which Borstal training is deemed not necessary. Such offenses are, exploding firecrackers when against the law, throwing stones at trains, and similar

* For an analysis of probation methods in England, see N. S. Timasheff, *One Hundred Years of Probation*, Part I, Fordham University Press, 1941, pp. 25-33.

"crimes" which, according to the judge, call for some definite form of corrective treatment. The maximum number of hours to be held in these centres is 60. Time of attendance shall not interfere with the child's school work.

4. *Howard Homes*—These are disciplinary centres for boys between the ages of 16 and 21. They must reside here under certain repressions, but may go to and from their work. It has been likened to a "hostel" to which an offender may be sent if the court considers that he is likely to benefit by strict supervision of his leisure, by severance of home conditions, or both. The maximum period of residence is six months. This is another substitute for sending the youth to Borstal.

(c) *Preventive Detention*: Preventive detention (extra sentence after the convict has served his regular court sentence) can be ordered for persons over 30 years of age if the court is satisfied that, in view of the offender's record and mode of life, such a sentence is expedient for the protection of the public. There is little change in this provision except the discretionary terms are, under the Bill, two to four years, in some cases, and from four to ten in others whereas the old law called for terms of from not less than five nor more than ten.

(d) *Hard Labor, Penal Servitude, and Prison Divisions*: The courts will no longer be empowered to order sentences of Hard Labor or Penal Servitude, those old hangovers from a more repressive day. In addition, the old "ticket-of-leave" is abolished and, it is hoped, a more worthy substitute provided, in a "positive aftercare" type of treatment. Since there is no "parole" as we know it in America, what new measures will be taken for supervising those discharged from prison is problematical. As it now stands, this work is done largely by private organizations with some state subsidy such as the Central Association for the Assistance of Discharged Convicts.

(e) *Corporal punishment*: No person shall be sentenced by a court to corporal punishment. However, the provision to inflict corporal punishment within the prison for mutiny, incitement to mutiny and gross violence to an officer of the prison, has been retained.

(f) *Offenses by the insane*: The term "State Mental patients," will be substituted for the term "criminal lunatics." State Mental Hospitals will take the place of Criminal Lunatic Asylums.[42]

As stated above, the delay in sending this Bill through the House of Lords, due to the confusion existing on the provision of abolishing corporal punishment sentences by the court, proved too much for the measure so that it was sidetracked for more important business after England entered the war. Friends of the Bill were willing to sacrifice the corporal punishment clause but to no avail. According to the Home Secretary, the complicated nature of the Bill would make too great a call on the services of parliamentary draftsmen and experts who were needed for work connected with the war. An editorial appearing in the *Howard Journal,* official publication of the Howard League for Penal Reform, London, seems to doubt this, by stating: "We suspect that in addition he (the Home Secre-

(42) The above material has been taken from a digest of the Criminal Justice Bill of 1938 by W. A. Elkin, appearing in the *Penal Reformer,* published by the Howard League of London, and reprinted in the *Prison Journal,* April, 1939.

tary) knew that some members of the House of Lords might press for other serious modifications of the Bill apart from the proposed surrender on flogging."[43]

It is important to quote further from this editorial concerning the Bill which met so unkind a fate when most intelligent persons in England were heartily in sympathy with its provisions:

> Opinions differ even among penal reformers as to whether the Bill was worth saving at the cost of abandoning the corporal punishment clause. Many believed that the provisions for Remand Centres, State Remand Homes, mental examination and treatment, Howard Homes and the like were in themselves a large and nourishing half loaf. Others argued that once this Bill reached the Statute Book, mutilated or not, we should have to wait another twenty years for a major measure of penal reform and that corporal punishment, condemned not only for its brutality but for its proved failure as a deterrent, would continue to disgrace our penal law for another generation.
>
> Prophecy is an idle occupation. The important thing now is to seize what good we can from the impetus which Sir Samuel Hoare's Bill gave to penal reform. Much can be achieved without legislation. No Court is compelled to flog or birch nor yet send young persons to prison. A little more support to and freer use of existing clinics, the Institute for the Scientific Treatment of Delinquency and the Child Guidance Council would save some mistakes now and build up a more solid body of experience in scientific handling of offenders . . . We look for another Criminal Justice Bill, which shall contain not merely all the good projected in the one we have lost, but shall put an end to flogging and the gallows. The Bill was acclaimed because the faith it embodied was in the minds of those with knowledge and experience of the problems. The next Bill will reflect the minds of those who stand behind it. It is the minds of the people that will count.[44]

In this rather lengthy discussion of England's system of penal discipline it is assumed that much is to be gained by scrutinizing its attempts to grapple with this aged problem of crime and the criminal. The English people have done remarkably well in abolishing the local political control over its jails and local prisons. As stated above, centralized control makes for efficiency and progressive policy. Those who have seen the system in operation are well pleased. As Professor Gillin, who surveyed the English system first hand some years ago says: "On the whole, one comes away from studying the English prison system with the feeling that, with all its drawbacks, it represents one of the great adventures of the modern world in the treatment of men who have not shown themselves to be amenable to the ordinary methods of social control. Many more steps must be taken, both inside the prison and without, before the problem of handling the poorly adapted individual is solved so as to readjust him to the social conditions under which men must live, in order that he may be a useful member of society."[45]

But all is not rosy in Britain. Most of the prisons are outmoded. In fact, only recently Home Secretary Herbert Morrison, in urging a sweeping reform of the penal system, stated that the prisons were so antiquated that he "would like to pull them down or blow them up."[46]

The annual report of the Howard League for Penal Reform for 1942-43 states that the war "has put the prison clock back almost to 1922."

(43)   Spring, 1940, p. 225.
(44)   *ibid.*, p. 226.
(45)   *op. cit.*, p. 256.
(46)   From a news report, March 29, 1944.

The shortage of officers and overcrowding have apparently made it necessary to curtail prison programs to a serious degree. Many classes in prison schools have been abolished and men are locked in their cells as early as 4:30 in the afternoon for the long night.

Especially to be deplored is the increase in the number of "birchings." In 1938 only 43 were flogged; in 1942 there were 300. Signs of reaction in juvenile courts may be seen by the increase in the number of young people sent to prison. In 1939 there were 123, and in 1942, 576.

This report from Britain is frankly quite pessimistic. This is in some contrast to reports here in America. Perhaps, though, we are too hopeful of penal reform in the postwar future.

THE HOWARD LEAGUE FOR PENAL REFORM

Students interested in the field of international penal treatment have long been accustomed to turn to the reports of the Howard League for Penal Reform for careful analyses by capable students of the field. This association has had a long and distinguished career, originally under the name of the parent organization, the Howard Association, and since 1921 under its present title. It was in that year that it became the joint society of the Howard Association and the Penal Reform League.

The original Howard Association was founded in 1866 and had for its secretary for many years the noted reformer, William Tallack (1831-1908). His book, *Penological and Preventive Principles,* published in 1896, was one of the earliest attempts to place modern penology on a dignified basis. His writings, in general, have been characterized as "discursive and somewhat confused but emphasizing wholesome principles." But this same criticism could be made of most writers in penal reform of that era. The purpose of the Howard Association, according to Tallack, was "to promote the best methods of the treatment and prevention of crime."

The Penal Reform League published annual reports and records from 1907 to 1920 when, after its merger with the Howard Association, the official publication became known as the *Howard Journal.* Not only has this publication been concerned with penal reform in Britain and the Dominions, but also throughout the world. There is no doubt that it has carried much weight, not only among laymen but also among public officials, in stimulating a deep interest in progressive penal measures. It has not hesitated to assume a militant role in crusading for intelligent and humane treatment of prisoners and, especially, of juveniles. Its long fight against flogging in Britain is worthy of special mention.

In 1927 an international bureau was created with its seat in Geneva. Its director was Miss Margery Fry and its secretary, Dr. Irma Hausmann. The purpose of the international bureau, during its operation, was to labor in the "international sphere for the right treatment of prisoners, and the prevention of crime and juvenile delinquency." It maintained correspondents and memberships throughout most of the countries of Europe, the United States and the British Empire.

The present war has restricted to a degree the work of the Howard League but it still publishes its annual *Journal* and continues to take a lively interest in progressive penal methods. Its secretary for many years has been Miss Cicely M. Craven and its president is Lord Mamhead. It is financed through private memberships.

CHAPTER II

PENAL THEORY AND PRACTICE IN THE BRITISH EMPIRE

THE PRISON SYSTEMS OF CANADA

In order to comprehend more easily the dual penal systems in operation in the Dominion of Canada, we herewith append a list of the institutions coming under the jurisdiction of the Dominion itself and those controlled by the various provinces.

PENAL AND CORRECTIONAL INSTITUTIONS OF CANADA

Federal Penitentiaries

British Columbia—New Westminster
   opened 1877—normal capacity, 581; population, 1942: 329 males

Manitoba—Stony Mountain
   opened 1877—normal capacity, 525; population, 1942: 774

New Brunswick—Dorchester
   opened 1877—normal capacity, 525; population, 1942: 439

Ontario—Kingston
         opened 1868—normal capacity, 920; population, 1942: 774
         males; 46 females (including alien prisoners of war)
      Collins Bay
         opened 1930—normal capacity, 335; population, 1942: 273
         males

Quebec—St. Vincent's de Paul, at Quebec
   opened 1877—normal capacity, 1186; population, 1942: 1013 males

Saskatchewan—Prince Albert
   opened 1911—normal capacity, 678; population, 1942: 504 males

Provincial Institutions

Alberta
   Lethbridge Provincial Gaol, Lethbridge
   Provincial Gaol, Fort Saskatchewan

British Columbia
   Industrial School for Boys, Port Coquitlam
   Industrial School for Girls, Vancouver

Manitoba
   Home for Boys, Rennie
   Home for Girls, Winnipeg
   Central Judicial Gaol and Female Prison, Portage la Prairie
   Provincial Gaol, The Pas
   Western Judicial District Gaol, Brandon

Detention Home for Men, Women and Boys, Winnipeg
Provincial Gaol, Headingly

New Brunswick
Interprovincial Home for Young Women, Coverdale
Boys' Industrial Home, East Saint John

Nova Scotia
Maritime Home for Girls, Truro
St. Patrick's Home for Boys, Halifax
Industrial Home for Boys, Halifax

Ontario
St. John's Training School for Boys, Toronto
Andrew Mercer Reformatory for Women, Toronto
Burwash Industrial Farm, Burwash
Training School for Boys, Bowmanville
Reformatory for Men, Guelph
Reformatory, Mimico (closed during the war)
Municipal Farm, Langstaff

Quebec
The Montreal Gaol
The Quebec Gaol
Hull Gaol (taken over for war purposes after construction)
Sherbrook Gaol (also county gaols at Bedford, St. Jerome, Three
Rivers and other county towns. Total for province, 21.)
No adult reformatories in province
Boys' Farm and Training School, Shawbridge
Girls' Cottage Industrial School, Sweetsburg

Saskatchewan
Industrial School for Boys, Regina
Female Gaol, Battleford
Provincial Gaol, Regina
Moosomin Gaol, Moosomin
Provincial Gaol, Prince Albert

It was in 1867 when the Canadian Dominion Government came into being and took over certain of the Provincial penal institutions. The most important institution to make up the newlyformed system of Dominion prisons was the penitentiary in the province of Ontario, located at Kingston. At the time it was erected, in 1853, it was considered a very superior institution. The Warden of the prison at that time, wrote:

> This extensive institution may be looked upon as protecting the community from the depredations of robbers, murderers, thieves, etc. I may also notice that previous to 1853, our gaols were occupied by wretches who were passing their time in idleness and sloth; and generally occupied in looking through the prison grating, and talking with persons attending the courts; as the court-rooms were generally overhead, and the cell situated beneath, thus they had a good view of persons passing and repassing. This was the most miserable state of affairs, as they passed their periods of imprisonment in indolence, etc., and it was not any punishment to this class of persons, particularly as liquor was frequently smuggled to them.[1]

(1) Quoted by C. W. Topping, *Canadian Penal Institutions*, Ryerson Press, Canada, 1929, p. 4, (*revised, 1944.*)

Other penal establishments located in the Provinces at an early date were those at Halifax, Nova Scotia and at Saint John, in New Brunswick. The former, known as Rockhead Prison, was erected in 1854. It is now a jail for the city of Halifax. It is a two story granite structure and contains about eighty cells. The institution of Saint John is surrounded by twenty-five acres of land. In 1867 there was enough machinery installed to keep eighty convicts busy making wash tubs, brooms and clothes pins. This institution still serves as a provincial jail.

The year 1911 is important in Canadian penal history, as it was then that the new penitentiary at Prince Albert, Saskatchewan, was projected. In 1912, a provincial jail was started, this one located at Montreal in the Province of Quebec. It cost approximately two million dollars. Some prison farms were also created in Ontario and British Columbia after 1912 and a provincial jail at Hull in Quebec, quite recently, which was immediately taken over for war purposes.

The penitentiaries operated under the Dominion are under the Department of Justice, with the Minister of Justice as the nominal head. The Deputy Minister, however, assumes the more active interest in the system together with an acting superintendent. As the system operates at present, the Government at Ottawa has charge of all prisoners throughout the Dominion who are on sentence of more than two years. The nine provinces have their own county or municipal jails, industrial farms, and, in two cases, Ontario and British Columbia, reformatories.

In the early part of the last decade, there was a movement set in motion by penal reformers to have a Royal Commission appointed to study the prison system. That commission reported in 1938 and urged many important reforms. A bill was passed soon after calling for the creation of an administrative commission for the penitentiaries to be substituted for the present one-man control. However, nothing has been done regarding this innovation, the present war being used as an excuse by the Dominion officials.

In 1919, the then Director of the Dominion Prisons, the late General W. St. Pierre Hughes, set forth fifteen specific recommendations which embraced his concepts of penology. In the following enumeration, we see what was contemplated for Canada's prisons at that time. They were: that the Canadian penitentiaries continue to maintain the high standards of the past; that the stone pile be abolished; that well trained medical officers be induced to enter the service; that a qualified, competent teacher be appointed in each of the penitentiaries; that library facilities be vastly improved; that work be arranged for the prisoners under the state-use plan; that better and more palatable meals be served the inmates; that the taxpayer be freed from paying for prisoners' tobacco through a system whereby those who wish it may purchase it from their wages; that employment for an inmate about to be discharged be arranged by a penitentiary official; that there be in each penitentiary a parole board dominated by the officers of the prison and to supply for each area a parole officer who shall make a thorough investigation of all cases, arrange for employment, and supervise each parolee; that inmates be paid wages for work well done; that the problem of the criminally insane be faced and dealt with by erecting a special institution for that purpose; that police officers be given a training course; and that the Penitentiary System be administered internally under the type of organization similar to that of the Royal Canadian Mounted Police.

Some of these recommendations were early achieved, but some failed of fruition. As we survey the Canadian penitentiaries today, we see that these principles need reaffirming as well as new ones adopted.

The problem of classification between penitentiaries is one which calls for a great deal of thought. Due to the large area included in the Dominion System, it is almost impossible to carry out much classification between prisons. We must recognize, also, that only so-called long term criminals are sent to the Dominion Penitentiaries. Speaking in 1935, the then Director of the Penitentiaries, General D. M. Ormand, pointed out the difficulties of classification. He stated that after much consideration was given the subject, a plan was adopted which called for classification within each institution of the following types:

1. Persistent offenders who have had previous penitentiary experience, and who are antisocial in their outlook and are not corrigible.

2. The large intermediate class having had previous experience in reformatories, jails and penitentiaries.

3. Convicts having had no previous conviction, over twenty-one years of age.

4. Convicts having no previous conviction, under twenty-one years of age.

He further stated that a special cellblock had been brought into use in Kingston, Ontario, penitentiary, for the use of 34 selected convicts who were labeled "star class" prisoners. These are naturally separated from the other convicts and are given special privileges. In addition to this provision, he recalled that in 1930, special new reconstruction at the St. Vincent de Paul penitentiary near Montreal together with the erection of the new penitentiary at Collins Bay, Ontario, made possible a classification for certain convicts who show signs of being reformable. He also pointed out that classification is almost impossible in the western provinces because of the great distances between institutions.[2]

It was not until 1933 that prisoners in the Dominion penitentiaries were permitted to converse. Prior to that time the silent rule was enforced, although association was found necessary. Even now inmates may only converse for a few specified periods, during the day. Quoting from the superintendent's remarks on this subject, we find:

Up to the present time this experiment has not indicated that any greater dangers to the security of the institutions have developed than existed before abolition of the silence rule. The Wardens point out, however, that the average conversation is of no reformative value to those taking part.

The well-behaved and studious convicts object to the noise and the interruption to their meditation and studies, and also object to the obscenities discussed by convicts. This change has not decreased offenses against prison regulations, and does not appear to have made prison administration less difficult.

It was also only in 1933 that compulsory education was introduced

(2) In an address before the First Canadian Penal Congress. Montreal, June 13-14, 1935. The new penitentiary just across the highway in St. Vincent de Paul, Quebec, opposite the old institution, is destined for the "Youth" group—16 to 21 years—already segregated in the main building, but construction proceeds slowly owing to lack of materials due to the war.

for illiterates. Those who are found teachable and are in the illiterate category are now taught grade school studies, up to the public school compulsory age. If any other convict wishes to study anything provided by the regular school, he may do so in his cell. However, he must furnish his own books and other material. Physical recreation is supervised for "not less than a half-hour" each day. Part of this is "rhythmic" and part of the type that provides "free movement exercise," such as volley ball, quoits and horseshoes. However, no exercise is permitted "which calls for competition between groups of convicts, or permits or calls for personal contact between them."

Wages are small indeed, but then, not much smaller than those found in many prisons in the United States. In Canada, the prisoner is given five cents each day he works, provided the work is satisfactory, his conduct is good, and he is not undergoing any form of discipline. Since 1935, convicts who use tobacco, must buy it with their own money. When a convict is released, he receives a sum of money at the rate of five cents per day for each day of remission of sentence, over and above seventy-two days. So, if he works at all, there is some chance that he will have a small "nest-egg" upon release.

Commenting on the Dominion penitentiaries, Professor C. W. Topping describes the type of inmates found in the various establishments. He states:

The inmate population has an individual stamp upon it in each penitentiary, even more than have the wardens. There is in the Maritime Provinces no institution between the county jail and the penitentiary; so that persons who in the other provinces go to a reformatory or to a prison farm, in Nova Scotia, New Brunswick, and Prince Edward Island are sent to the penitentiary at Dorchester. The lack of the large cities in the area is also a selective factor, so that one may also say that there are no real "criminals" at Dorchester. The same statement would apply to the institution at Prince Albert, except that in the Province of Saskatchewan jails are in fact prison farms and can be used as such in lieu of the reformatory which does not exist in the province. St. Vincent de Paul penitentiary is located in a small suburb of the city of Montreal and gets the criminal from the city "jungle," making it probably the hardest of any institution in Canada to control.

The inmate population at Kingston, in Ontario, is highly selected and is largely major crime "material," because of the existance in Ontario of one reformatory and three prison farms. Stony Mountain, in Manitoba province, gets the man from the Winnipeg "jungle," but he is an amateur in contrast to the Montreal product. New Westminister, located in British Columbia, gets the seaport riffraff, the dope peddler, and the smuggler, and ranks next to St. Vincent de Paul in difficulty of control. The institution at Dorchester, New Brunswick, on the other hand, is the most easily controlled, as far as the inmate population is concerned, of any penitentiary in Canada.

The six penitentiaries are very much alike in government, in plant, and in results achieved. The individual wardens vary considerably, as do the inmate populations, but the uniformity in regulations, in general organization, in housing and in activities, and still more, the dominating personality of the Superintendent of Penitentiaries, offset these two differentiating factors. Individual differences do show up, however, such as the superior buildings at Prince Albert, hospital at Dorchester, farm and school at Stony Mountain, morale at New Westminster, officers' club-rooms at St. Vincent de Paul, and vocational work at Kingston.[3]

(3)   ibid., pp. 43-48, (passim). Since the publication of Mr. Topping's book, a new penitentiary was built at Collins Bay, Ontario. It was erected with the view of having it used for a "preferred class" of inmates. Owing to pressure on all penitentiaries at this time, due to the war, it has been necessary to use it as an overflow from Kingston. More recently some "preferred" inmates have been sent here which indicates that the classification by institution is being tried for adult first offenders as well as for junior offenders.

The population in the seven penitentiaries of Canada in 1942 was 3,818 males and 46 females. However, by July 23, 1943 this total was reduced to 2,980 due to the fact that many special paroles for war work were granted. There are annually about 67,000 men, women and children discharged from all Canadian prisons, including jails and penal farms. In July 1943 there were approximately 75,000 prison and jail inmates throughout the Dominion.

The Canadian systems of conditional release are somewhat similar to those in practice throughout the penal world. These are expiration of sentence, less "goodtime"; by parole, or ticket-of-leave; and by extramural employment. We in the United States are familiar with the first two types, but the third type is somewhat novel. It is in practice in the Ontario prisons only. Its object, according to Dr. A. E. Lavall, then Chief Parole Officer for the Province, was "to find out whether prisoners, without changing their status in any way but merely the environment, could, without imperilling custody, be employed outside an institution to the advantage of the prisoner, the family and the public."[4]

The man who is given this privilege must sign a statement that he thoroughly understands his responsibilities in going outside the prison to work. He may sleep in his own home on a sort of "confinement to barracks" system, or in the city jail. He must be off the streets by eight o'clock at night. He may keep all he earns except any maintenance he may require at the jail. This plan makes it possible for the convict to support his dependents and also go through a process of "regeneration" under the supervision of prison officials or those delegated for the purpose.

Preparation for parole is none too adequate in Canadian prisons and supervision thereafter is practically nonexistent since parolees must report to the police. Parole or conditional release as it actually exists is somewhat as follows: The Remission Branch of the Department of Justice at Ottawa has the power to recommend conditional release for any prisoner in penitentiaries or provincial jails. In addition, Ontario has a provincial parole board which operates for reformatories and jails and, in order to so operate, has adopted the indeterminate sentence. This, however, is not used for Federal prisoners. The Federal parole is based merely on the idea of clemency. This being so, conditional liberty on ticket-of-leave is granted by the Governor General through the Secretary of State though the recommendation is made by the Minister of Justice, for whom investigations are made and advice given, by the Remission Branch of his department. The present system was adversely criticized by the Royal Commission of 1938 but, according to agreement, there was to be no action taken by the proposed administrative commission of the penitentiaries.

Probation is a provincial matter and is in general use in the juvenile courts wherever established. Ontario and British Columbia have established adult probation, the first probation law going back to 1889. But as one reads reports and statements from conferences on penal treatment the impression is gained that many of the more progressive concepts in the field of penal treatment are lightly engaged in, if at all.

The prison aid societies are quite active and are constantly on the alert to bring about a more advanced philosophy in the Dominion control.

(4)   Quoted by Topping, *op. cit.,* p. 78.

The Salvation Army and the Jocists (Jeunesse Ouvrière Catholique), the latter operating in Quebec among the French speaking population, do much constructive work. Then, too, some lawyers volunteer their services through the prison aid organizations.

The common jail evil is a menace in certain of the provinces of Canada. This is particularly true in the Maritime provinces where there are to be found no reformatories or jail farms. As late as 1931, a commission was appointed to study the jail situation in Nova Scotia. They reported: "There is not a single well equipped continuously busy shop in all the provincial jails." There are 26 jails scattered through that province. The industrial farms in the provinces where they are located are, however, doing a reasonably good job in the type of work for which they were conceived. Unfortunately, though, three of the provinces do not even have these in their penal set-up. These three are the so-called maritime provinces, New Brunswick, Nova Scotia, and Prince Edward Island.

A description of one of the industrial farms is hereby appended. It is probably typical of this type of institution in Canada.

Oakalla farm is located at Burnaby, in British Columbia. It is beautifully situated between Vancouver and New Westminister, a little off the main travelled road and comprises 207 acres. The lake covers two acres of this, the buildings, fifteen, farm land, eighty, hay, pasture and wood land, forty-five;—the remainder in ravine and woods. About seventy acres are surrounded by a 10 foot wire fence (not electrified). The buildings are of four wings; one wing houses short term prisoners, another those awaiting trial and appeal, the third, longer term prisoners; and the fourth, the workshop. Youths are separated from the more hardened offenders and special attention is given first offenders, but admittedly classification is incomplete. There is a 900 volume library, a chapel and a recreation room also.

There are 472 cells each with two bunks. Unless unusually crowded the second bunk is never used. There are no dungeons, but cells may be darkened for disciplinary purposes. The average number of inmates is about 421, of which about 16 are females. There are shoe shops, tailor, blacksmith shop and laundry. Farming and vegetable gardening are carried on by the inmates. Auto license plates are also made in this institution.[5]

Concluding this section on the Canadian penal system, we might state that much work must be done to bring it to a comparable state found in many countries of Europe as well as in some states of America. Many of the ideas that are working fairly successfully in European countries and the United States are well known in Canada, and, in many instances, are in their incipient stage of development. It is possible that after the current war, a more constructive program might be initiated which will include such standard devices as adult probation, parole units operated by the Dominion, the Voluntary Defender, strict separation of the young offender from adult institutions, and others we might mention. It is not our purpose here to find fault with Canadian practices. We have much to abolish in the States and still more to initiate before we can be justified in throwing stones. But we feel that since Canada finally abolished the old silent system—not until 1933, however—it will take considerable time to develop

(5) From remarks made by Judge Helen MacGill, of Vancouver, B. C. at the First Canadian Penal Congress, Montreal, 1935. For further description of Ontario's institutions. see A. E. Lavell, *The Convicted Criminal and His Re-Establishment as a Citizen*, Ryerson Press, 1926.

a program that measures up with our own Federal System or those found in a few of our more progressive states.[6]

The Canadian prisons, like those of this country, have been of great assistance in the war effort. At the outset of the war, in 1939, the prison aid societies, through their linking organization in Montreal, the Canadian Penal Association, made representations to the Minister of Justice at Ottawa, as well as to the provincial authorities urging use of prisoners in war work and a more liberal policy of permitting those inmates who were fit and ready for enlistment to do so. As a result, production in the prisons increased, prisoners were enrolled in the services and blood banks were enriched. Agricultural production has also been greatly increased. In Quebec a bill was passed in 1943 enabling the government to employ jail inmates outside on a much wider basis than heretofore.

AUSTRALIA'S PRISONS

The Commonwealth of Australia is made up of six separate States on the mainland and the island State adjacent to it, Tasmania, for many years known as Van Diemen's Land. Each has its own system of penal treatment and its own gaols and penitentiaries. We shall briefly discuss the most important features of each.

1. *New South Wales,* capital, Sydney. During recent years Australia, in common with most civilized countries, has introduced several modifications and improvements in methods of prison management. Under the old system, punishment partook more or less of the character of reprisal for wrongdoing, and the idea of constituting the prison as a reforming agency was in the background. Reformatory methods and philosophies are conspicuous in the state of New South Wales. Scientific classification and restricted association of prisoners, with special treatment of inebriates have been the objectives of the system here during the past few years.

The passage of the Crime Act of 1924 called for the placing of misdemeanant repeaters into the "habitual" class and thus be liable to "reformative detention." Classification of various types of offenders is made possible by placing them in various institutions within the State. Productive employment is the keystone of the reformative program. Young first offenders are sent to the Emu Plains Prison Farm and the same type, over twenty-five years of age, are employed at the Prisoners' Afforestation Camp, at Tuncarry, on the Manning River. Both of these employment projects have given satisfactory results. The total area set aside for afforestation is 3,380 acres, of which about two-thirds have been planted. At present, over two million trees have grown to maturity since this work was started in 1926. Another large area, at Mila, Bombala, has been set aside for young offenders to pursue this same type of work. New South Wales has a total of 22 gaols and prisons in which are housed about 1,100 prisoners. In 1915, a special institution at Shaftesbury was developed for the treatment of noncriminal inebriates. In time, suitable cases from the Long Bay prison were sent here. No inmate suffering from a contagious disease may be released until cured. Mental cases are placed in the observation ward of the penitentiary and given proper treatment.

(6)   We are indebted to Mr. John Kidman, of the Canadian Penal Association, Montreal, for much of this information concerning the Dominion penal system.

In the past few years, various types of recreational activities have been introduced into the prisons to relieve the monotony of the nonworking hours of the inmates of prisons. These take the form of educational classes, libraries, musical concerts and the like. Special attention is also paid to the diet of prisoners.

There is a Prisoners' Aid Association in New South Wales which functions privately and which has branches in all the towns and country districts of the State. These groups deal with the discharged prisoner, assisting him in finding employment, and, in general, maintaining a friendly supervision over him during the period of his conditional release.

2. *Victoria,* capital, Melbourne. In Victoria there is an excellent system of classification and allocation of prisoners in various grades to different gaols, while at the important penal establishment at Pentridge prison in Melbourne, careful segregation of several classes is carried out. First offenders are placed in the "special" division and it is said that very few of this class are ever reconvicted of an offense upon their release. An afforestation camp known as McLeod Settlement, French Island, is maintained which carries on the same type of work as the camps in New South Wales. Prisons are maintaned at Ballarat, Geelong, and Castlemaine. The latter is a reformatory. In all, there are twelve gaols and prisons in Victoria with a population of about one thousand inmates.

Conditional release as well as the administration of an indeterminate law are handled by the Indeterminate Sentence Board. Released prisoners are turned over to the care of voluntary associations and the Salvation Army. Socialized programs are featured in the various prisons, similar to those instituted in the system of New South Wales.

3. *Queensland,* capital, Brisbane. The prisons of Queensland have been considerably modernized in recent years. Among the most prominent is the establishment of an institution at Brisbane for long term prisoners and the extension of the principle of classification and separation. All juvenile offenders, between the ages of 16 and 21, are kept rigidly apart from older inmates. Emphasis has been placed on training the prisoners in the trades, as studies made in this State show that very few skilled workmen become criminals. The penal settlement at St. Helena has been converted into a farm colony, and well conducted prisoners are afforded special privileges during the latter stages of their incarceration.

Excellent work for discharged prisoners is conducted by the Salvation Army, and the "William Powell Home" also renders services to this group. Queensland operates six prisons with a total population of about 275, including all classes.

4. *South Australia,* capital, Adelaide. This state has fifteen gaols and prisons. The present prison system was drafted along English and European lines and brought up to date with modern concepts of penal discipline. The largest prison in the State is the Yatala Labor Prison. Here the inmates are graded into three classes—first offenders, second offenders, and old offenders, all classes being kept apart. Chronic inebriates are first placed in the Adelaide Gaol and then transferred to the special institution dealing with such cases, located at Gladstone. A small monetary return is afforded to most prisoners, a part of which must go to dependents who need support. Additional money may be earned by working in the cells at night. Under

the Prisons Act of 1924, prisoners who have served one-half of their sentence are eligible for release. Special probation officers have been appointed who visit and supervise all persons placed on probation by the courts. Supervision of discharged prisoners is undertaken by voluntary organizations such as the Prisoners' Aid Association and other types of welfare societies.

5. *Western Australia,* capital, Perth. A royal Commission in 1911 recommended the adoption of a number of reforms in connection with the prison system of this State. Most of these were carried out, including the extension of the principle of separate treatment, improvement in diet, more satisfactory arrangements in regard to remission of sentences, better working conditions, and leaves of absence for staff members. Fremantle Prison is the main State prison, a part of which has been set aside for a reformatory. First offenders are kept apart from more hardened inmates. A farm was set up at Pardelup to which good conduct prisoners are transferred from the Fremantle prison. The "mark" system of penal discipline is maintained in the prisons of Western Australia, but it has been remodeled from time to time to keep abreast of new conditions. The Indeterminate Sentence Board has all jurisdiction over conditional release and probation. Care of discharged prisoners is assumed by the Prison Gate Committee. This State has 19 penal institutions with a population of about 260.

6. *Tasmania,* capital Hobart. There is only one gaol in Tasmania, located at Hobart. In recent years it has been remodeled so that a more complete segregation of types can be carried out, in addition to furnishing the maximum amount of employment. Youthful offenders are cared for separately in the institution.

7. *Northern Territory,* capital, Darwin. There are three prisons in this section of the country with few prisoners incarcerated.

* * * *

Much attention has been paid to the intelligence of prisoners in Australia. Studies have been made in Hobart and Melbourne by psychologists and visiting physicians which tend to support the thesis that the bulk of those sent to prison are "mentally and morally under the age of discretion."

Relative to capital punishment, Australia executes very few criminals. In earlier days, however, the rate was distressingly high. Today, in the various States, only murder is generally capital. In a few States, however, rape is still capital, but the extreme penalty is very rarely carried out for this offense. Seldom are there more than two or three criminals executed in any one year.

Australia holds the distinction of being the first country to establish special children's courts. The first was created in 1895 in South Australia. Since that time special courts have been set up in all the states. Their object, according to the report of the courts in the Year Book, is "to avoid, as far as possible, the unpleasant surroundings of the police court."

Probation came relatively early in the various states of Australia stimulated, no doubt, by its adoption in England. Queensland adopted it

in 1886, South Australia and Victoria in 1887, Western Australia in 1892,
New South Wales in 1894 and Tasmania in 1898.[1]

Little information on Australia's penal system reaches this country.
We gather, however, that the disciplines followed in the various states
are simply modifications of the British system. The above information is
meagre, indeed, but it does give some clues as to what the authorities of
that continent are attempting in order to carry on concepts of modern
penology.[2]

It must not be forgotten that Australia served for over a half century
as Britain's penal colony. The first boatloads of convicts were sent there
in 1787 and the system did not come to an end until 1852. One of the
main reasons for the gradual abolition of transportation was the strong
opposition of the colonists as time went by. A discussion of this phase of
Britain's penal history may be found in any textbook on penology.

Mention has already been made of Alexander Maconochie's brilliant
experiment on Norfolk Island following 1840 which led the way to the
Reformatory System and the indeterminate sentence. Australia must be
given credit for this contribution to progressive penology.

PENAL INSTITUTIONS IN NEW ZEALAND

New Zealand was colonized by the Maoris, the native race, as early
as 1350. They remained unmolested for some three hundred years, or
until they were discovered by the Dutch navigator, Tasman. Due to a
massacre by the natives of several of the crew of Tasman's expedition, they
were left in peace until Captain James Cook rediscovered them in 1769.
Immediately, colonization by the British took place, so by 1840, the island
was proclaimed a part of the Mother Country.

It was then that local jails and prisons were established. We shall not
discuss penal conditions in the early days of New Zealand, but proceed to
the year 1880 when it was found advisable to develop the colony's system
of prisons according to the British system. Accordingly, one Captain Hume,
from Dartmoor Prison in England, went out to New Zealand and set
up the separate system of confinement. A disciple of the old rigorous tradition of penal servitude, hard labor and expiation, Captain Hume did
accomplish many good reforms. For example, he was a great believer in
the classification of prisoners. To this end, he saw that the district prisons
were enlarged, that children were treated separately from adults, and
that a system of largescale tree planting be inaugurated.

Captain Hume retired in 1909 and the prisons were taken over by
the Department of Justice. Due to the large areas of uncultivated and
waste land found in New Zealand, a system of agricultural and land
development was introduced which is carried on to this day. Thousands
of acres were reclaimed with farming, animal husbandry, dairying and
other agricultural pursuits included in the prison program at present. In

(1)   For details, see N. S. Timasheff, *One Hundred Years of Probation*, Fordham University Press, 1941, Part I, pp. 33-42.

(2)   The above material is taken partly from the Australia Year Book of 1929, with
some supplementary information furnished by the Australia Bureau of Information,
New York City.

addition, much industrial work is carried on in the prisons located in or near the cities of the island colony.

Persons serving long sentences are confined in the Mount Eden prison at Auckland which is what might be called a maximum-security institution. The other prisons are quite small, on a minimum-security basis, many of them resembling camps, where small units of differentiated prisoners are housed and employed. Sexual perverts may be found in one prison undergoing special treatment; the old and senile offenders isolated in a special institution with work which they can do, provided, and accidental offenders who are considered trustworthy sent to the various farms and camps, where the honor system is in operation.

Counting the various jails, New Zealand has fourteen prisons and reformatories, three Borstals for young offenders and twenty-three minor prisons for offenders of both sexes. In 1940, there was scarcely more than a daily average of 870 persons in custody. All prisoners are productively employed, provided they are physically and mentally able to work. While the law stipulates that the prisoner sentenced to hard labor has no claim to wages, he is nevertheless given some compensation. Part of this is defrayed for the care of his dependents and part reserved for him on the day of his release. The state-use system of prison labor is in operation. Prisoners work on an average of eight hours per day.

Various educational courses, including technical and industrial, are provided the inmates, in the evenings. Aftercare of discharged prisoners is similar to that in England—under the jurisdiction of voluntary societies. There is nothing outstanding in the New Zealand set-up except that every prisoner who can, is provided remunerative work, much of which has real social value. Aside from the tree planting and reclamation work, other types of work are the manufacture of boots, road work construction, quarrying, bookbinding, printing, and general farming.[1]

New Zealand clung to the death penalty and flogging for many years, although there was much concerted opposition from the reform elements. However, in the Fall of 1941 both of these barbaric hangovers from the dismal past were abolished. In addition to these sweeping reforms, New Zealand has recently launched forth on a comprehensive program of delinquency prevention. The Child Welfare Branch of the Department of Education realizes the importance of research in this field. A recent report from that part of the world states: "Segregation in a suitable environment where necessary and treatment of young offenders, based on a recognition of all of the causes, including psychological factors, is being undertaken."[2]

New Zealand has had probation since 1886, being the first of the British Commonwealth of Nations to adopt, through statute laws, the philosophy as conceived in England. In 1920 a law was passed which modified the earlier provisions to a considerable extent. The earlier statutes permitted probation in any offense, whereas since 1920, only those offenses punishable by imprisonment call for probation.[3]

(1) Much of this material is from "The New Zealand Prison System," Edgar C. Baldock, *Journal of Criminal Law and Criminology*, vol. 29, pp. 216-225, July-August, 1938.

(2) *Howard Journal*, autumn, 1941, pp. 67-69.

(3) Cf. Timasheff, *op. cit.*, pp. 33-37, 80-81.

PENAL REFORM IN THE UNION OF SOUTH AFRICA

Following 1934 the Union of South Africa experienced a complete metamorphosis in its prison system. The most important phase of this change dealt with prison classification.

The various types of offenders were placed in special institutions as follows: Those offenders who commit petty statutory crimes are segregated; first offenders with a sentence of less than two years are isolated in the gaols from hardened criminals; recidivists and those sentenced indeterminately are segregated from all others; and native offenders are housed in camps where they are employed in roadmaking.

In addition, Europeans are accomodated in the Central Prison at Pretoria and Negro prisons are established at certain points throughout the Union.

Reformatories were transferred from the Department of Justice to the Department of Education. This made possible many new improvements in dealing with the young delinquent and preparing him more adequately for release.

The Probation Association of South Africa is very active in working with official organizations. It has its headquarters at Johannesburg with branches at Capetown and Durban and enjoys the support of all leaders in social work. It acts as a connecting link between the various charitable and social activities and is thus able to influence public opinion to a considerable degree.

The Association has also started a depot for the employment of women at Johannesburg. Formerly dependent on the state, they are made selfsupporting by training them in the garment trade. There is also a brickyard maintained to assist in the rehabilitation of discharged prisoners.

One of the most outstanding actions contemplated by the Government is the amalgamation of social work. It was stated that if this plan worked out Governmental support would be forthcoming. A person conversant with prison practice in South Africa stated: "South Africa has perhaps been late in reorganizing its penal system and social welfare activities but evidently amends are now well underway."*

AFRICAN CROWN COLONIES[1]

Seldom do we read or hear of penal conditions in those areas of the globe in which native cultures are controlled or at least appreciably modified, by the white man's culture. However, in those colonies that are under the jurisdiction of the big imperialist nations the natives find themselves in somewhat of a quandary. They must subscribe to the age old primitive sanctions of the native culture and at the same time submit to the more "civilized" methods of punishing criminals. We see such an illustration in the Crown Colonies of Nigeria and Kenya, owned and controlled by Great Britain, and the mandated colony of Tanganyika.

Primitive African society has no criminal laws as such. In the great majority of crimes, reparation was the method of treating the offense, that is, the offender was obliged to make some form of compensation to the

* This material is from E. Jones, "Progress in the Union of South Africa," *Howard Journal*, 1934, pp. 78-79.

(1) For a statement regarding crime among primitive cultures, see Arthur E. Wood and John Barker Waite, *Crime and Its Treatment*, American Book Co., 1941, pp. 446-451.

victim. Even murder could be "paid for" by the killer or his relatives. If a stranger was guilty of murder and could not raise a sum of money to meet the claim against him, he was slain. The welfare and perpetration of the social group was the dominant motive of the type of penal treatment provided.

Much of this primitive code had to be abandoned or modified with the gradual infiltration of the white man, whose penal concepts were much different, and were difficult for the native to comprehend. Even now much confusion exists. The following description of penal conditions in the above mentioned colonies is of interest since it shows the difficulty of translating nonmaterial culture traits of a conquering people into the mores of a more primitive group.

In 1934, there were some 90,000 prisoners in the jails and prisons of the African Crown Colonies. Due to the size of these colonies and the serious difficulties of transportation, little centralization can be accomplished. The result is that only the long term prisoners are sent far from the scenes of their crimes and trials. Each district must maintain a "lock-up," known as a thirdclass prison for short term offenders. These institutions vary from stone buildings to wood and thatch makeshift structures in the more isolated areas of the colonies.

Since the native African cannot fathom the white man's laws, he tends to infringe upon its provisions, often unwittingly. His problem manifests itself when, instead of being called on for reparation to right the wrong, he is informed that he must be locked up in prison. Then, too, he cannot understand why he is called upon to work for the government rather than for the man he has wronged, or his relatives. He accepts his penal incarceration in an apathetic manner. He cannot profit by imprisonment like his white companions may. The latter may take advantage of library facilities, of interviews with staff officers and welfare agencies; the native merely sits out his time, doing the work he is called upon to do. However, upon release, he does not experience the stigma of a prison sentence as does the white prisoner. He returns to his native village, none the worse for his incarceration, unless he has learned some criminal knowledge from the white inmates. He has probably been bored with his imprisonment since he could not have women, beer or dancing, which he thoroughly enjoys when at home.

There have been many reform measures suggested for these colonies. Probably the most important has to do with a sort of classification program. The short sentence, especially for minors, has been deplored. Detention camps for young delinquents, together with the possibility of utilizing the old tradition of tribal responsibility in disciplining the young have been suggested. There is a definite move underway to separate the "technical offenders" from the "real" criminals. Improvement in personnel, the abolition of the old "lock-up" except as a pure house of detention, the use of prison visiting—all are on the agenda of improvements which, it is hoped, might be realized in the near future.*

* This material is from "The African Prisoner," G. B. Orde Browne, *Contemporary Review*, vol. 151, pp. 577-582 (May, 1937). For other articles substantiating the above, see "Crime in Southern Rhodesia," by G. R. Agar, *Howard Journal*, 1934, pp. 76-77; "Ugandi's Prison Problem," by Julius Lewin, *ibid.*, 1936, pp. 409-410; and by the same author, "Crime and Punishment in Africa," *ibid.*, Spring, 1940, pp. 245-248.

THE PRISONS OF INDIA

In olden days in India, offenders were beheaded at the whim of their Muslim or Hindu rulers or officials. Beheading, trampling to death by elephants and poisoning were only a few of the methods for ending the lives of evil doers or those who incurred the hatred of their masters. Maiming of the most hideous sort was also practiced.

However, the East India Company, under the authority of the British Government, after 1704, pursued an energetic policy of establishing law and order as interpreted by English concepts. By 1836, a large number of jails, accommodating 72,000 prisoners, were erected. In that year also, road making, which had been inaugurated for prison labor, was abandoned, because of the high mortality among the convicts, and in its place, forms of intramural labor adopted.

In 1836, also, a system of classification was conceived, developed on the basis of the character of the offense. The concepts advocated by the great English prison reformer, John Howard, met with enthusiastic reception in India so that by 1856, her penal system was far in advance of that of Great Britain. However, it is not to be implied that India escaped many of the mistakes made by England in penology. For example, the old tread-wheel and crank were used; floggings were plentiful; and transportation to outlying places was adopted.

As early as 1787, four years after Britain assumed control of India, Indian prisoners were sent to Bencoolen, in southwest Sumatra. It is a coincident that in the same year, 1787, the first shipload of convicts left England for Australia. The first batch of convicts sent to Bencoolen were employed in jungle clearing and road making. A few were hired by the local planters.

It is reported that many of these convicts married, settled down and were loath to return home to India. In 1823, when Bencoolen was taken over by the Dutch, the convicts then there were transferred to the island of Penang which, by that time, had become the second penal settlement. Two years later, this colony was closed and the one at Singapore opened. Another colony was operated in the Straits Settlement from 1825 to 1873. Also, in 1867, several life convicts were taken to the Andaman Islands and after the closing of the Straits Settlements, the convicts there were taken to the Andamans. Here they were quartered in barracks and villages around the large harbor of Port Blair or on one of the small islands adjacent to it. By 1910, there were about 11,000 convicts in the Andamans. Contagious diseases were prevalent at that late date, but due to inadequate medical service being supplied from India, nothing could be done except to close the settlement. This was recommended in 1924.

Prior to the current war the settlement was still being used for some transported convicts, but none were obliged to go without their consent and if they measured up to the rigid requirements necessary, such as good health and ability and willingness to become good workers and good citizens. We quote from a description of the convicts sent there as late as 1941:

The convicts are quickly drafted out into semi-free stations or villages of the Settlement; they are encouraged to marry and to have their families with them; they can secure full tenure of their land; they are provided full facilities for the observance of their own religion and there are excellent schools and dispensaries throughout the Settlement. Malaria and dysentery have . . . been reduced to one tenth of what they were formerly and all cases of tuberculosis or other serious disease are repatriated to India as soon as diagnosed.[1]

The real starting point of modern penal reform in India is dated from 1919-1920. A Report of the Indian Jails Committee brought about such new concepts of treatment as the Borstal System, Children's and Probation Act, and aftercare of ex-prisoners. These reforms were acted upon slowly in many of the Provinces, although some adopted them without question.

One of the most perplexing problems confronting India is the thousands of criminal tribes marauding the countryside. No other country in the world has anything which compares with this scourge unless it might be China which, for many years, was menaced by thousands of bandits. A word about these criminals who are so indigenous to India should be of some interest here.

Over forty thousand men, women and children in as many as forty-six tribes are literally "tied" by their religion to a life of crime. They prey on the law abiding citizens in their frenzy, committing robberies wholesale, murdering without hatred or qualms of conscience, to a degree that would shock people of western civilization. Their activity presents one of the most serious menaces confronting the government and, so far, they have not been checked. As one writer describes their lawlessness:

They bump off their victims without the least malice and then disappear into the constantly moving, strange underworld which has its own code of honour. They are sworn to lead a life of crime, but it is unpardonable to "squeal" or give up a pal.

Any person belonging to the criminal tribes who transgresses this unwritten code and co-operates with the police in solving a crime, however petty, in which a member of the fraternity may have been involved, is excommunicated by his own people and spends the rest of his life cowering under the shadow of a sudden and violent death.[2]

In one year alone, over 34,000 cases of burglary and 3,400 cases of cattle stealing were recorded. Each criminal tribe has its own acknowledged chief who lays down the law for his people. He receives a "tithe" from the illgotten gain of each marauder and in return sees that the family of any criminal receives support if he is apprehended and sent to prison. The members of the tribes are usually selfsupporting; the men rob and the women make and sell bead work, wicker baskets, collect strange herbs and peddle them, and in some cases, work as domestic servants.

The origin of these tribes is shrouded in mystery. There are several theories advanced by ethnologists. All that is really known is that they are an entirely distinct race from the ordinary inhabitants and also from the settled aboriginal stock who inhabit the more wooded and wilder regions of the interior of India.[3]

They are characterized as follows:[4]

1. The apparently neglected and uneducated strata of society
2. The diverse castes and creeds from which they come

(1) F. A. Barker, "Twenty Years of Penal and Prison Reform in India," *Howard Journal,* autumn, 1941, pp. 52-59.
(2) S. N. Ghosh, "Criminal Tribes—Gigantic Problem Awaits Solution," *The Penal Reformer,* October, 1941, pp. 212 f.
(3) *ibid.,* p. 212.
(4) Abul Hasanat, "The Nature and the Future of the Criminal Tribes of India," *ibid.,* pp. 216 f.

3. The scattered areas they cover
4. The width of the range of their operations
5. The repetition by them of almost the same form of crime
6. The specialization in skill
7. The almost inevitable drift of practically the entire progeny of the classes to crime
8. The difficulty with which they can be treated and
9. The apparent hopelessness of any attempt to reform them.

Commenting briefly on these points, we find them to be woefuly uneducated and neglected by respectable people; that they come from both Muslims and Hindus, mostly from the innumerable castes and subcastes under the latter; that they are found all over the vast reaches of the country and not in any isolated region as is so frequently the case with neglected and lawless groups in most countries; that they are highly mobile, ranging all over the country, aided largely by the railway system of the country; that they all tend to commit the same crimes which fact leads students of the problem to the conclusion that "the precepts and examples of the elders prepare the youngsters" for their lives of depredation; that their specialization and skill in committing crimes is uncanny; that the children are doomed to lead a life of crime; that due to "their wandering nature, their shirking agility, their bluffing skill," all combine to make them exceedingly elusive; and that "it seems almost hopeless that anything can be done to reform them."

Professor J. L. Gillin has admirably discussed the serious problem confronting Britain and the Indian authorities presented by the activities of these criminal tribes. We refer the reader to his treatment of these gangs of native robbers.[5]

By a series of acts which had for their purpose the control of these tribes, various powers were given the Provinces to hunt down the criminal families and place them in settlements. There are four different types of settlements described by Professor Gillin: (1) the industrial settlements near some large plant such as a cotton mill, railroad shops, or a large tea plantation; (2) agriculture colonies, in which the settlers are permitted to cultivate the land at a nominal rental; (3) forest settlements, where the convicts work at getting out timber and reforesting the land for government or private owners; and (4) reformatory settlements, for those who cannot be trusted and who attempt to escape. However, these measures apparently have been ineffective since the problem seems to be as acute today as it was when Professor Gillin visited India, fifteen years ago. Students of the problem are convinced that it represents a long and serious uphill fight on ignorance, the caste system, poor economic conditions and inefficient penal methods before India will be able to rid herself of this constant menace.

On the advent of the Provincial Self-Government of 1936, immediate attention was given to the subject of penal and prison reform. Not much, however, was done except the compilation of reports and the utter-

(5) *Taming the Criminal,* Macmillan, 1931, chapters iv and v. *The Penal Reformer,* Indian publication, devotes its entire issue of October, 1941, to an analysis of the criminal tribes.

ance of brave words. However, from 1920 India has made some progress in bringing her penal system up-to-date.

The prisons of India are of all types. On the whole, however, they follow a horizontal pattern, rather than vertical, as in Britain. Described by one writer, a prison may spread over from one hundred to two hundred acres, with plenty of gardens and flowers. These buildings are usually of one story and the sleeping accommodations are in association. Not more than twenty per cent of the convicts are housed in cells. On the whole, prison architecture is far less depressing than in Britain. Young custodial officers have recently replaced the old type guard, most of them coming from good families. Ex-military reservists usually have the preference for such positions. Paid teachers are now being provided in the larger jails.

Many reforms under the headings of Physical, Educational, Moral and Labor have been introduced in recent years. Sanitary measures and physical training are scrupulously cared for by the authorities. Diets are scientifically drawn up and are under daily medical observation. Education is largely reserved to teaching illiterates. Both paid teachers and literate inmates are delegated to this tremendous task. Newspapers and library books are available for those who are able to read. Moral and religious training is beset with great difficulty in India due to the constant strife between sects. No combined religious service or singing are allowed in jails, except in the European wards where Christian services are held. Even this concession has prompted Hindu and Muslim "agitators" to demand the abolition of such services or be permitted their own observance of religious services.

Labor is becoming less penal in character. To supply government demands, the various crafts have been introduced into the prisons. These include carpentry, blacksmithing, tinning, painting, wool and cotton spinning, brick making, masonry and construction work. Since most prisoners are agriculturalists, large gardens are connected with most jails and prisons. The work program also attempts to teach trades or to make better farmers out of those who are thus inclined.

Flogging has decreased in India in recent years, only a few cases being reported annually. The death penalty, however, flourishes and is favored by practically every police officer and district magistrate in the country, as well as most civilians. This attitude prevails, according to an ex-penal administrator, because of the number of violent crimes in India. He says: "There is more violent crime in the Punjab and North-West Frontier Province than in almost any other country, and life is held very cheap. Only about 20 per cent of the murderers are brought to trial at all, and of these not more than 25 per cent are sentenced to death. Yet, in spite of this, in the Punjab alone, there are usually 2,000 or more executions a year, a figure exceeding the total for 35 years in the United Kingdom.[6]

Prior to 1920, there were no "Discharged Prisoners Aid Societies," but, with the formation of them in Bengal and Bombay, they soon spread throughout the country. Now practically every prison in the Central Provinces and the Punjab have such an organization connected with it. Specially appointed Assistance Officers are appointed to "keep a kindly

(6)   F. A. Barker, *loc. cit.*, p 59.

eye on ex-prisoners scattered throughout the countryside." Adolescents are cared for through the Borstal System. Probation Acts are in operation in the Madras and the Central Provinces and are under consideration in several other Provinces.

Advisory Boards are a feature of most administrations. These Boards meet at stated intervals and review the sentences of prisoners. In suitable cases they recommend to the Government the release of prisoners before the conclusion of their normal sentence. In the Punjab, Advisory Boards have been replaced by *The Good Conduct Prisoners' Provisional Release Act,* by which well conducted prisoners may be provisionally released and sent to work either in Government farms or colonies or as servants or laborers to suitable employers. Their work and conduct are supervised by "Reclamation Officers."

Here, then, is India and her penal program. She has been under the influence of Great Britain, but, at the same time, she has had to adapt western penal measures slowly and carefully. There is no doubt much room for improvement, but, in general, she is at least not standing still in working out a rational and even progressive penal program in the light of the problems brought about by the clash of cultures which has been responsible for so much unrest in that wide and expansive country.

CEYLON'S PRISON SYSTEM

The Prisons of Ceylon as well as those of India are quite a contrast in architecture to those familiar to Americans and British. Instead of Bastille-like fortresses, reminiscent of the middle ages, they are dazzling white buildings of simple structure, surrounded with gay tropical flowers and shrubs, workshops frequently open to the air with roofs to protect the workers against the sun. There is no silence rule and little actual confinement.

We shall first examine Ceylon's prisons. According to Professor Gillin, who visited this island crown colony of Great Britain, in 1927-28, there are six convict prisons under unified control with all local jails. They are all under the jurisdiction of the Inspector-General of Prisons. There are rudiments of modern classification theory, although this is accomplished on the basis of length of sentence, rather than on crimes committed.

The Welikada prison, located at Colombo, is the classification depot. It also serves as a place of detention for short term offenders from the city of Colombo. In addition, the prisoners found here include: all male first offenders sentenced for two or more years; all juveniles under twenty-three for their first offense; and all females, except short termers from other cities of the island.

The Bogambara Prison at Kandy houses: first offenders sentenced by the local courts for a month or less, and all prisoners sentenced for less than two years; special class prisoners who are selected from reconvicted offenders with sentences of over two years; and those sentenced to preventive detention. This latter class is made up of habitual criminals who have had extra time added to regular sentences.

The Mahara institution handles chiefly reconvicted prisoners of the worst type but who have not yet been sentenced to preventive detention. These are subjected to hard labor and close confinement. The Jaffna prison has four classes of prisoners: prisoners of bad repute, such as leaders of gangs and escaped prisoners who have been apprehended; prisoners from other prisons who have been unruly; short term prisoners of less than six months; and those sentenced from courts who are guilty of petty offenses. In reality, we find in this prison, hopeless convicts and those for whom nothing constructive can be done, even though their offenses were not serious. The Nagombo prison is for convalescent inmates from all other institutions. The Anuradhapura prison receives first offenders sentenced from between six months to a year.[1]

The Ceylon authorities have planned carefully in carrying out their system of imprisonment, with all that it implies. There was, for example, a thorough overhauling of prison industries, started in 1924, which continued until there developed a progressive system based primarily on state-use philosophy. It is not only based on economic production but rehabilitation of the inmates as well. Clothing, printing, road material, making of mail bags, as well as the traditional trades are all carried on in Ceylon's prisons. A small wage is given all first offenders and special classes. The educational work and the standards of medical service are both high in the prisons. For example, education for all under the age of twenty-four is compulsory. English, commercial techniques and regular elementary education are all taught in the prisons.

Ceylon has the English system of preventive detention. Those convicted for serious offenses may be sent to the detention prison for from three to five years in addition to their regular sentence. While this group is considered the worst type of criminal, all hope for their rehabilitation is not abandoned. They are induced to learn a trade and are inducted into industrial parties. The authorities are none too optimistic, however, but the point is that sincere efforts are being made to help them.

It is significant to note from the report of the inspector-general of the prisons, quoted by Professor Gillin, that this group looks upon all treatment measures, as well as privileges, merely as relaxation from their more onerous tasks. They show little interest in lectures or educational measures. But, in spite of this observation, the administration does offer rewards for good behavior, including compensation for work well done.

(1) We have taken this material from Professor Gillin's inclusive work, *Taming the Criminal*, The Macmillan Company, 1931. Grateful acknowledgment is hereby accorded.

CHAPTER III

THE PHILOSOPHY AND ADMINISTRATION OF PRISONS IN LATIN EUROPE

BELGIUM

In less than a hundred years, three distinct stages have succeeded each other in the Belgian prisons. The first was the workhouse type of prison created in 1773. This movement, so well known to students of penology, need only be mentioned here. Its practical application embraced the enlightened penal philosophy of Hippolyte Vilain in the *maison de force,* or *Rasphuys,*[1] at Ghent, in Flanders. This institution, like its sister institutions in Britain as well as on the Continent, served primarily as a place of forced custody and labor for adults. Its inmates included vagrants, beggars, and prostitutes and, as thus, has often been identified as a part of a realistic social welfare program. Nevertheless, the workhouse was distinctly a penal institution. Hard work was the essential motif.

Vilain has often been called "the father of modern penitentiary science." His objective was reformation, and the means was hard work. He recognized the importance of trade instruction in order to put the inmate in condition to earn an honest living upon his release from prison. Vilain's vision was uncanny, for in many respects he anticipated the leading concepts of modern prison labor.

In his *Rasphuys,* Vilain provided medical treatment, inaugurated an excellent classification program—felons were separated from miscreants, women and children from male offenders—and kept a meticulous record of each inmate. It is well known that the prison at Ghent strongly influenced the development of the penitentiary system in America, both architecturally and administratively.[2]

In 1838, following the movement that was influencing students of penology all over Europe, Belgium adopted the Pennsylvania System of separate confinement. The Belgian economist and penal reformer, Edouard Ducpétiaux (1804-1868), had visited America and had written on the system.[3] He strongly advocated the system and in 1845 the new and famous prison at Louvain was erected and became the model separate prison in the same sense as the Pentonville Prison in England. We need not elaborate on this system for its many features which attempted reformation of the criminal are familiar to all. The system persisted for many years in Belgium. In fact, the use of the face-mask was not discontinued until 1920, when M. Emile Vandervelde was Minister of Justice.[4]

(1) English *rasphouse,* so called because its inmates labored at rasping wood, that is, grating it into a powder.
(2) For an account of Vilain's penal philosophy, see John Howard, *State of Prisons,* Dutton, 1929, pp. 114-118.
(3) *La Reforme Penitentiare,* 3 volumes, 1837-38.
(4) Sidney and Beatrice Webb, *English Prisons Under Local Government,* Longmans, Green, 1922, p. 189 n.

48

The third and present stage resulted from the recognition of the inadequacy of the cellular régime, a greater understanding of crime and the criminal, and a better knowledge of prison therapy. The plan in operation during the past several years has a scientific basis. Its aim is to do away with the uniform treatment of convicts and to create institutions designed for definite categories of delinquents, so as to specialize and individualize their treatment. Following are the types of institutions provided for:[5]

A. Special institutions for normal convicts
    1. Prison school for delinquent adolescents
    2. Reformatory for adults—reformable class
    3. Prison-factory for improvable convicts
    4. Prison for hardened recidivists
    5. Institution for social defense for incorrigible recidivists incarcerated for the protection of society.

B. Special institutions for abnormal convicts
    1. Asylum for the criminal insane
    2. Prison-asylum for abnormal psychopathic cases
    3. Prison for those subject to convulsions
    4. Special prison for those condemned for sexual crimes and offenses of a pathological character.

C. Special institutions for those physically ill
    1. Prison hospital, surgical clinic
    2. Prison-sanitorium for the tubercular
    3. Penal section for inebriates (bad cases of alcoholism and drug addiction)

The new system is based on two principles. The first is the scientific examination and observation of the prisoners and their systematic grouping; the second is the specialization and individualization of treatment. All recidivists or those sentenced for more than three months are sent to the laboratories for examination. Each laboratory is under the direction of a psychiatrist well versed in criminal anthropology. In 1920, at the instigation of Emile Vandervelde, Minister of Justice, following the lead of Jules Renkin, a previous Minister, who founded the first laboratory of criminal anthropology, similar clinics were established in the ten important prisons of the country.

Examinations in these clinics include medical, neurological, and psychological tests and finally a psychiatric analysis. Social assistants also are called in to make a thorough examination of the offender's social case history. These analyses embrace "moral influences," educational measures, family situation, medical treatment, prison labor, and vocational training.[6] These studies and analyses result in the classification or transfer of the

(5) A Delierneux, Jr., "Evolution of the Prison System in Belgium," *Annals of the American Academy of Political and Social Science*, in "Prisons of Tomorrow," edited by E. H. Sutherland and Thorsten Sellin, September, 1931, pp. 181-182.

(6) See Professor Thorsten Sellin's statement regarding this in the *Journal of Criminal Law and Criminology*, vol. 23, p. 129.

prisoner to an institution adapted to his physical and psychic needs. The report of the investigation and examination is sent to the Forest Prison at Brussels, so that should the subject be reconvicted after his release, his complete record can be sent to the penitentiary in which he is to serve.

The requirements of the personnel are a high intellectual and social standing, special schooling in professional training, and apprenticeship already served along the line of specialization.

The Belgian prisons are run for state-use, so that all of them must be occupied on public works. As M. Delierneux says: "Prison work is oriented toward production with the object of decreasing the cost of maintenance of the prisoners and toward their vocational training to facilitate their reinstatement in society."[7] There is a central Bureau of Labor which directs and coordinates prison work. While prisoners have no right to wages in Belgium, they do receive compensation which is approximately ten per cent of the wages which are paid to free labor.

Most of the newer institutions are located in the country. The institution located at Merxplas is perhaps the most famous of Belgian penal colonies. Located thirty miles from Antwerp, it consists of about 2,800 acres. Here are several specialized institutions and hospitals. These include, (1) a prison agricultural school for young delinquents, (2) a prison for convicted epileptics, (3) a prison sanitorium for convicted tuberculars, and (4) a prison asylum for the feebleminded. The last three are for the purpose of placing in safe custody, and for special treatment, those who are suffering from mental and pathological disorders who are considered dangerous to society. The agricultural school for young delinquents is not for punishment, but rather for moral regeneration and social readaptation. This school has its counterpart in the industrial school at Ghent for those delinquents who are better adapted to trade than to farming. There are ten large prisons in Belgium, located in Brussels (Forest), Louvain, Gand, Anvers, Liege, Mons, Bruges, Namur, Charleroi and Merxplas.

At Merxplas is found the famous colony for vagrants and beggars. This has been in existence since about 1870 and has made a signal contribution to the knowledge of caring for this group of constitutionally weak individuals. Those sent here for such offenses as begging and vagrancy are not considered criminals. They are, however, under the administration of the Minister of Justice and are detained in the colony on the theory that it is the duty of the state to prevent the degeneration of this class, from which criminals are recruited. They are given work and studied as individuals, the training having the objective of reclaiming them for the free society from which they have fallen. Originally, this colony attempted to be agricultural, but in time, it was found that most of the men sent here came from the cities, so industrial work gradually took the place of farming for this group. Then, too, Belgium is primarily industrial.

Hardened criminals and adult recidivists are sent to the old separate prisons in existence since 1845. Younger men are given much attention in the Belgian scheme of penal discipline, since it is they who tend to become the criminals of tomorrow. In both the prison industrial school at Ghent and the agricultural school at Merxplas, young offenders go through

(7) *loc. cit.*, p. 183.

various stages of reclamation. There are four categories: (1) Les Meilleurs; (2) Les Bons; (3) Ceux en Observation ou d'Epreuve; and (4) Les Pervers ou de Punition. The inmate passes from one to the other by means of accumulating points for good conduct, neatness, showing an interest in economy, for diligence, for maintaining silence, application in school, application at work, and other efforts at selfimprovement.[8]

In the two higher classes, "Les Meilleurs" and "Les Bons," much confidence is placed by the authorities. More and more freedom, as well as responsibility, is extended these groups. Individual conferences are provided for, in which problems confronting the boys are freely discussed. Guidance is a cardinal feature of the program of reclamation. Commenting on the importance of this interesting experimental work with young offenders, Professor Gillin says:

> This system of prison schools comprising the industrial institution at Ghent and the agricultural school at Merxplas, is an experiment quite different in many respects from that to be found in any young men's reformatory in this country . . .This advance is marked in the first place by the separation of those who are to be trained for trades and those who are trained for agriculture. It is marked also by the special study which is given to the incoming inmates by every device known to modern science. Again it is marked by individual treatment, such as is rare even in our best reformatories in this country. Finally, it emphasizes once more the importance of having first class, understanding men at the head of such institutions who see that mere mechanical treatment *en masse* cannot perform the task of readjusting these young men, victims of their own heredity and their circumstances, to a normal social life. Here is to be seen an experiment, an adventure in the endeavor to reconstruct distorted personalities, an adventure in which is combined all that science has to teach as to personality with all the art of personal adjustment can contribute to this great task.[9]

A word about the Belgian Penal Code is now in order. Belgium functions under the code passed in 1867, which is Neo-Classical in its theory.[10] While it is concerned with the overt act committed by the offender, it makes a signal attempt to apply the theory of individualization to him. Belgium's conditional release law goes back to 1888. By the provision of this act, an offender incurring a penalty of not more than six months can have the benefit of a reprieve. The law of 1891 has to do with vagrants. Professional vagrants can be sentenced to a work colony for a term from two to seven years. Occasional beggars and vagrants are sent to the *Maison de Refuge* for a short term. If they can find work, however, they may be released on the decision of the Minister of Justice. The penal code of 1867 gives the judges discretion in exercising the minimum-maximum type of sentencing and, in 1919, an act was passed giving the judges even more latitude. For example, a crime punishable by death, might be punishable by a short term in prison, if extenuating circumstances so warrant.

Among the more important of the reforms in the Belgium penal jurisprudence are those dealing with the protection of the child. In 1912, a special department to handle children's offenses was set up, calling for a juvenile court in each of the twenty-six judicial districts, to be presided over by a special magistrate familiar with the treatment of the complex

---

(8)   See John L. Gillin, *Taming the Criminal*, pp. 190-201.
(9)   *ibid.*, p. 200.
(10)   See Louis Vervaeck, "Evolution in the Treatment of Belgian Delinquents and Mentally Ill," *Journal of Criminal Law and Criminology*, vol. 24, May-June, 1933, pp.. 198-217.

manifestations of youthful offenders. The age for these culprits was set at sixteen, but in case of vagrancy, the limit was extended to eighteen. To assist the judge in his task, "deputies for juvenile protection," usually volunteers, are appointed to supervise those brought before the court. It was this law of May 15, 1912, that definitely separated juvenile delinquency from the penal law proper. The judge's authority is limited, however, in that he may not question criminal responsibility of minors.

Postinstitutional treatment in Belgium is in charge of the *Comité de Patronage* and other similar quasipublic organizations. The former organization has been functioning since 1894 when it was founded with royal approval. It is a private group of male and female members, having branches all over the country. They focus their attention on the social re-adaptation of those released from prison, provide protection to juvenile offenders, and also aid the mentally ill, the blind and the aged.

Another such organization is the *Office de Réadaptation,* founded in 1932, functioning in Brussels, especially, and more recently, expanding to a few other cities. Still another society which deals with ex-convicts, and is especially interested in mental hygiene, is the *Ligue belge d'hygiene mentale.* This league was founded in 1922 by Dr. Louis Vervaeck and Dr. Auguste Lay. It disseminates information regarding the causes of mental ailments and hopes to make possible effective cures for those suffering from such diseases.

Belgium enacted laws dealing with probation as early as 1888, holding the distinction of being the first continental country to make such provision.[11]

Another vital part of the Belgian program of treatment is that embraced in their Observation Centres. These are a combination of child guidance clinics and institutions since their function is both to diagnose and to train the juvenile offender. They were established as early as 1912 by law. Progressive standards are scrupulously maintained by the several Centres throughout the country. They handle cases involving dependent, neglected and delinquent children. The two largest and, perhaps, best known are St. Servais, formerly at Namur, for girls, and Moll, for boys. They are commodious, well equipped and well staffed. The one at St. Servais is composed of a dozen villas or pavilions and is operated by nuns.

Other institutions are the Institute St. Elisabeth situated near Risensart which is a medico-pedagogical Centre for girls and small boys, and a farm-school at Waterloo, provincially supported, for both boys and girls.[12]

Belgium shows every indication of a modern and scientific grasp of the problems of delinquency, vagrancy, crime and mental disease. She has been fortunate in having a large number of well trained and public spirited professional men who have made many contributions to the various fields we have mentioned. It is indeed unfortunate that the present European tragedy has eclipsed the efforts of these outstanding scientists and humanitarians and it may be hoped that they still find the opportunity of carrying on their work in their respective fields.

(11)   Cf. Timasheff, *op. cit.,* Part II, 1943, pp. 8-9.
(12)   See Flora Kennedy, "Belgian Observation Centres; Their Aims and Methods," *Howard Journal,* 1933, pp. 73-78.

THE FRENCH PENAL PROGRAM

HISTORICAL BACKGROUND

Much drama and romance are associated with the prisons of medieval France. Perhaps the most famous of all of them was the Bastille, which originally was not a prison, but one of the city's fortified gates. It became a prison in 1417 after the city had grown far beyond its early limits. Here were thrown hundreds of unfortunate wretches without trial and held at the pleasure of the French kings of the seventeenth and eighteenth centuries. It finally came to an end when it was stormed and destroyed on July 14, 1789, the opening battle of the bloody French Rovolution.

Another famous prison was the Conciergerie, which was an appendage of the Palace of Paris. It derives its name from *Concierge,* the abode of the royal porter and door keeper. It is from this famous prison that Marie Antoinette went to her doom. Robespierre, who was the soul of the Reign of Terror, was also incarcerated here and he, too, went to his death from this gloomy prison. Other prisons, almost equally famous in story and poem were the Temple, reputed to be the strongest of all the Paris prisons and torn down in 1811; For-l'Evêque (*forum episcopi*), an ecclesiastical prison, built about 1611, with dungeons or *oubliettes,* under its towers, which was used as a prison until 1780, and which no longer exists; Bicêtre, famous now as a "lunatic asylum," but once serving as a "catch-all"—a hospital and almshouse, as well as a prison, and from which the galleyslaves, as late as 1835, went to their endless drudgery; and Saltpêtrière. This latter prison derived its name from the fact that it was built for the manufacture of gunpowder. It soon ceased to be used as an arsenal and was turned into a hospital for beggars. Many are the gruesome stories emanating from these medieval prisons.[1]

Aside from these medieval fortress-prisons, when one thinks of France in connection with penal treatment, he usually visualizes the faroff penal colony of Devil's Island. Hundreds of thousands of the more serious offenders of this country have been sent to this hell-on-earth since its development in 1851. However, as in former times, pure caprice has all too frequently cast the deciding vote as to who might be spirited away to this colony, so far away that few return. It is not our purpose to discuss here the penal colonies of France as many books and articles have been devoted to them.[2] Rather, we shall attempt to describe the system which is carried on in Continental France—at least prior to the occupation of the Nazis.

No history of penology could be written without mention of a number of outstanding scholars and reformers who focused their best thoughts upon the concepts of penal treatment. The names and contributions of La Rochefoucauld, Moreau-Christophe, de Beaumont and de Tocqueville, Bonneville de Marsangy, Charles Jean Marie Lucas, Frédéric Auguste Demetz and Guillaume Blouet at once come to mind.

(1) See Major Arthur Griffiths, *The World's Famous Prisons,* privately printed, The Grolier Press, London, (undated, circa, 1908), vols. 6 and 7.

(2) See Barnes & Teeters, *New Horizons in Criminology,* Prentice-Hall, 1943, pp. 447-451, for discussion of both Devil's Island and New Caledonia colonies. See also Rene Belbenoit, *Dry Guillotine,* Dutton, 1938, and *Hell On Trial,* Dutton, 1940; also Aage Krarup-Nielsen, *Hell Beyond the Seas,* Vanguard, 1936.

In any discussion of the conflict between the Pennsylvania (separate) and the Auburn (silent) systems of penal discipline, the reports of the various commissioners sent to America by France to make an evaluation of the two systems present themselves for scrutiny. The first of these, by de Beaumont and de Tocqueville, was somewhat lukewarm on the merits of the separate system. But the second commission, composed of the judge, Demetz, and the architect, Blouet, endorsed it. However, France was unable to adopt the system until about 1875, and even then, due to the great expense of changing over from the old congregate type of prison discipline, never fully effected it in all its details.

In France the penitentiary establishments are divided into three distinct classes: (1) the departmental prisons; (2) the central houses; and (3) institutions or colonies for young offenders. These latter are divided into public and private. We shall defer our treatment of them until later. All institutions are under the direction of the Minister of Interior.

The departmental prisons are designed for those arrested on suspicion, those awaiting trial, and for individuals serving short terms of less than a year and a day. By request, some long term prisoners may also serve their sentence in a cell in one of these prisons. There is a departmental prison in every district (*arrondissement*).

To the central houses are sent all those condemned to long sentences, exceptions being made to those sent to long terms at hard labor. In due season, many of those sent to the central houses are transported to a penal colony. Prior to debarkation, they are all sent to a depot to await the sailing of the convict ship. This place is known as the Dépôt de St. Martin-de-Ré.

The colonies, or institutions for young offenders, receive minors convicted prior to the age of sixteen or those whom the judge feels need special attention, even though not convicted of a delinquency. As we stated above, they are both public and private.

We shall now describe in more detail the various types of institutions falling within each category.

DEPARTMENTAL PRISONS

During the period between 1871 and 1874, a number of investigations of prisons were undertaken by official order, which culminated in the law of June 5, 1875. The purpose of this law was to substitute in the departmental prisons the system of separate confinement for the older congregate methods then in operation. Provisions were also made in this law to subsidize the departmental prisons by the State in order to assist the transformation from the congregate to the separate system, so that rigid separation could be carried out uniformly.

In 1881 another act was passed, stipulating the degree of separation to be observed in the thirty-nine departmental prisons. It stated that all communication between prisoners was to be prohibited during the entire period of their imprisonment, regardless of their class. Individual separation was provided for in the receiving cells, the cells designed for rest, the cellular yards and, in addition, the mask had to be worn when the prisoners walked through the interior of the prison. An additional law, passed in 1893, made it possible for the State to condemn any departmental prisons that failed to subscribe to all provisions of the previous act, as to separation, sanitation, hygiene etc.

The departmental prisons are grouped in districts, each embracing two or more departments, and are administered by a director under the authority of the prefects of the departments concerned. The departmental prisons are classified as follows:

The houses of detention where are confined those arrested and held under a writ of twenty-four hours duration.

The houses of justice where are confined persons accused of crimes and who are to be brought to trial.

The houses of correction for convicts serving a sentence of one year or less (associated type of institutions).

The houses of correction, on the cellular plan, for those condemned to imprisonment for a year or more and who have premission to serve their term in cells.

Special prisons handling those imprisoned for debt, certain civil and military transients, cases of physical restraint, etc.

The houses of detention, of justice, and of correction of the same district usually occupy separate quarters in the same building. However, in some of the larger cities, they may be found each in its own special building. Some of the departmental prisons are quite large. Those in Paris, the Santé, and the Fresnes-les-Rungis can house about 3,000 prisoners each. The practice of pronouncing repeated short sentences exists, or rather, did exist for many years in spite of many objections of competent men who saw in it a tendency to recidivism. In 1891, increased penalties for recidivists were permitted and favorable results were soon observed. The act passed that year also provided for a diminution of penalties for first offenders.

CENTRAL HOUSES OF HARD LABOR AND OF CORRECTION

The central houses of hard labor were established by a decree passed June 16, 1808, and were placed under the jurisdiction of the Minister of Interior. These institutions are divided into two groups: central houses of hard labor (*de force*), and central houses of correction. In the former, prisoners are subjected to strict separation; this is likewise true of females. In the houses of correction, sentences may be served from one to ten years and are congregate. There are ten central houses for men in France and three for women, as follows: for men: Poissy, Melun, Beaulieu, Gaillon, Fontevrault, Rion, Nimes, Thouars, Loos, and Clairvaux; for women: Clairmont, Rennes, and Montpellier.

Punishments in the central houses are the usual type found elsewhere. Reprimands, deprivation of reading matter, visits from members of the family, or extra food, may be imposed, and in serious cases, the use of irons. Labor in both the central houses and the departmental prisons is compulsory, although it has never been considered punitive. There is much handicraft work which lends itself to cellular confinement. All labor is on the state-use plan and no commodities may be sold on the open market. The prisoners are paid a slight wage, graduated on the basis of their previous criminal record.

France has always been keenly interested in the education of its convicts. Libraries, schools, discussion groups and religious activities are amply supplied in all institutions. Discharged prisoners come under the influence of "societies of patronage," scattered throughout the country and partly subsidized by the State. Conditional liberation may be obtained from French prisons upon the manifestation by the inmate of good conduct, sustained industry, and "repentance." He must, in order to secure the benefits of such release, have served at least half of his sentence, if he is a first offender, and two-thirds if he is a recidivist. He must have employment upon his discharge. Revocation of this conditional freedom is effected if the discharged man fails to measure up to the conditions of his release.

The law of May 27, 1885 provides for "relegation," or transportation to a penal colony of those convicts who have committed, within ten years, crimes or misdemeanors whose number and nature are enumerated in the law. It is regarded as an accessory penalty and is pronounced by the courts. It is questionable, however, just how far equity and justice are employed in deciding what cases shall be "relegated."

A word about prison personnel may not be amiss. Each applicant is subjected to a rigid examination, preference usually given to veterans of the army. Since France has always had a form of compulsory army service, this fact is not so startling as it may sound to Americans. Candidates are more likely to be chosen if they can teach trades. Schools for guards are maintained, elementary in their nature, but in Paris, a higher school is maintained for those who wish to advance in the service. The teaching staff is chosen from the inspectors in the service. The course of instruction includes hygiene, taught by the physicians, anthropometrics, and elements of criminology.

The supervision of women convicts is in the hands of members of that sex. It is interesting to note that the personnel is chosen from widows and daughters of officers who have died in the service, or from members of religious orders (congréganistes).

TREATMENT OF YOUTHFUL OFFENDERS

The history of the treatment of dependent and delinquent children in France is equally as fascinating as that of adults. In 1568 new and vigorous measures were taken to control minor delinquents and mendicants. Boys and girls of tender years, who "gave themselves to mendicancy" were shut up in the asylum-prisons of Bicêtre and Saltpêtrière. The whip was used as the official means of correction. Children who could not be controlled by their parents or who were "disrespectful, lazy, or inclined to debauch" were summarily sent to these places and whipped into submission.

The decree of September 25, 1791, took a more humane attitude toward minors and stated that "special education" should be substituted for "chastisements." The question of moral discernment was also opened in this act. It furthermore stipulated that minors under the age of twenty-one incarcerated for paternal correction, were to be placed in the house of correction. Prisons of those days were regarded as unfit places for children. One account states that prisons were "unclean sewers, where women and children, young and old men, of all ages, all conditions, innocence and criminality, were mingled in monstrous confusion."[3]

The French law of that day assumed that children under sixteen years of age were not responsible for their acts, but stated that the judge might use his discretion in asking the child whether or not he acted with discernment. It is illuminating to note that, if he had acted with discernment, the penalties were to be as follows:

> If he has incurred the death penalty, hard labor in perpetuity, or deportation, he shall be condemned to a penalty of ten to twenty years' imprisonment in a house of correction. If he has incurred the penalty of hard labor for a time, he will be condemned to be incarcerated in a house of correction for a period equal to at least a third and at most one-half of that for which he might have been condemned. In any case, he may be placed under the surveillance of the police at least five years and at ten years at most.[4]

In 1830 the Government began the study of a project for constructing a central establishment for the treatment of youthful offenders. However, nothing was actually accomplished since the mode of treatment was causing a great deal of debate. It was generally agreed that field work and life in the open were more favorable to the moral and physical regeneration of children than institutional experience.

From that time forward we find a large number of private, as well as public, institutions opened for the care and treatment of dependent, neglected, and delinquent children. The first of these was founded in Paris in 1827 by the Abbé Ausoux. However, it did not continue for any length of time. In 1839, three similar establishments were created: (1) the house of correctional education at Bordeaux, organized by the Abbé Dupech; (2) the same type of school opened by the Abbé Fissiaux; and (3) the famous colony of Mettray, founded by Messrs. Demetz and Bretignières, of Courteilles, who were inspired by the experiments in the United States, known as the Houses of Refuge.

From that time, a still larger number of private schools were opened for the same purpose. M. Charles Lucas founded such a school with his own funds in 1865. His was an agricultural colony, located at Val d' Yevre, near Bourges, which in 1872 was taken over by the Government. In addition to these private schools, the penitentiary administration made special provision for children in a number of the central houses. By 1850, it was felt that new laws should be passed to create children's establishments. Accordingly, in that year, a law was formulated which prescribed especially that minors, both boys and girls, were to receive moral, religious, and professional education and that: (1) a distinct quarter must be set aside for children in houses of detention and trial; (2) children acquitted because they acted without discernment should be conducted to a reformatory colony, where they should be subjected to strict discipline with agricultural and mechanical training; and (3) special institutions created for those considered insubordinate. In 1885, an additional law was passed making it compulsory that all minors be completely segregated from adults.

(3)   Much of this material is taken from Charles Richmond Henderson, *Modern Prison Systems*, (House Document 452, 52nd Congress, Second Session, 1903), pp. 235-270, *passim*.

(4)   *ibid.*, p. 235.

By the turn of the century, a large number of private and public schools were in operation, both for boys and girls. These featured mainly agriculture, horticulture and mechanical trades.

The law of July 15, 1899, was farreaching in its effects regarding the form of treatment in the French children's schools. An interesting system of rewards and punishments was decreed, accompanied with the philosophy that repression should yield to more humane principles of education. Among the rewards for industry, good behavior, and accomplishment were: (1) inscription of one's name on a tablet of honor; (2) supplementary food; (3) places of honor and trust; (4) the right to a special repast at a "table of honor"; (5) an engagement in the army or navy; and (6) return to one's family. The act, in delineating punishments, specifically prohibited corporal punishment or the use of handcuffs. Among the penalties for bad conduct or breaking rules were: (1) privation of recreation; (2) loss of badges or special tablets of honor; (3) privation of visits; (4) isolation at specified periods; and (5) punishment cell with restricted diet. In severe cases of incorrigibility, the child could be sent to a correctional colony.

The French have gone far in dealing with children in correctional institutions. The abolition of corporal punishment is something that American reform schools might well copy. The ultimate objective of these schools is reform, but it is questionable that this can ever be achieved in an institution.

France adopted probation in 1891 after many years of preliminary study. As probation is conceived in France and Belgium, particularly, from which the Franco-Belgian concept is derived, the suspension of the execution of the sentence rather than the suspension of the imposed sentence is its essence. It is this system that has gained favor in many Latin American countries where it is referred to by that term.[5]

ITALIAN PENAL PHILOSOPHY

Penal reform in Italy goes back to the year 1655 when the attention of the public was earnestly called to the subject by Scanaroli of Modena, an archbishop, in a work entitled *De Visitatione Carceratorum,* which dealt with the matter of prison visiting. However, prior to that date, there were many organizations having as their object the visiting of convicts.

As early as 1431, Pope Eugenius IV had ordered that it was the duty of an officer of the courts, together with the superintendent of the poor to visit the prisons twice a month to examine into the conditions of the prisoners, hear their complaints and remedy their grievances. They were even authorized to abridge the term of imprisonment when, in their opinion, the circumstances justified it.

In 1519 Julius de Medicis, afterward Pope Clement VII founded the *Arch-confraternità de S. Girolano,* an association dedicated to prison visiting. In nearly every Italian town organizations of a similar nature

(5)   For an historical account of probation in France, see Timasheff, *op. cit.,* Part II, 1943, pp. 3-7.

were developed so it may well be stated of Italy that many of its citizens were more than casually interested in prison reform.*

In any discussion of Italian criminology the names of Beccaria, Lombroso, Garofalo and Ferri instantly come to mind. It was Cesare Beccaria (1738-1794) to whom the major credit is generally given for stimulating significant reforms in criminal jurisprudence. This he did by the publication of his *Essay on Crimes and Punishments* in 1764. He is also known as the father of the Classical School of Criminology.

In the following century, the nineteenth, we find the rise of another school of criminology which also had repercussions throughout the world. This was the Positive or Italian School, the founder of which was Cesare Lombroso. Generally associated with this intrepid physician are Enrico Ferri and Raffaele Garofalo, all of whom made valuable contributions to the science of criminology.

While it is impossible to discuss the contributions of these men in this short survey, it should be stated that in a sense Italy, through their work, can be called the motherland of penal reform and of scientific criminology. The influence of these pioneers spread all over the world and even today much of criminal jurisprudence and scientific investigation reveals their philosophy and concepts regarding the criminal. We shall discuss their influence below.

Italy was long the exponent of separate confinement, but like so many other European countries in more recent times, she has gradually abandoned it or, at least, diluted it in some manner. As recent as 1936, Sanford Bates, formerly Director of the Federal Bureau of Prisons in this country, found separate confinement in a prison at Florence. Quoting him, we find:

> I remember standing with the warden . . .looking over the exercise yard, which was cut into small cubicles. When I explained to him that in an American prison of 2,000, men would be permitted to congregate in the yard he showed great surprise and said it would be considered dangerous to follow that system.[1]

Penologists have long pointed to the Hospice of San Michele, established in Rome in 1704 by Pope Clement XI for wayward boys, as the precursor of solitary confinement. But many years prior to this, the ecclesiastical influence of solitude and penitence manifested itself in the great prison erected in Rome by Pope Innocent X in 1655. It had been dedicated to "Justice and Clemency" for the "more secure and better custody of criminals."

The Hospice at Rome was designed by the architect, Carlo Fontana. The object of the institution was reformation by hard work and strict silence. Over the door was an inscription which read: "SILENCE: it is not enough to repress the wicked by punishment, it is necessary to make them honest by good treatment." The institution was enlarged in 1733 by Pope Clement XII to include the incarceration of females.

John Howard, visiting Italian prisons in 1778, found them horrible. He saw in Venice "the strongest prison" he had ever seen. Many of the prisoners were confined in "loathsome and dark cells for life." Upon inquiry, he found that all preferred to go to the galleys rather than to

---

* An interesting article on early Italian penal philosophy may be found in the *Journal of Prison Discipline and Philanthropy*, January, 1845, pp. 51-55.

(1) *Prisons and Beyond*, 1936, p. 85. By permission of The Macmillan Company, publishers.

be cooped up in these horrible cells. At least, in the galleys they could enjoy pure air and sunshine. In general, he found conditions fair to good in the smaller prisons at Florence, Padua and Leghorn, in so far as the quality and amount of food were concerned, but the convicts were all heavily shackled most of the time when they worked. They were otherwise humiliated by the degrading garb they wore, made of bright colored cloth.

Italy, at that time, also pursued the galley system for the punishment of prisoners. Howard described the condition of the slaves forced to work therein as particularly severe, although there was evidence that they were well fed and cared for when sick. None under twenty years of age was subjected to the galleys.

He found the two prisons in Milan which "do honour to the country." They were La Casa di Correzione and L'Argastro. Except for the most "atrocious" among the convicts, who were chained together and worked on the streets, the inmates of these two establishments were kept busily employed, learning trades, so that they "will become useful members of society which should be a grand object in all such houses."

After the separate mode of confinement became prevalent in Italian prisons, it was rigorously enforced for certain types of prisoners. In these categories were: prisoners "on trial" during the period of instruction; prisoners "on trial" who preferred seclusion; prisoners who must expiate their crimes without seclusion, but who nevertheless wished that form of treatment. All other types of prisoners were placed in solitary cells at night, but were not permitted any communication during their daily labor. Dr. Giovanni Novelli, Director-General of Penal Institutions, stated in 1931, that separation today is "largely a disciplinary, hygienic and sanitary measure,"[2] although the penal code inaugurated in that year abolished it for general use.

For many years, prior to 1921, Italy showed definite signs of being dissatisfied with its old penal code (the Zanardelli Code, 1889-1931), so in that year, she called on Enrico Ferri, staunch old advocate of the positive school of criminology, to draw up a new one. This he did in a courageous and thoroughgoing manner in which he expounded the positivist tradition by renouncing "moral responsibility." His code was rejected as being too radical by the Fascist state.[3]

Other attempts were made through the following decade, under the direction of former Minister of Justice Rocco, so that by 1931 a new and comprehensive code was adopted. It was no easy task since Italy has long been influenced by two opposing schools of thought. It must be remembered that the father of Classical Penology, Beccaria, was an Italian, and also, those exponents of the Positive School, Lombroso, Garofalo and Ferri left an indelible impression on their native country. The two philosophies were diametrically opposed regarding the question of "freedom of the will." Hence, the commission was obliged to straddle the issue.

The new penal code, "Regulation Governing Penal and Preventive Institutions," called for the retention of moral responsibility but at the

(2)   "The Prisons of Italy," *Annals of the American Academy of Political and Social Science*, September, 1931, pp. 208-220.
(3)   See Gigulio Battaglini, "The Fascist Reform of the Penal Law in Italy," *Journal of Criminal Law and Criminology*, vol. 24, May-June, 1933, pp. 278-289.

same time focused much of its attention on the study of the criminal rather than the offense. As Professor Nathaniel Cantor says regarding this code: "The classical and positivist points of view are combined in one criminal law. The net result is clear-cut confusion."[4] In another connection, he adds: "The essential and avowed aim of the prisons is to chastise, to punish. The betterment of the inmate plays only a secondary role. . . . Despite the positivist elements incorporated in the new law the dominant classical tendencies remain entrenched. . . . One either supports the traditional classical system with its central doctrines of moral responsibility and matching offense with punishment or else accepts the positivist's view of protecting society by sanctioning measures of social defense against those who are declared *legally* responsible. . . . The difference in point of view will have far-reaching implications in the institutional treatment of inmates."[5]

We quote this largely because it explains the dual nature of the new code with its lack of logic and general confusion. Yet, in spite of these handicaps, there is a serious attempt to classify, punish and rehabilitate, all of which are either explicit or implicit in modern penal programs. We shall now attempt to explain this new code and describe how it affects prisons and prisoners alike.

In the code we find the terms punishment and treatment used again and again. There is an attempt made to distinguish between the two. In punishment, detention in an institution is considered an essential element; whereas in setting up measures of public safety, detention is used not only for custody, but treatment and reeducation. Interpreters of the code contend that even in punishment, there is a genuine attempt to reeducate the criminal. However, such social treatment must not interfere with punishment which "consists in chastising," to quote Dr. Novelli.

In order to protect the state against recidivism and the activities of the mentally abnormal, and to discourage the young from developing into criminals, "measures of social defense" are taken. The penal law recognizes two special groups of offenders to whom such measures may be applied: the habitual, the professional, and the criminal "through tendency," and those who suffer from "some grave psychic infirmity, or are deaf and dumb, or victims of chronic alcoholism, or drugs."[6]

The habitual offender is one who has been committed for three major offenses and who shows that he makes his living by criminal pursuits; the "criminal through tendency" may be a single offender, but must show by observation and intensive study that he cannot help being thus inclined.

In the type of treatment which employs "measures of public safety," we find fewer restrictions placed on the prisoner so that reeducation may result unhampered. The indefinite sentence may also be employed in such cases. But those undergoing "punitive" detention are denied the indefinite sentence. Temporary freedom is also extended those who fall within the category of "public safety." This privilege is also denied those undergoing punishment "since the continuity of detention is a characteristic and perhaps a fundamental element in the effectiveness of punishment." It is obvious

(4) *Crime and Society*, Holt, 1939, p. 216.
(5) "The New Prison Program of Italy," *Journal of Criminal Law and Criminology*, vol. 26, 1935-36, pp. 216-227.
(6) *ibid.*, p. 221.

that punishment is to intimidate the individual and to act as a deterrent on the civil population.

Since there are these two forms of detention, differentiated treatment in special institutions may be seen for those sentenced for punishment, or imprisonment, and those detained under "measures of security." Cantor describes the treatment of the two groups, calling them (a) condemned and (b) detained:

> The condemned are known by a number while the detained are called by name. For the condemned, work is always considered an element of punishment while under the measures of security it is essentially a means of reeducation and readaption. The condemned must pay their maintenance, the court cost of the legal proceedings and the damages resulting from their criminal act. The detained retain all of their wages except the expense of maintenance. Both the condemned and the detained may buy extra food rations but the former are limited in the amount they may spend. (The wages are approximately three to four cents a day. The detained receive approximately a cent more per day than the condemned). The detained have wider privileges in letter-writing and visits, as well as the privilege of the temporary freedom (which is rarely exercised). The detained may be released when their "social dangerousness" has ceased to exist but the condemned are under a definite sentence.[7]

The most significant functionary in the Italian penal system is the "surveillance judge" who is extended many powers of interesting significance. In each district may be found such an official who has close supervisory authority of all prisons and prisoners within that jurisdiction. He is naturally a member of the judiciary and among his other duties, which are legion, he protects the rights of the prisoner. In order to minimize conflict between this official and the heads of the prisons, precise provisions are set forth by the Code defining very sharply the provinces of each. Here are the powers of the surveillance judge, as presented by Giovanni Novelli, Director-General, Penal and Preventive Institutions of the Ministry of Justice:[8]

> Transfer from one special institution to another during the period of penal treatment.
> Admission of prisoners over eighteen years of age into special sections.
> Provision for prisoners serving a sentence who are not adapted to congregate imprisonment.
> Assignment to institutions of social re-adaptation, and its abrogation.
> Transfer of prisoners to a disciplinary prison and from this to the ordinary institution.
> Transfer of prisoners to a prison with severe regime or to an institution for physical or mental defectives.
> Transfer of a prisoner who is suffering from a mental disease to a criminal insane asylum, to a sanitarium, or to a house of custody.
> Admission to the work in the open (all' aperto), and revocation of this privilege.
> Rejection of a request for conditional release obviously unfounded.
> Complaints concerning maintenance expenses of a sick inmate.

And, in addition, the surveillance judge renders an opinion on the granting of "conditional release" and on cases of pardon. In short, he is the last word on all subjects of discipline, classification and parole, as understood in this country.

(7)   This material is quoted by Cantor from Novelli, "L'esecuzione delle misure di sicurezza detentive" in *Rivista Di Diretto Penitenziario,* March-April, 1932, pp. 17f. See Cantor, *loc. cit.,* p. 224.

(8)   See "The Prison Program in Italy," *Annals of the American Academy of Political and Social Science,* September, 1931, in "Prisons of Tomorrow," pp. 208-220.

In performing his many duties, the surveillance judge is constantly moving from one institution to another checking up on prisoners, prison officials and looking into transfers.[9] Because of their many duties the judges tend to be overworked, which makes for a superficiality which is unquestionably detrimental to the system. As Professor Monachesi points out: "It is no secret that the majority of the surveillance judges are extremely overworked and must necessarily become 'rubber stamps' to the administrative personnel of the penal institutions." He demonstrates this by quoting from a report which showed that the surveillance judge of Florence had under his supervision in 1931-32, 650 offenders in four different establishments. Of this number some 300 had to be transferred from one institution to another. Aside from dealing with these problems, he had to spend the greater part of his time with individuals subjected to measures of security. There were 210 such cases. Monachesi found the same situation with the judge of Genoa. He states further:

Case loads are by far too heavy to permit anything but superficial work. The time at the disposal of the judge is too brief to allow him to make a thorough examination of the response that each individual offender makes to treatment, and consequently he must rely upon the opinion of the directors of the institutions for information on this question.[10]

The director or warden of the prison has control of the internal administration of his institution while the judge, to quote Professor Cantor, "is really a type of penal magistrate with powers of examination, decision and recommendation in the execution of both punishments and the measures of prevention." Further, he must decide when the inmate's "social dangerousness" has ceased to exist and whether he is ready for discharge. This is done through examination of the inmate at the expiration of his minimum sentence. If the result is unfavorable, the judge fixes a new date six months later for re-examination. In theory, the judge assumes the responsibility for the decisions but, in practice, the administrator of the institution or some other official on his staff makes recommendations which carry considerable weight.

As Professor Cantor describes the institutions, we see a sort of classification which probably seems satisfactory to a nation that admittedly wishes to perpetuate the concept of punishment:

The penal institutions have been specialized in order to realize the aims of the prisoners' classification. Special sections have been provided for prisoners over 18 years of age, disciplinary prisons for those who persist in the violation of prison rules, special institutions for lifers, for those mentally or physically infirm, agricultural colonies, and "institutions of social re-adaptation."

Prisoners serving long terms may be transferred to the "institutions of social re-adaptation" after having served a certain fraction of their sentence and having classified as "good" for more than three years. The theory is that a long prison term has made the inmate unfit to resume normal social activity. Hence, the discipline and regulations in this institution are less severe and the director of the institution may alter the general regulations with regard to those privileges which tend to foster sociability. Thus, even within the system of punishment, an attempt is made to overcome the evil effects of prison life.[11]

(9) Cf. Elio D. Monachesi, "The Italian Surveillance Judge," *Journal of Criminal Law and Criminology*, vol. 26, 1935-36, pp. 811-820; also Nathaniel Cantor, "The New Prison Program of Italy," *ibid.*, pp. 216-227.

(10) *ibid.*, p. 819.

(11) *loc. cit.*, p. 222.

Those who do not fall within the category calling for subsequent "measures of security," that is, those not habitual, professional or otherwise "dangerous," serve their sentence imposed by the court. However, if their sentence does not exceed five years, they may be sent to a special institution of "social re-adaptation," the function of which is to ease them back gradually into society. They must, however, have served at least one-third of their sentence and be considered a "good" prisoner by the authorities. The code describes the purpose of these institutions, as follows:

> In institutions of social readaptation the treatment to which the inmates are subjected must aim to consolidate and to foster in them the qualities of sociability which they have already shown in preceding institutions, in order to prepare the prisoners for their return to a life of freedom.[12]

Those who are believed dangerous to society are expected to serve out their regular sentence, after which they are subjected to "measures of safety." Special institutions are provided for all types of potentially dangerous persons, mentally diseased, chronic alcholics or drug addicts. The measures for others are either detentive or nondetentive. That is, the individual may be further detained in an institution or permitted to return to the free community under supervision. The purpose of these various measures is to prevent further law infractions on the part of those whom the judge feels are "socially dangerous."

Upon conditional release, the discharged convicts are placed under the community control of special Councils of Patronage. These groups are supported in part by fines collected by the courts. The Italians have little faith in prison aid societies or the efforts of other private organizations. In general, too, they frown on prison visiting. As described by Professor Cantor, these quasi-official bodies represent an interesting departure from traditional methods used in many other countries. Each judicial district sets up a Council of Patronage and is presented with a "judicial personality."[13]

These Councils are composed of "representatives from the court, prosecutor's office, the district health officer, the directors (wardens) of the penal institutions within that district, representatives from the National Association for the Protection of Maternity and Infancy, the provincial industrial, agricultural and commercial labor federations, the Church and two outstanding lay figures, one of whom must be a woman.[14] The members are appointed by the Minister of Justice for a term of three years and receive no remuneration. Each Council is supported by both private and public funds as well as legacies. It meets bi-weekly to discuss cases of both prisoners not yet released and discharged convicts. The two most important functions imposed on these bodies by the State are to provide employment for the ex-prisoner and to make any assistance to his family that is deemed necessary.

Investigations are made into the prisoner's family and relative to his prospects for work upon release. Since there is the usual difficulty in securing work, which is not peculiar to Italy, the Councils have ventured forth on a daring experiment since their organization. They have

(12)   Article 228, quoted by Novelli, *loc. cit.*, p. 217.
(13)   See Nathaniel Cantor, "The Councils of Patronage," *Journal of Criminal Law and Criminology*, vol. 24, pp. 768-773, (November-December, 1933).
(14)   *ibid.*, p. 769.

established industrial establishments in their respective districts for the exclusive employment of ex-prisoners who signify a desire for such help.

The city of Palermo, in Sicily, created the first such establishment, known as *Assistenziario Per I Liberati Dal Carcere* (Institute for the Aid of Discharged Prisoners) which was opened in 1931, erected by funds raised by private and public subscriptions. Since that time, similar institutions have been established in Rome, Milan, Florence and Naples.[15] About a month prior to the prisoner's release, the prison notifies the local Council of this fact. The secretary of the Council then writes to the inmate inviting him to discuss his plans with representatives of the organization. The inmate is free to accept or reject this offer. If he chooses to take advantage of work in the institution for discharged prisoners, he is provided work but permitted to remain in his home at nights. He works at some trade which he feels fits in with his aptitudes and inclinations, receiving a wage slightly less than the prevailing wage in the community. Whenever he wishes to quit he may do so. During his stay at the institution, the Council concerns itself with his various problems, attempting to assist him in making his adjustment to free life.

While this is an interesting innovation, it is problematical if the effort is worth much. Certainly, in America, such projects have long been discouraged since they tend to carry over into the community, the social stigma pinned on the convict. It would be much more healthful if the Councils made more serious gestures to place each discharged prisoner in various trades along with free men, difficult as that undoubtedly is. No one has yet found a rational solution to this baffling problem of finding employment for discharged prisoners, but Italy is making a practical gesture in this direction.

Whether the inmate accepts work or not in such an establishment, he must report periodically to the Council which in turn makes reports to the surveillance judge who, in the last analysis, has control over the discharged prisoner until he is finally released from all surveillance. Thus we see the circle of imprisonment completed.

One of the interesting features of the Italian penal system is what is known as labor in the open, *"All' Aperto."* There are two such types of employment: (1) workshops in the open and; (2) mobile groups of prisoners who leave the institution to work and return at night. The first type includes agricultural colonies set up by the system in Sardinia and in the Tuscan archipelago. In Sardinia there are five such colonies covering altogether about 10,000 acres; in the Tuscan archipelago there are three colonies. Novelli enthusiastically describes these colonies, as follows:

Few foreigners know of these marvelous Italian penitentiaries inclosed by the sea, high mountains, and green pastures, in which the work done with love and pleasure by the prisoners in the elevating atmosphere created by the free life of the field helps to expiate their crimes in a splendid way. The surveillance of prisoners is reduced to an indispensable minimum. They wander through the vast fields almost entirely without supervision and, in spite of this, there has been a truly negligible number of insubordinations and escapes.[16]

(15) *ibid.*, p. 773.
(16) *loc. cit.*, p. 214.

The second type of open labor, mobile units from the institution, has proven satisfactory but more expensive due to the need for greater vigilance. All prison work is remunerated in Italy. The compensation is divided into two parts; one is reserved for the prisoner, cannot be less than one-third, and cannot be pawned or attached; from the other part, the following items are deducted: (1) sums due as payment for damages, (2) expenses for maintenance during the sentence, and (3) money due the court for prosecution of the case.

In each prison, there is an educational program, although it is on no higher plane than that found in America. As Professor Cantor says concerning this activity: "The usual elementary subjects are presented. The libraries do not excite admiration. As for personnel in charge of moral and social education the problems in Italy are . . .not different from other countries. One finds a large group of indiscriminate guards with no particular aptitude or training and a few outstanding higher officials who are exceptional."[17]

Dr. Novelli contends, however, that all prison officials must attend the school of Penal Law at the University of Rome where special courses in criminal anthropology, psychology, biology and similar subjects are offered. Custodial officers are expected to take a six month course in a special school in Rome where they are taught the principles of the penal code and the code of criminal procedure, the legal and social aims of treatment and a knowledge of institutional rules. In short, all officers in the prisons, both for men and women, must have specialized training.[18]

Children under fourteen years of age are not held responsible for their acts. There is also a strong desire to prevent adolescents from entering prison, but in some cases it is found necessary to commit them to "preventive custody" or regular sentence. But in all cases of adolescents, extreme care is taken in providing treatment. Institutions for such persons are not at all like prisons—there is no uniform garb and they are supervized by plain-clothes specialized agents. School work and recreation make up a large share of the daily program. Everything, in short, is aimed toward re-education. Sociability is developed through association of those inmates who are deemed worthy. Much emphasis on classification of young offenders and aftercare treatment is attempted. Probation, however, is very poorly organized in Italy.

To understand and evaluate the new penal code of Italy we must see it as an integral part of the framework of the now defunct Fascist philosophy. As Cantor puts it: "According to the Fascist philosophy the right to punish is the right of conserving and defending the State 'born with the State itself' which assures and guarantees the fundamental and indispensable conditions of life in common."[19] This is opposed to that philosophy which inspired the French Revolution of 1789 and which gave rise to the penal code of 1791 which served as a model for the old Italian code in operation between that era and 1931. In addition to this swing away from liberalism, the new code, as we stated above, is an attempt to carry water on both shoulders so far as the recognition of both the Classical and Positive schools of thought are concerned.

(17)   *loc. cit.*, p. 225.
(18)   *ibid.*, p. 209.
(19)   *loc. cit.*, p. 220.

While it is true that a real attempt is made at classification of types of offenders with corresponding types of treatment provided, Italy's insistence on preserving the concept of punishment as "chastisement" and for purposes of deterrence, with an oldfashioned notion of expiation thrown in, makes it obvious that little of a progressive nature can be expected to emanate from that country. Both Cantor and Monachesi, who have visited Italy since the new code went into effect, are not especially enthusiastic about the penal system. Cantor's chief criticism, hinted at throughout this section, is the confusion that exists in the dual nature of the code. And Monachesi states: "these will be little more than paper innovations unless conditions are created which are favorable to their practical realization."[20]

We cannot close this section on Italian penal methods without commenting on the work done in the field of criminal causation by contemporary students in that country. All students of criminology are familiar with the great achievements of Lombroso and Ferri. These men made a tremendous impression on Italian students who came after them and there is no doubt that their great work continues to stimulate the unusual amount of interest manifested today in the criminal and his behavior.

Lombroso did not devote all of his attention to "morphological anomalies" as is generally thought. He did accept the importance of both sociological and psychological factors in crime causation.[21]

Certainly Ferri gave quite as much emphasis to sociological factors as he did to biological. Today, the emphasis on criminological research in Italy accepts both opposite concepts. As Monachesi so clearly points out in a scholarly article, these students have attempted to ascertain the relationship between "degeneracy and criminality, neuropsychoses and criminality, psychopathic personalities and criminality, alcoholism, narcoticism and criminality, and disease and criminality."[22] As a result of these studies there has developed a school known as the "constitutional school of criminology." The thesis of this group is that the real criminal, aside from the occasional offender, is born with certain constitutional defects that make him quite susceptible to certain environmental influences which result in antisocial behavior. Consequently his heredity makes it impossible for him to react in a normal manner to social conventions and legal sanctions. It is therefore the purpose of the research undertaken to inquire into the origin of these constitutional weaknesses and to attempt an understanding of how they respond to environmental influences.

Italian research can best be summed up by the hypothesis held by one of Italy's representative students in the field, Nicola Pende, the well-known endocrinologist. According to Pende, the morphological, psychological characteristics of the individual are due to specific properties of the components of the individual's heredity. These components, or factors, in combination determine the body type of the individual, as well as his capacity to adapt and react to the stimuli furnished by the environment. The individual's constitution, therefore, is determined by his heredity prima-

(20) loc. cit., p. 820. This material, of course, was written before the invasion of Italy by the United Nations.
(21) See Lombroso's work, *Crime: Its Causes and Remedies*, English translation, 1911.
(22) Elio D. Monachesi, "Trends in Crininological Research in Italy," *American Sociological Review*, vol. 1, 1936, pp. 396-406.

rily, and, accessorily by the disturbing actions of the environment operating on this heredity.

The Italian anthropologists and psychologists contend that any abnormality of the individual, inherited by him, would obviously dispose him toward antisocial or pathological behavior. This might be offset by segregation or treatment before he would succumb to certain environmental conditions that would produce such behavior. Many Italian scholars, including such distinguished persons as Ottolenghi, DiTullio, DeSanctis, Morselli, Colella, Michel, Saparito and Aisencitat,[23] emphasize specific abnormalities and attempt to create the concept of the "delinquent constitution." Their research has been focused on two problems: (1) factors responsible for the original abnormalities in the personality of the individual; and (2) the factors in the external environment which, operating on the delinquent constitution, result in criminal behavior.

A word about some of these studies is undoubtedly of consequence although we cannot take the space to elaborate on them. Ottolenghi and his student, DiTullio, are both convinced that the "real" criminal is a biological phenomenon. The former's lectures at the Royal University of Rome, in which he used prisoners for demonstration purposes, emphasized exclusively biological principles. He even reverts to Lombrosian hypotheses by pointing out the significance of scars and tattoo marks on the criminal. According to him, they have great value in giving knowledge of the individual's morality, sensibility and attitudes. In one study he made of forty-two "real" delinquents he found without the slightest doubt, that forty of them had degenerate heredity. DiTullio's studies of alcoholics and murderers show that most of them also are victims of degenerate heredity.

The work of Jacob Aisencitat revolves principally around children. Of 1,680 neglected children, he found 1,400 abnormal. Michel, in another study of 249 felons, found that 177 were offspring of parents who suffered from mental and nervous diseases, alcoholism or criminality. He states that such offspring are ill prepared to cope with the exigencies of normal social life. Saporito, following Lombroso, studied criminality and mental illness among soldiers. Such persons, according to his findings, are retarded in their physical and psychological development as a result of defective heredity. This same observation has been made by De Sanctis and Ottolenghi. The association between tuberculosis and criminality has been noted by others of this group of research students, mainly Morselli and Colella, as well as by Ottolenghi, DeSanctis and DiTullio. These authors are agreed that tuberculosis, with its auto-intoxication, stimulates delinquent tendencies. They further add that encephalitis and syphillis act in a similar manner.

One could continue with a discussion of other similar studies of this group of men—of their work with persons suffering from traumatic cerebral conditions, emotional disorders and glandular disturbances—but enough has been said to show the trend of the Italian research students. Practically nothing has been done with environmental "causes" of crime. Then too, as Monachesi points out in his evaluation of the work accomplished by this school, criminological research can only be fruitful when biographies of "normal" individuals are presented, so that a more scientific comparison can

(23)   Mentioned by Monachesi with appropriate bibliography.

be made with those of criminals. This has been utterly neglected in Italy just as it has, to a lesser degree, in America.

PENOLOGY IN SPAIN

CONDITIONS IN EARLY SPANISH PRISONS

In early days members of the royalty maintained their own private *cárceles,* or detention prisons, a custom which gave rise to serious abuses. Later this privilege was abolished and the crown took over the control and care of prisoners. They were farmed out to hunters who were charged with their safekeeping. At night they were kept in stocks. In these early days there were no underground dungeons in Spain, an evil found all too frequently in most European countries during the medieval period. Women were usually placed under the supervision of the monasteries.

In 1329 King Alfonso XI showed some interest in the condition of prisoners and insisted that they be well treated by their jailers. Keepers of detention quarters were obliged to maintain cleanliness and to provide clean water for drinking and bathing. Nevertheless, those detained or imprisoned were obliged to pay for their keep, the rate depending on rank. Poor boxes were much in evidence throughout the countryside for the solicitation of funds to care for poor prisoners. In fact, the jailers themselves appointed their own solicitors to collect such funds. Gambling was permitted in the jails and the sexes were not segregated until 1519. The youth were not segregated until 1785.

At the end of the sixteenth century, Cristobal de Chavés, in his work *Jail of Seville (Relación de la cárcel de Sevilla)* denounced the concessions that were in operation outside the jail which were demoralizing to free citizens and prisoners alike. Prisoners with money could buy whatever they pleased and, in fact, could sleep outside the walls of the jail. As early as 1500, however, there was an organization of twenty-four "gentlemen of Salamanca" dedicated to ameliorating the abuses of the *cárceles.* Later, in 1572, another such society was formed in Seville.

During the sixteenth century, condemned criminals were sent to the galleys as was customary throughout western Europe. In 1749 it was decreed that those convicted of crimes should be sentenced to work in the mines of Almaden and out of this practice grew the so-called *presidio minero* or mine-prison. Out of this type of prison as well as the military establishments erected at Oran and Ceuta grew the idea of productive prisons.

In his *Pragmatica* of May 12, 1771, Charles III classified crimes according to the nature of those committing them. There were only two categories, those considered degenerate and those not coming under such category. Those committing the former were sent to the arsenals of Cadiz, Ferrol and Cartagena and were subjected to the hardest and most servile type of work. The others were sent to the *presidios* or prisons of Africa and were not permitted to be mistreated. In no case could one of this class be subjected to more than ten years labor.

By the end of the eighteenth century, the welfare of the convicts of Spain compared favorably with those in other countries. At least corporal punishment was not permitted. Certain types of onerous and degrading labor were abolished. Several charitable organizations showed a special concern for the welfare of prisoners.

In 1779 the Royal Association of Charity was founded. It had as its head the Count of Miranda whose statutes were approved by royal edict. In 1787 a society of women was organized to visit jails. The natural pity and the religious fervor of the Spanish people decreed that there should be no spectacle made of human suffering as was so frequent in many other countries of Europe.

Early prisons in Spain were constructed with patios in the center which were usually embellished by fountains. As shade was necessary in such warm climate, prisons were well supplied with long low corridors. While torture was rarely resorted to in most of the early prisons, dangerous convicts were always chained. A quaint custom arose whereby magistrates pardoned certain prisoners on holy days. Another unusual custom at this time—the fifteenth century—was the provision which made it possible for sentences to be altered by visiting advisors who made the rounds of the prisons.

The House of Correction movement spread to Spain during the eighteenth century somewhat belatedly. It was based on the principles of religion, education, order and work. Beggars and vagrants were kept in the *Casa de Corrección de San Fernando*, not far from Madrid. Separation of the sexes, cleanliness, adequate provisions and care of the sick were its features. Each inmate was expected to work. This edifice was constructed on the Panopticon pattern. The *Hospicio de Madrid* was another model institution dedicated to the principles of segregation of the sexes and productive labor.

In the beginning of the nineteenth century a number of outstanding students of penology published materials dealing with penology throughout the world with adaptations to Spain. Among these were: Jacobo Vilanova Jordan, *Cárceles y Presidios (Madrid,* 1819); Ventura de Arquellada, who translated the work of La Rochefoucauld on the Walnut Street Jail of Philadelphia, 1804; Marcial Antonio López, who described the prisons of Europe and America, and Hernandez, who gave to the press his *Principios* on prisons in 1820. The penal code of 1822 made provision for work on roads, public works, canals and provided inside work for those not permitted to leave the prisons. Those who worked outside the walls were chained two by two.

In 1834 the prisons were placed under what was then called the Minister of Patronage (Home Office). The general characteristics of the penal system as of this date are as follows: 1. Classification of the prisons into three classes: (a) *depositos correccionales,* where were confined those prisoners sentenced to two years; (b) *presidios peninsulares,* from two to eight years; (c) *presidios de Africa,* over eight years. 2. Separation inside each jail or prison of those of less than 18 years of age and those who were considered "infamous." 3. Continual communication (association) of prisoners day and night. 4. Obligatory work applied to the needs of the state. 5. Military discipline. 6. Auxiliaries or helpers chosen among the prisoners themselves (trusties).

During the nineteenth century three illustrious penologists appear in Spain. These were Ramón de la Sagra, Col. Manuel Montesinos, and

Baltaser Anduaga y Espinosa. The first of these was commissioned to visit the prisons of the United States and of many of the European countries. Upon his return he founded a society which was influential in having constructed a model prison, a special prison for women, a department for youth in the *Saladero de Madrid*, and factories for the "salvaging of youth." Sagra made numerous speeches on penal reform and in 1843 published an atlas of the principal jails and prisons of many of the countries of Europe.

The outstanding work of Montesinos is well known to penologists. In 1835 he was appointed governor of the prison at Valencia which at the time contained about 1,500 prisoners. He organized his establishment on a semimilitary basis with inmates as inferior officers. One reason for his success was that each inmate could earn one-third reduction from his sentence by good behavior and positive accomplishments. This was revolutionary at the time and preceded by five years the indeterminate philosophy of Alexander Maconochie on Norfolk Island in Australasia.

It is significant that when the law under which Montesinos worked was repealed, his system collapsed. He resigned in disgust and in 1846 published a pamphlet expounding his views on penal treatment. He contended that severe punishments were pernicious and fatal to reform and that selfrespect was one of the most powerful sentiments of the human mind. This, he contended, could be obtained only by introducing within the prison a form of treatment that would "receive men idle and ill-intentioned and return them to society . . . honest and industrious citizens."

Some of the chief characteristics of Montesinos' system were: separating the "good from the bad" prisoners; never altering the discipline; hard and never ending work for all inmates; rewards and punishments distributed equally; thorough study of each prisoner—"vices, instincts, culture, education, moral state and religion"; treatment with paternal solicitation. While he loved his men he was a stern disciplinarian and every prisoner worked in complete solitude.

Baltaser Anduaga y Espinosa translated and commented on the civil and penal works of Jeremy Bentham, the distinguished British reformer, and on his *Panopticon* type of prison with variations adaptable to Spain.

Other distinguished students of penology of the nineteenth century were Doña Concepción Arenal (1820-1894), Francisco Lastres and Pedro Armengol.*

It was Doña Concepción Arenal who, in 1879, wrote the following indictment of Spanish prisons to Enoch C. Wines, the distinguished American penologist of that day:

Such is the state of the prisons of Spain, set forth with exactness, which ought never to be smoothed over by a pretended patriotism, because of the love of country, so pure and so elevated, cannot take the form of a lie. No, a genuine love of country speaks the truth, which shines like an aureole for Spain. Her honest children ought to make her understand this, to the end that she may correct what is wrong; that she may blush on hearing the accusatory voices which come from beyond the mountains and the seas, accompanied by noble examples which she ought to imitate. The greatest evil and the greatest offense that can be done a people is to flatter it: and those who are ready to

* Most of the above material is taken from *Enciclopedia Universal Ilustrada*, vol 43, Madrid, 1922.

sacrifice themselves for their country will never sacrifice the truth in her supposed interest.[1]

According to Wines, writing at this time, Spain's penal legislation showed a progress far in advance of her penal practice, that is, in her mode of applying punishment. As he states:

> Codes are easily translated. But to build prisons, which require large disbursements; to adopt systems, a knowledge of which can be acquired only by profound study; to have a *personnel* of great moral and intellectual elevation; to give to the penitentiary work the indispensable succor of a loving devotion—it is necessary that the idea which looks upon the reformation of the convict as possible and rational, and that the sentiment of pity and compassion toward him penetrate society far more deeply that they have hitherto done. All this demands a public opinion enlightened and powerful, capable of overcoming the numerous obstacles which oppose penitentiary reforms, and of accepting the sacrifices which they exact. Whoever, therefore, would form an idea of the penal justice of Spain must distinguish between penal legislation and penitentiary practice.

The punishments inflicted in Spain, as of 1879 were: death (capital punishment was abolished here in 1932); hard labor for life, hard labor for a term (*travaux forcés à perpétuité, travaux forcés à temps*); reclusión (transportation) for life, reclusión for a term; the greater penal servitude, the lesser penal servitude (*presidio mayor, presidio menor*),— the *presidio* being a convict or central prison; correctional reclusión, correctional prison (*reclusión correctionelle, prison correctionelle*); forced arrests, simple arrests; banishment for life, banishment for a term; exile to an assigned place; exile.

1. *Hard labor for life, hard labor for a term.* This punishment was undergone in the convict prisons of Africa, of the Canaries, and of Outre-Mer. Those thus sentenced worked for the State at hard and painful labor. They wore a chain, of a foot length, suspended from the girdle. The youthful and the aged were relieved of some of the rigors of this type of punishment.

2. *Reclusión for life, reclusión for a term.* This was applied in establishments situated either within or without the peninsula. The convicts were subjected to hard labor for the benefit of the State.

3. *The greater or lesser penal servitude.* The first of these was undergone in the peninsula, or the Canaries, or the Balearic Islands, and the second in the peninsula. In this type of punishment, prisoners could earn some money to take with them upon release.

4. *The convict prison and the correctional prison.* The first type of imprisonment was undergone in the peninsula, or on the Balearic Islands, the second within the jurisdiction of the court which pronounced the sentence. The prisoners here worked to their own advantage at employments of their own choice, so far as possible.

5. *Forced arrest.* This was undergone in a special establishment which existed for the purpose in the local capital.

6. *Simple arrest.* This was undergone in the mayor's office, or some other house set apart for the purpose, or even in the prisoner's own home.

Women never wore chains; they were never sent away from the peninsula, and they never worked outside the penal establishment.

In spite of all these forms of punishment, in the prison establishments one could find convicts serving a wide variety of sentences. They might

(1) Enoch C. Wines, *State of Prisons and Child-Saving Institutions in the Civilized World*, 1879, p. 365.

have different dormitories, but they worked in association during the day. As Wines states: "The honest citizen, who has broken the law in a moment of passion, and the cruel, depraved, and incorrigible criminal."[2] He continues: "Neither the legislator nor the administration nor public opinion takes notice of the injustice and the absurdity that result from the fact that the code ordains, and the sentence pronounces, that which can by no possibility be reduced to practice."

Conditions in the detention prisons were deplorable except for those who were able to pay for better quarters and some comforts. Aside from the segregation of the sexes, there was no classification. Wines wrote of the exploitation of the accused or suspected prisoners by the guards in these prisons. He says: "This is exercised in an infinite number of ways by those who are charged with the maintenance of order, who, by menaces, by violence, by vexations of all sorts, compel even the poor prisoners to contrive ways of getting money to buy off ill-treatment."[3] Privileges that might be bought ranged from entire liberty of action within the prison to that of going out on promenade or to visit in the *café*, granted even to prisoners accused of serious offenses. The personnel in these detention prisons was of a low order, without any special qualifications. As one judge of Madrid wrote: "One of the causes (perhaps the most potent) productive of crime at Madrid is the state of the detention prison for men; that is to say, the organization, the discipline, the staff, the vices and customs of the *Saladero* (prison)."

Of the prison (*presidio*) buildings in Spain, they were designated "bad" and "worse"; none was fit for a penitentiary, according to Wines. In the prisons: "the vast number of convicts carries demoralization and disorder to the highest point." Food, at that time, was supplied on contract. The rations were insufficient and of inferior quality; convicts slept on mats—a piece of tissue of Spanish broom—with a thin coverlet over them. The dormitories were ill ventilated and were called "stables" by the inmates. Classification was impossible since there were no physical facilities to make this possible. More than half of the convicts were idle which led to discontent and immorality. There was no remuneration for labor performed. There was a class of convicts who were given custodial authority. They were called *caporaux á verge* (sergeants of the birch) and did no work except to preserve order among the others. Other convicts were used wherever their services could be utilized. Many were clerks in the prisons. They were chosen because of their ability to do specific tasks and regardless of their offense. Religion was a mockery. In a prison of 1,100 convicts, there was one chaplain who, because of his low salary furnished by the state, was looked upon as a mere overseer by the inmates.

Wines, commenting on Spanish penology, states: "The punishment undergone in these conditions is neither exemplary nor correctional, and it mortifies in the inverse ratio of the convict's perversity. If the punishment does not intimidate, neither does it reform; and one of the rare cases in which all Spaniards are of the same opinion is, that the convicts leave the prison worse than they entered it." Recidivism, at that time, was low in Spain because police methods were poor, the administration of

(2) p. 367.
(3) p. 369.

justice very imperfect, and criminal statistics very inexact. To the abuses found in the prison régime, may be added the even greater abuse—right of pardon. These were obtained through pure chance or favor. Not only was this true, but commutation of punishments was bestowed in honor of political days, which are called *fastes* (lucky days).

Major Arthur Griffiths, writing on Spanish prisons twenty years later, reiterated every word of condemnation uttered by Enoch Wines. Irons, chains, and other modes of restraint were much in evidence wherever convicts were assembled. The novelist Cervantes, writing three hundred years earlier, describes Don Quixote meeting a dozen men chained by the neck, *ensartados como cuentas,* strung together like beads on a rosary, all handcuffed, some with leg-chains and others with waist-chains. Griffiths states that there were many laws and regulations prescribed as to the kind of fetters to be used on criminals, as well as their application. There were shackles, fetters, halters, *guarda amigo,* the "hold-friend," similar to the English "come along with me" double handcuff.

Indicting Spanish prisons in realistic fashion, Major Griffiths nevertheless paid high tribute to that outstanding penal administrator, Manuel Montesinos at Valencia, whose work has already been reviewed.

Every conceivable building which by a wide stretch of the imagination could be adapted for the housing of convicts was used in Spain. Griffiths stated that of the 456 correctional prisons of the country, only 166 could be deemed suitable at all for that function. Some of the more ancient had once been palaces, some fortresses, one had once been the *abattoir* and salting place for pigs. This prison was described as follows:

> It was the most meagre, dark, and dirty place imaginable, although it had a deeper depth, the dungeon known as "hell," which was so pitch-dark that when new-comers arrived, the old hands, to make out their faces, struck matches which they had made out of their linen steeped in grease saved from their food. When this prison was emptied, it was found impossible to clean the filth encrusted through long years upon the floor, and the whole place had to be swept away before the new buildings were begun. But the new prison was little improvement on its predecessor; lighted but dimly, having had but just enough air to keep the pork from being tainted. . . Children and youth were lodged in a windowless loft open to all weathers. They were kept half-starved and nearly naked; they were denied the name as well as the rights of human beings, and were known as *micos,* or monkeys.[4]

This prison was erected in 1883. It was situated in Madrid and known as the Saladero.

The prison colony at Ceuta, on the African coast, was Spain's contribution to the system of penal transportation. This penal settlement was thriving at the time Major Griffiths wrote of Spanish prisons. While it was somewhat of a show place for the Spaniards, Griffiths had little of commendation to say regarding it. Doña Concepción Arenal, mentioned above as one of Spain's crusading penal reformers, described the Ceuta colony prisons, as follows: "In them it is justice which is punished— or, more exactly, crucified—and with it hygiene, morality, decency, humanity— all, in a word, which every one, who is not himself hateful and contemptible, respects. It is impossible to give the reader any idea of the state of the *cuartel principal,* or chief barrack of Ceuta; we can only refer to its terrible and revolting demoralization."[5]

(4) *Secrets of the Prison House,* London, 1894, vol. I, p. 338.
(5) Quoted by Griffiths, *ibid.,* pp. 350-351.

Other prisons condemned by Major Griffiths in 1894 were; the citadel prison, Hacho, where the men, numbering 800 to 1,000, "were clad only in soldiers' tattered red breeches, or as often naked to indecency, and tottered in and out of their wretched sheds they called their homes, devoured and quarreled like hyenas over their insufficient fare; smuggled knives into the fortress, and fought and killed one another like wild beasts"; and a "still worse prison, the Presidio del Campo, the 'Field Prison' in which the chain-gangs still employed on public works were detained, in filthier hovels, with less food, greater ruffians in the majority, and more general demoralization." He further quotes a Spanish officer: "They are not *presidios*, but dens of fornication and nurseries of thieves."[6]

Thirty-five years later, in 1928, an English writer, Mr. Stacy Aumonier, tried for three months to gain permission to enter a Spanish prison in order to observe its internal functioning. He tried every conceivable channel and influence possible but to no avail. He was told by one influential resident that "the authorities were, as a matter of fact, a little ashamed of their prisons." Being unable, therefore, to see inside of a prison, Mr. Aumonier did the next best thing: he interviewed a reputable English business man, manager of a big red ochre works in Malaga, who unfortunately, was obliged to spend a night in prison for accidentally running over a child with his car. This was in 1928. The following description rivals those presented earlier by Wines and Griffiths:

> The prison was built, like most Spanish and Arab buildings round a central patio. In this case the patio was just a prison yard in an indescribable state of filth. It was by this time past ten o'clock, and the prisoners had been shut into their cages. There were six of these cages, each holding fifty prisoners. A "cage," indeed, was the only name that could have been applied to them. They had three solid stone walls with no windows, a stone ceiling and a stone floor. The fourth side was a thick iron grille, with a padlocked iron door opening on to the central patio. Collins (the detained manufacturer) said the night was intensely sultry. . . He wandered around the patio and peered into the cages, but the smell emanating from them was almost overpowering. . . After a while he went up to one of the cages and called into it. He wondered if by any chance a fellow countrymen might be in one of these poisonous holes. After a minute or so he said that he saw three or four weird figures advance toward the door of the cage. They were all stark naked. . .He discovered afterward that the majority of them were gypsies. Moreover, owing to their confinement and the vile nature of their treatment they were either mentally deficients, or little removed from animals. They stood there scratching themselves and jibbering at him.
>
> He learnt also that the prisoners in these cages are given nothing in the way of mattresses. They sleep on the stone. If one has money, he may buy a mattress when he goes in, but it is a doubtful advantage, for the mattress has a way of attracting all the vermin in the cage, and after a week or two it almost walks away from him. The food is so inadequate that the prisoners would starve to death but for outside charity. In the yard is one water tap for the 300 prisoners, but no means of taking a bath. A man may be there for years without having a bath or a change of linen.
>
> There is no discrimination between the prisoners, a youth and first offender is herded into the same cage with hardened criminals and moral degenerates. There are priests connected with the prison, but they only appear in the gallery above the yard, and offer up prayers and solemn masses. They never mix with the prisoners, who are left almost entirely to their own devices. Once in prison there is no appeal (to the authorities). No one takes any notice. Without money or influence you may languish there for years untried, or with your sentence undetermined.[7]

(6) *ibid.,* pp.. 352-353.
(7) "A Prison in Spain," *Fortnightly Review,* vol. 124, July-December, 1928, pp. 243-249.

The author of this account states that during Holy Week, when one of the religious processions passes the prison, one of the convicts is freed, which is, as he states: "a very beautiful idea."

SPANISH PRISONS UNDER FRANCO

It has been very difficult to procure much reliable information regarding the penal system in Spain immediately prior to and since the Spanish Civil War. As an aftermath of that bitter struggle overcrowding of the worst sort has marked the penal régime. Food and material shortages have had their effect upon conditions in Spanish penal institutions as well as in the concentration establishments where hundreds of thousands of political prisoners have been incarcerated.

It is not relevant here to discuss or describe the wretched conditions existing in the prisons for political prisoners.[8] Suffice it to say, however, that there has been a decided trend in releasing the number of those considered enemies of the new régime from prison. For example, the official number of prisoners reported in all Spanish prisons in 1933 was 12,574. In 1939, when Franco assumed control of the country, the number of all prisoners amounted to 100,000. By January, 1940, there were 270,719. In January, 1941, there were 233,328 and in January, 1942, 159,392. At the present time it is reported that there are some 93,000 prisoners of all kinds, exclusive of interned or detained refugees entering Spain without proper papers. Of this number, 49,000 are said to be political prisoners who were tried by tribunals of military jurisdiction.*

The number of penal establishments of a permanent type operated under the central Spanish government is said to have increased from 12 before the civil war to 27 at the present time. These are as follows:

Alcalá de Henares (penitentiary with workshops) with a penitentiary for women also; Alicante (reformatory); Almaden; Burgos; Calzada de Oropesa (for women); Celanova; Cuellar (sanatorium); Dueso (penal settlement); El Puig (for women); Figueiredo; Gijón; Guadalajara; Hellín; Santa Rita, Madrid; Yeserias, Madrid; Ocaño (reformatory); Pamplona; Pastrana (military); Puerto de Santa Maria; Segovia (hospital-asylum); Santander, for tuberculars; Santiago de Compostela; Totana; Talavera de la Reina; San Miguel de los Reyes, Valencia; and Chinchilla. Fifteen of these 27 establishments have been constructed since the Civil War.

In addition to the above, the administration under Franco has established a fluctuating number of penal institutions in buildings originally created for other purposes. There are also local prison camps as well as local prisons under provincial authorities.

From recent publications of the Franco régime, notably *La Obra de la Redención de Penas* (1941), we find that much emphasis is placed on the necessity of keeping all prisoners productively employed. Convicts are

---

(8)   The reader is referred to articles by Ernest Scheuer, "Spanish Women in Prison," *Free World* November, 1942, pp. 134-137, and Klaus Dohrn, "Franco's Prisons," *The Commonweal*, December 31, 1943, pp. 274-276, for descriptions of conditions in Franco's prisons for political prisoners.

* These figures have been disputed by some critics of the Franco regime who now reside in this country. Due, however, to the recent weakening of the dictator's position, it is quite possible that most political prisoners have been released. Some 8,000 additional prisoners were released at Christmas 1943.

assigned to the prison closest to the point of conviction and assigned to one of the following types of work: 1. Inside the prison in workshops; 2. Outside on government projects and with other convicts; and 3. In private industry. This is based upon the seriousness of the crime with the provision made for passing from one grade of labor to another. If the prisoner is not familiar with a trade he is taught one in the prison workshop.

Much is made of painting and sculpturing in Spanish prisons. The impression is given that many inmates spend much of their time in these forms of cultural pursuits. When work is scarce in the penal establishments, those (a) with the lightest sentences, or (b) with professional aptitudes, or (c) with dependent children, or (d) who can exercise speed, are given preference. Each day of work is the equivalent of two of the sentence; hence, work is much sought after. Wages are strictly controlled by the administration even though the prisoner works for a private concern. The amount of wages depends on the ability of the prisoner as well as the number of dependents he has.

Education within the prisons is primarily of a religious nature and is conducted by priests and nuns. This is especially true of women's institutions. Civics and political indoctrination are provided by the government; all other instruction is in the hands of the church. The priest teachers also take charge of illiterates. The painting and sculpturing is also in the hands of the priests.

In some prisons there are no cells whereas in others each man has his own cell. The former institutions are made up of dormitories. There is a free and easy association of prisoners, especially in recreation and religious functions. On religious holidays there are special festivals under the direction of the prison administration and church at which time relatives and friends are permitted to visit the inmates.

There does not seem to be any type of guard training in the present-day prison régime. There is a sort of conditional release which provides for release to well behaved prisoners whose sentence is about to expire. Those thus released must behave according to certain rules and must report to the prison administration.

One gets the impression that there is much room for improvement in Spanish penology. For example, only rudimentary probation exists. A law was passed in 1908 introducing certain conservative features of probation such as making it applicable only to first offenders and then only when certain offenses were committed. Juvenile courts were not established until 1918 but they were restricted to the larger cities.[9]

Regardless of the status of penal philosophy or prison administration of a country, there is likely to be considerable and lively research in criminological matters. This often carries over into penal research as well. Spain has been no exception in this. Within the past fifty years as well as at present many distinguished students have made definite contributions to the fields of both criminology and penology, but more especially to the former. One need but mention a few of these whose works are well-known in both of the Americas, North and South.

Perhaps the best known students of general criminology are the critic,

(9) For details on probationary measures in Spain, see Timasheff, *One Hundred Years of Probation*, Part II, Fordham University Press, 1943, pp. 23, 49.

C. Bernaldo de Quiros, Dorado Montero, and Julio Aramburu. A great authority on penal law is Luis Jiménez de Asúa who is now in Argentina. Interested in the etiology of delinquency has been Eugenio Calon, while Quintiliano Saldaña has made extensive contributions to the field of criminal law and criminal anthropology. Perhaps the best known student of the field from this country was Rafael Salillas, author of the noted work *El delincuente espanol,* 1898, and who was for many years the head of the official School of Criminology in Spain.

It is, therefore, essential that Spain be recognized first for the rise of prison labor and the indeterminate sentence, at the hands of Montesinos and second, the eminence of her later scholars in the progressive study of the law which accounts, to no little degree, for the progressive concepts of criminal law in Latin America. Actual penal reform, however, has been retarded primarily by reactionary political and economic conditions as well as the social upheaval in that unhappy country.

THE PRISON SYSTEM OF PORTUGAL

Little information regarding Portugal's penal system has reached this country in recent times. Professor Arthur E. Morgan, who visited Portugal some years ago, was quite impressed with the *Colonia Penal Agricola de Antonio Maciera* located near Sentra,[1] and V. S. Pritchett enthusiastically described the large modern prison in Lisbon.[2] The latter writer was impressed with all of the features of this Lisbon prison except the régime of separate confinement which Portugal still maintains.

For many years Portuguese authorities recognized that its system of penal treatment needed a complete revision. The number of penal institutions, as well as the nature of those already in existence, was considered insufficient for the needs of the country in curbing crime. The decree of May 28, 1936 was a conscientious attempt to remedy these shortcomings.[3]

This decree was realistic and comprehensive. The items covered were: types of institutions needed; construction and equipment necessary; types of punishment and treatment to be invoked; means of individualizing punishment; means of gradually adapting the prisoner to eventual freedom; forms of conditional liberty; organization of work for prisoners; organization of bureaus and other services to insure consistency in prison administration; and the selection and training of prison personnel.

The decree is thoroughgoing in so many particulars that it unquestionably ushers in a new dispensation in Portuguese penal philosophy. To what extent it has been put into operation, however, is not known.

At the outset the decree recognizes the importance of both insuring the measures of security by setting up suitable punishment for those considered social menaces, and developing a régime that will result in the readaptation of the criminal to a free society. It provides for individualization of treatment by differentiating the various penal units for special classes and for special treatment for minors.

Aside from the local jails for detention, there are two types of insti-

(1) *Prison Journal,* January, 1932. pp. 22-24.
(2) "Spring in Lisbon," *Fortnightly Review,* June, 1932, pp. 703-706.
(3) This material is a digest of an article on Portugal's prison system appearing in *Recueil de Documents en Matiere Penale et Penitentiaire,* vol. IX, No. 2, November, 1940, pp. 133-143.

tutions: the prisons and the establishments for security (*éstablissements de sûreté*).

The prisons are divided into the following categories: departmental (for punishments up to three months); central (for longer periods); and penitentiaries (for long term imprisonment, *réclusion*). The decree also provides for other special prison institutions for the observation and treatment of special types of criminals. These are prison schools, prison hospitals, maternity prisons, asylums for abnormal criminals, and penal colonies outside the country for habitual criminals and political prisoners.

The establishments of security include hospitals for mental criminals, workhouses for mendicants and alcoholics, and special institutions for delinquent minors.

The decree adopted the cellular type of prison construction so that there may be isolation of the inmates at least during the night.

Article 19 provides for *preventive detention* in either complete isolation or association during the daytime. The sentence of *arrest* calls for complete isolation but with certain modifications of exercise in the fresh air and work in association, to be carried on in departmental prisons.

The punishment of *imprisonment* is carried on in the central prisons. It begins with a three month isolation period with exercise. This initial period may be prolonged if the attitude of the prisoner warrants it. Its purpose is for observation. During this period the inmate is visited by the physician and social workers who determine when the prisoner may be ready to pass to the next stage of treatment.

The decree adopted the progressive system of penal discipline. After the period of cellular isolation, the prisoner passes to another degree in which he may worship, go to school or work under the rule of silence. His meals are served in his cell and he sleeps alone. After the inmate has served one-third of his sentence, or at least three months, he may be passed to the third degree which is in association except at night. After one-half of the sentence is served, or at least six months, he is passed to the fourth degree where he may have certain concessions.

The transfer from one degree to another, together with retrogression to a lower degree, is ordered by the director of the prison on the advice of the Technical Council of the prison. In cases of doubt the Institute of Criminology may be consulted. If the prisoner fails to make an adequate adjustment he may be transferred to a penal colony for habitual or difficult criminals.

The sentence of *réclusion* is served in its initial stage in cellular isolation from three to six months with daily exercise in the open air. If an institute of criminology functions near the prison the inmate may be sent there for observation. The time spent in the various grades or degrees is similar to that in the central prisons.

For young offenders Portugal created specialized prison schools and correctional colonies a long time ago. These institutions also house children up to the age of sixteen sentenced to prison. In addition, separate sections are provided for those between the ages of 16 and 18 who have been charged with begging, loitering, drinking and other such minor offenses. The regular group of delinquents between those ages is sent to correctional colonies, for minors.

The purpose of the prison school is educational. It is divided into four sections: observation, limited responsibility, complete responsibility, and semiliberty. During the observational period, the young delinquent is placed in a cell; in the next two phases he enjoys association except at night. The last stage continues until the director and the council decide on his release. However, he may not be kept in this institution after he has reached the age of twenty-five.

The decree of 1936 also provided for prison sanatoria or hospitals for tuberculars and others suffering from serious diseases calling for long medical treatment. Maternity prisons for female delinquents who have children up to the age of three have also been provided. If the mother has not been released from prison by the time her child reaches three years of age, a tribunal for minors assumes charge of the child and takes appropriate measures after social investigation.

Special prisons are created for the habitual criminal. The period of isolation is double that served in other establishments and the progressive stage system is applied in corresponding fashion. If the prisoner shows a tendency to reform he may be transferred to an ordinary prison. Some of these institutions are outside the country. Political prisoners are also sent out of the country.

Workhouses and agricultural colonies have been created to house and treat mendicants, vagabonds, alcoholics and others of this type. The time sentence ranges from one to six years.

In the prison asylums may be found those suffering from mental diseases. These are annexes to the regular prisons and are in charge of physicians in consultation with the director of the prison.

The capacity of the prisons in Portugal, according to the decree of 1936, is limited to 500 for the most part and 200 for those caring for misdemeanants. A Commission of Construction for prisons functions under the Minister of Public Works.

The execution of the penal sentence, according to the decree, must be such that it will preserve the fundamental idea of deterrence but at the same time maintain the philosophy of readaptation of the criminal to the free society. Treatment that is either inhuman or unproductive is forbidden. The decree states that not only should the submission to the prison rules be considered but also the aptitudes and abilities of the prisoner be recognized and encouraged.

Justice and humanity are essential in penal administration. Prisoners must not be humiliated or be made to suffer by treatment that will militate against reformation. Objectives of treatment should involve specifically a sense of order and respect for the law, interest in work and a sense of responsibility for the general welfare.

Recreation and amusements not in harmony with penal treatment and which might prevent reformation are forbidden. Those suggested are lectures or moving pictures which exercise a wholesome influence.

Prisoners must be given periodical examinations—psychological, anthropological and vocational. Definite provision as to dress, medical care and types of food to be furnished the prisoners are all set down in the decree.

All prisoners are obliged to work according to their ability and strength. Those charged with crime but who have not yet been tried, as well as political prisoners, may choose a type of work providing it is compatible with the institutional management. They may engage in intellectual work, even though it is unproductive. All other types of prisoners must do work assigned to them which must be productive in nature. When assignments are selected it is necessary to consider not only physical, intellectual and professional abilities of the inmate but also the possibilities for use in the future after his release.

Working hours in the prisons depend on age, sex and the type of sentence but are greater than those of free laborers. Various systems of prison labor have been worked out. In no case is work to interfere with the internal order or discipline of the prison nor with the fundamental objective for which the sentence was imposed; nor should the measures of safety be placed in jeopardy.

Compensation of prisoners is divided into four parts: to defray the cost of maintenance; to pay an indemnity for the crime; to assist dependents; and to build up a reserve (*pécule*). This reserve may be applied toward the day of release.

Prisoners may follow their own religious beliefs and may be visited by their own spiritual advisers but in no case may any form of religious service be made compulsory. In addition to religious advisers, teachers and social workers are charged with the moral instruction of the prisoners. They serve to stimulate the inmates in their work and to assist in their family problems; they also help them secure work upon release.

So far as education is concerned, Portuguese prisons provide classes for the illiterate and attendance is mandatory for these. Advanced courses are provided for others which are optional. Inmates are separated while attending school. Libraries are also provided.

Visitors are permitted under certain restrictions. They are supervized by a prison attendant. Correspondence is also strictly regulated.

When a prisoner is released from prison, without condition, he may ask for a testimonial on his abilities and conduct from the Association of Patronage without prejudice of imprisonment. Conditional release is granted by the Minister of Justice on the qualified recommendation of the Director of Prisons. This official, in turn, must act on the advice of the Institute of Criminology and the Superior Council of Criminal Services. The release ranges from two to five years with successive renewals of two years and with ten years the maximum. The obligations placed upon the prisoner depend on his case. These may include: reparation of damages to his victim, forced residence in designated regions, the exercise of a profession or trade, and a pledge of good conduct. If he can find no employment he may be obliged to go to a home for the unemployed or by act of the Minister of Justice sent to an oversea colony. Certain types of released prisoners may request to be sent to these colonies at state expense. If the conditional release is revoked for some violation the prisoner is returned to the prison for from six months to two years.

The conditionally released prisoner is turned over to the care of social workers or placed under the supervision of the police.

Pardon may take the form of *grace* (outright) or commutation of sentence but in either case it is subordinated to the regulations governing conditional release. The applicant for a pardon petitions the Minister of Justice on the advice of the Director of the prison.

The Association of Patronage functions throughout Portugal with funds supplied by both private and public sources controlled by official decree.

The general supervision of Portugal's prisons is under the Minister of Justice operating through the Director General of Prisons. Numerous functions relating to the prisons are granted to a Superior Council which advises the Minister. Prison inspection is carried on as frequently as the authorities see fit. The Council is composed of the Minister of Justice who presides, the Procurer General of the Republic, a judge of the Court of Cassation, two professors from the school of law, the president of the Supreme Council of the Society of Lawyers, the Director General of Prisons, the Director General in charge of minors, and three laymen.

The personnel of the prisons must be trained so that they may be charged not only with custody but training of prisoners as well. Each prison must be supplied with an ordained minister, the denomination depending on the faith of the majority of the prisoners; one or two physicians, a psychologist, social workers of either sex, some of whom are paid and some volunteers. The personnel is appointed by the Minister of Justice, with or without civil service. A school is set up to train personnel.

A technical council operates in each prison presided over by the Director and composed of a physician and one other person designated by the Minister. In addition, there is an Administrative Council composed of the Director of the Budget and the Prison Director. The Institute of Criminology is also a part of the penal system.

As early as 1852, Portugal provided for an incipient form of probation. The penal code of that year made it possible for judges to replace punishment by a reprimand if the offender had previously led a law-abiding life. However, if such an offender committed an offense later he was treated as a recidivist.[4]

A law passed May 27, 1911 created a Board for the Protection of Children whose duties were similar to those of the juvenile courts in the United States. Probation work is carried on by agents of the National Federation of Institutions for the Protection of Children.[5]

(4)   Timasheff, *op. cit.*, p. 12.
(5)   *ibid.*, p. 39.

CHAPTER IV

PENOLOGY IN HOLLAND AND SCANDINAVIA

THE PRISONS IN HOLLAND

In any discussion of the prison system of Holland, attention must be called to John Howard's several visits to that little country. He was much impressed with conditions then existing in the prisons and workhouses there. He wrote in 1775: "Prisons are so quiet, and most of them so clean, that a visitor can hardly believe he is in a gaol. They are commonly white-washed once or twice a year; and prisoners observed to me how refreshing it was to come into the rooms after they had been so thoroughly cleaned. A physician and surgeon is appointed to every prison: and prisoners are in general healthy."[1]

He noted with great satisfaction that in every prison criminals were given a room to themselves, thus making for complete separation. However, in the rasphouses or spinhouses, prisoners were in association, but kept diligently employed. He described the great prisons at Rotterdam, Middleburg, Amsterdam, Zwolle, Leeuwarden and Utrecht with keen satisfaction. While the Dutch were capable of extending severe punishment, especially in capital crimes, they accepted their responsibility of training prisoners for later life with a thoroughness so characteristic of that country. The following statement from Howard's remarks bears out this observation, which could be made even today: "I leave this country with regret, as it affords a large field for information on the important subject I have in view. I know not which to admire most, the neatness and cleanliness appearing in the prisons, the industry and regular conduct of the prisoners, or the humanity and attention of the magistrates and regents."[2]

William Penn, a hundred years earlier, was also much impressed with the houses of correction which he visited in the Netherlands. They served as a model for that which he hoped to establish in his new colony in Pennsylvania. The workhouse at Amsterdam was a rival to the famous prison at Ghent, operated by Vilain, in carrying out progressive ideas on penal treatment.

The philosophy of separate confinement as exemplified by the Pennsylvania System, was formally inaugurated by law in Holland in 1851, although separation was not unknown for certain offenders much earlier. In 1854, corporal punishment and branding were abolished by the Dutch, and in 1870, capital punishment as well. The last execution took place in 1861.[3]

The outline of the present system of penal institutions in the Netherlands was fixed by the Penal Code of 1886. At that time, the entire system of penal establishments was put under the control of the Minister of

(1) *State of Prisons*, E. P. Dutton, 1929, p. 47.
(2) *ibid.*, p. 61.
(3) For a treatment of penal law in Holland, see W. A. Bonger, "Development of the Penal Law in the Netherlands," *Journal of Criminal Law and Criminology*, vol. 24, May-June, 1933, pp. 260-270.

Justice, appointed by the King. He delegated his authority to two officials; the inspector-general, who is in general charge of the prisons, and who deals with penal legislation and represents the government; and a "referendary," who has charge of the administration directly and also handles all accounts.

In the early days of the Penal Code of 1886, all prisoners sentenced to five years or less, were placed in separate confinement. All over that period were placed in congregate labor after serving that part of their sentence in separation. However, separation longer than five years was optional.

As early as 1823, an organization was established to care for released prisoners. It was known as "The Society of the Netherlands for the Moral Amelioration of Prisoners," and exerted a great influence on the development of the prison system. Writing in 1903, Professor Charles Richmond Henderson, stated:

> The organization has given special attention to instruction and religious help, and that at a time when these matters were regarded by the Government as mere accessories and were not treated in a manner worthy of their importance. They have rendered valuable aid to young offenders. It has several local branches, all under a central bureau, so that it is made up of a federation of societies, all working under one regulation for a common purpose, and directed from a central office. The statutes of the society express one purpose—in the prisons to uplift the prisoners, and outside to aid those discharged, and especially to protect the young offenders.[4]

The penitentiary system of the Netherlands in its early days did not recognize penal labor, as such, calling it "useful work" only. This is significant since work for prisoners in many systems throughout the world was degrading and arduous. While hard work has always been imposed, the prisoner was permitted somewhat of a choice. Much of it was hand work and wages were always paid. Punishments were decreed by the code of 1886 and were more in the nature of deprivations, although a bread and water diet and a "stretch" in a dark cell were also provided for more refractory inmates.

We shall now turn to the prison system as it operated before the current war. There are three special prisons, viz: Leeuwarden, for men serving sentences of at least five years' penal servitude; Rotterdam, for women serving like sentences; and the Hague, for tubercular prisoners, old men, prisoners under observation, and those who refuse to do military service. There are, also, twenty ordinary and eight emergency prisons corresponding to English local prisons, and twenty-one Houses of Correction. In addition, there are three labor colonies—Veenhuizen and Hoorn for men and Gorinchem for women. Vagrants, beggars and drunkards go to Veenhuizen and to Hoorn are sent what we might call recidivists. Here the discipline is more severe.[5]

As we stated above, Holland, like so many European countries, adopted and studiously maintained the system of separate confinement, patterned after the Pennsylvania plan. Only within recent years have modifications been introduced to break this monotonous and outmoded form of discipline. In 1924 the Minister of Justice sent out a request to

(4) *Modern Prison Systems*, 1903, p. 105.
(5) The material used here is from *The Howard Journal*, October, 1928, article on Holland's prisons by M. H. Moll, pp. 242-245.

all prison governors asking their advice as to how this system could be tempered. Acting on some of the suggestions received, he ordered the following: (1) Certain privileges to be introduced after thirty days, such as use of the library and the canteen; greater facilities for seeing friends; and permission to attend prison lectures; (2) More privileges to be introduced after four months. These are: permission to read a newspaper; restricted censorship, and in some cases, free correspondence; more visitors; windows of transparent panes in the cells and painted instead of whitewashed walls; use of pictures and permission to have pets in the cells; permission to stay up later at night; permission to shave themselves and to wear their own clothes on Sundays and holidays; permission to smoke; and provision for outdoor exercise.

There has continued a strong desire on the part of the Dutch authorities gradually to abolish the strict form of the solitary prison and permit more open air work, in association. This was tried with favorable results in the prison at Veenhuizen. Labor seems to be plentiful in the Dutch prisons. Among those trades taught are weaving, printing, bookkeeping, tailoring, leather work, sail making, shoemaking, brush making, the manufacture of sacks and firelighters, and the usual conventional trades of carpentry and furniture manufacturing. In addition, there is a form of school to be found in each prison.

A strong effort is made by all judicial authorities to keep as many persons out of prison as possible. This is done by extending the use of the fine. If the fine cannot be paid, sometimes the offender's goods and income are confiscated rather than to be sent to prison.

In 1931, through the efforts of Dr. Frida Katz, a member of Parliament, a study was made of female offenders of which there are very few in Holland. A report was issued in 1935. Prior to that date women were housed in sections of the men's prisons. The report of that year urged that all women should be housed in one institution with facilities provided for their reclamation. It is not known whether this recommendation was acted on. In 1936 there were two institutions for girls. These were well equipped and managed on a high level.

The Dutch authorities also maintain an "Association for Education of Prison Staffs." Members meet regularly, lectures are held, books and magazines are read aloud and discussed.

What has taken place in Holland since the current war, we are unable to state. It would seem, however, that the authorities were making serious atempts to effect reforms in their penal discipline. No doubt this effort will continue after hostilities cease and the normal processes of life once again are restored.

PENAL PHILOSOPHY IN SCANDINAVIA

One of the most enlightened penal philosophies in Europe, judged in the light of the temperament and social philosophy of the people, is to be found in the Scandinavian countries, Norway, Sweden and Denmark. All three countries were definitely influenced by the Pennsylvania System of separate confinement—introduced in Sweden by King Oscar in 1840, in Denmark in 1846, and Norway in 1851—and all of them still carry on this form of treatment, however diluted it may be in certain cases.

As we survey these countries today, noting their progressive concepts in every realm dealing with the welfare of humanity, we can scarcely understand that these same people, during the time of John Howard, were meting out the most barbaric forms of corporal and capital punishments to the wayward. True, this was prevalent all over Europe, but the Scandinavian countries were doubtless even more bloodthirsty and severe. This may be accounted for by the fact that the old Norse traditions of blood vengeance merely reflected the harsh climate they had to withstand. However this may be, these three countries have swung over to a more rational and humane penal philosophy to a surprising degree.

John Howard tells us that at the entrance to many towns in Denmark one could see the whipping-post; on gibbets and wheels the bodies of unfortunate wretches dangled where all might see and profit thereby. Some of the more heinous crimes were punished by being broken on the wheel, although the usual form of execution was with the axe. He reported that there were many child murders and the penalty was work in the spinhouse for life with a severe whipping annually. This was considered the most severe of all punishments. The descriptions he gives of the unsanitary conditions found in the prisons of Rendsburg and Copenhagen are revolting. All of the horrible conditions found in most gaols and prisons throughout Europe ensued in Denmark.

In Sweden, Howard observed that private homes were much cleaner than in Denmark. Hoping this would be true with the prisons as well, he was quite unprepared to find the same filthy conditions existing, especially in the men's apartments. He visited the three prisons in the city of Stockholm and was sickened by the sights he saw. Scurvy was prevalent, due to "the want of cleanliness, to close confinement, and to the use of saltfish and other salt provisions." Men convicts were loaded down with irons but he was told that this type of treatment was never inflicted on the women. They were kept busy with needlework.

He happily found that many of the prisoners were employed at spinning and he was pleased also that some were able to make money if they did more than their "stint." Diligence to work further gave them time off their sentence. There were hours for prayers and for recreation, but, in general, the inmates were kept at their tasks most of the time.

Sweden operated on a penal code formulated in 1734, draconic in nature, down to the year 1864. This latter code drastically mitigated the old penalties, among which was a diminution of capital crimes, and the elimination of such revolting practices as death by torture followed by "the infamous treatment of the corpse."[1] As the years progressed, Sweden became more progressive insofar as punishments were concerned. For example, in 1890, the old penal servitude for life sentence in larceny cases was abolished; the death penalty was abolished in 1921, and, perhaps more noteworthy, the revamping of the laws regulating the amounts of fines to be paid. Here it was decreed that individuals were to be fined according to their ability to pay.

Today these three northern countries are, in many respects, quite similar in their philosophy and in their treatment of the offender, whereas

---

(1) See Olof Kinberg, "Criminal Policy in Sweden during the Last Fifty Years," *Journal of Criminal Law and Criminology*, vol 24, May-June, 1934, pp. 313-332.

in others, they differ, but never to any great degree. This is undoubtedly due to the likemindedness of the people who live in these three enlightened and literate states.

One of the major features worthy of special consideration, found in all three countries, is the progressive attitude taken toward those awaiting trial. While they must remain in seclusion, without benefit of bail or visits from friends, they are housed in commodious rooms, rather than cells, each one completely segregated from any other prisoners. To quote Mr. Viktor Almquist, formerly Director-in-Chief of the Board of Prisons of Stockholm, Sweden:

> According to the Scandinavian point of view, it was held that the accused should, during the preparation of a trial be held in isolation, enjoying certain comforts, but under such conditions that he could not communicate freely with individuals outside of the personnel of the court or of the prison . . .Each cell [is] furnished with regular doors . . .with a window of its own . . .which made the room somewhat more pleasant as a living quarter.[2]

The reforms in these countries have started from the point of considering the person's civil rights prior to his trial. As early as 1864, it was decreed that "detention shall be of such a nature that it is not dangerous to the health of the person detained, nor shall several people be placed in one room when it can be avoided . . . and finally, a person arrested must not be detained (in any case) in company with one who is serving a prison sentence."[3]

In order to care properly for detained persons awaiting trial, these countries have supplied themselves with many local places of detention, each local unit having its own. In Sweden there are 178 such detention houses, used for that purpose exclusively; over a hundred in Norway, and 101 "arrest houses" in Denmark. However, in the latter country, these detention centers also house a large number of persons serving sentence. This dubious concession has made it possible in Denmark to limit her state prisons to four.

In Sweden, there is a large detention house in Stockholm in which offenders unable to pay fines may also be kept. This, however, is limited to the capital of this country. In Sweden, the larger state prisons are called central prisons, *centralfängelser*), prisons, (*strafflängelser*) and crown prisons, (*kronohäkten*). There are thirty-four such institutions in addition to special prisons caring for criminals with limited responsibility, recidivists, tramps, and vagabonds. Aside from the local houses of detention, which belong to and are administered by local districts, all prisons are under centralized control of the State, through a Prison Board.

Before we discuss the prisons and classification as existing in the three countries, a word about personnel is important. Something similar to our civil service is in operation so far as all members of the administrative and custodial staffs are concerned. The top ranking men are appointed for their knowledge of penal affairs regardless of political party. In most cases, these men have served with distinction within the prison system, moving up through the ranks on the basis of merit and achievement. Aspirants to the higher positions usually qualify by taking special training

(2) "Scandinavian Prisons," in the *Annals of American Academy of Political and Social Science*, "Prisons of Tomorrow," September, 1931, pp. 197-207.
(3) *ibid.,* p. 198.

courses, including social and penal subjects. A college degree is not necessary, however. Sweden and Denmark are more exacting so far as training of the lower types of personnel than is Norway. As Mr. Almquist says regarding this subject:

> In the Scandinavian countries the view has become more and more accepted that a good prison system depends relatively little on excellent buildings and a well worked-out system, as compared with a well-trained personnel of a high morale level and with humanitarian views. The securing of such a personnel should be one of the highest goals for the effort of all prison administrators.[4]

In all three countries, the long term prisoners start out their imprisonment with solitary confinement, especially in Sweden, where it seems there are plenty of cells provided for this type of treatment. While in their individual cells the prisoners are provided with the type of labor peculiarly suited to such a condition. Gradually they are given work in association, but under the silence rule, except where communication is necessary relative to the nature of the work. Still later, more association is permitted, until the prisoner is allowed free association except at night, when either he occupies a cell alone, or is placed in a large room with not more than three other prisoners. Short term prisoners usually spend their entire time in seclusion.

The labor policy is similar to the state-use system in America. It is interesting to note, however, that it is optional rather than compulsory, at least in Sweden. Public bodies must first investigate if they can be supplied by the prison and bids may be accepted from the institution, a trifle less than from free contractors outside. Prisons manufacture shoes and clothing for the army and navy, cabinet work and furniture for the military barracks and printing for governmental agencies. Prisoners are given "premiums," these varying according to skill. Part of such premiums may be used by the prisoner for his own needs and part for the maintenance of his family. The remainder is placed in trust for him upon release. In the larger prisons of all countries there are agricultural pursuits carried on outside the institution enclosures. Reclamation work is a feature of some of the prisons located in the proximity of land that needs such treatment. If the prisoner demonstrates that he can be trusted he may join small units where life approaches that of the free man. In Sweden, especially, this type of limited freedom has shown excellent results. Some men live in these camps without any supervision whatsoever. Since 1938 Sweden has been experimenting with institutions similar to the English Borstals. Young offenders from 18 to 21 are sent to these "prison-schools" for a four year period of training.

The educational work of the prisons is on a high level even though compulsory education laws insure practically no illiteracy in Scandinavia. Libraries are unusually ample and they are moved about from prison to prison so that a maximum of the prisoners may take advantage of a larger selection. Musical participation is encouraged and most prisons have their choral work which is thoroughly enjoyed by the inmates.

In all Scandinavian prisons, the first classification is that which involves the mentally deficient. The insane and subnormal are weeded out and segregated in "internment" institutions. Constant observation by psychia-

(4)   *ibid.,* p. 201.

trists and physicians is a routine procedure in all prisons. Complete written records are kept on all inmates, including family history, earlier occupations and criminal record. Classification of short term offenders consists only of progressing from one set of privileges to another on a higher level. They do not share in the "progressive" stages afforded the long termers. Recidivists and others considered socially dangerous are, in general, sentenced indefinitely. They are not released until it is determined that their dangerousness has disappeared; for example, with the onset of old age.

Conditional release, or parole, scarcely exists as we understand it. Release depends upon the prisoner's good conduct and upon the length of sentence he has served. In Sweden, the time element is at least one year and two-thirds of the sentence. Such release is granted on order from the King. In Norway, the time element is at least six months and two-thirds of the sentence but in Denmark there is no such provision. Here they must serve out their sentence or receive the very rare conditional pardon.

We shall now take up in more detail the prison system of Denmark as it is especially interesting.

The principle of solitary, or separate, confinement is fairly well adhered to in the Danish prisons, especially for first offenders. Ingenious accommodations are resorted to in maintaining this outmoded feature of penal discipline, many of them smacking of nineteenth century English practice. For instance, the prisoners work and even exercise in some prisons in cleverly arranged pens. Following is a description of these circular workshops and exercise yards from the pen of the late Roy Calvert, noted British penal reformer:

> If you can picture a huge cart wheel about 60 feet in circumference turned on its side, and think of the rim and spokes as walls about eight feet high, and the hub a raised platform, you will get a fair picture of what these open air workshops are like. Each prisoner is confined in one of these segments, shut off from others but within sight of the supervising officer, who stands on a raised platform at the center.
> Even the exercise is taken in solitude, each man being allowed to cease work and exercise in his open air segment for half an hour twice daily. [In the prison at Vridsloselille] each three-cornered exercise yard has its own three-sided path, its triangular bed of grass and its flower bed in the center[5]

In addition to exercise twice daily in these little cubicles, gymnastics are required twice each week. Here again, the activity is performed on the principle of separation. Specially constructed gymnasiums in which eight men, each unseen by the others, go through strenuous calisthenics under the watchful eye of the instructor who can see them all. In church, the hundreds of little cubicles make it impossible for the men to see or communicate with one another. Yet the rector can see them all as he stands before them. It might be interesting to quote Calvert on the persistence of the principle of separate confinement by the enlightened country of Denmark:

> I am sure Denmark must soon learn the lesson so bitterly learned in this country of the evils of solitary confinement. The Danes are a kindly people, and no doubt they practice solitary confinement in their prisons because they sincerely believe it to be the best method both for society and the prisoner. I am sure it is a mistaken conviction. There *are* real difficulties, as the Danish officials say, about the association of prisoners. It is doubtful, however, whether they can

(5) E. Roy Calvert, "Prisons of Denmark," *Howard Journal*, June, 1929, pp. 301-306.

approximate the evils of solitary confinement. Perhaps both judges and jailers in
every country must learn the bitter lesson that confinement in a present-day
prison, under a solitary or any other system, is hardly likely to reform anybody.
It will no doubt be necessary to incarcerate law-breakers for the protection of
society, but the most we can hope from their confinement in any prison is that they
shall come out no worse than they went in. For prison is a substitute for, and
only a very poor substitute for, alternative treatment of a reformative and
educational character.[6]

The Danish penal administrators give as their reason for clinging
to this principle, dropped so long ago in America and England, that since
theirs is such a small country, prisoners could almost never live down
their incarceration and escape subsequent blackmail imposed by other ex-
prisoners who might become acquainted with them in prison. This is one
of the early reasons advanced in Pennsylvania for the adoption of separate
confinement but seldom do we hear it in these days. Recidivists and long
term prisoners may work in association since they have little to lose if
they are recognized by other prisoners. It is strange, too, that women, who
are incarcerated in a wing of the local Vestre Faengsel prison in the suburbs of Copenhagen, are permitted association.[7]

One of the interesting features of all Danish prisons is the work
program. Prisoners are paid fairly good wages and the products are mainly
toys, sold on the open market. However unique this system of work, it is
doubtful if it has any real constructive value upon release. Classification
of prisoners is on the intraprison principle, similar to that practiced in
Sweden and Norway. This is accomplished by a gradation of privileges.

The Nyborg prison for young offenders, situated on the island of
Fyen, was built for an institution similar to that of an English Borstal.
However, it is used as a penitentiary for offenders under 26 years of age
and is operated on the solitary line, with some exceptions. Prisoners are
worked and exercised in squads, in association, but with limited opportunities to recognize each other. The prison located at Vridslöselille was erected
in 1859 and accommodates about 350 prisoners. It is for offenders who have
been sentenced from six months to three and a half years. All prisoners
are in solitary, except some recidivists who work in association. Cell work
in the form of operating lathes or sewing machines is maintained in this
institution. When it is necessary for prisoners to leave their cells to attend
lectures or classes, they wear brown masks which they pull down over
their faces permitting only the eyes to show through.

Prisoners undergoing sentences of life imprisonment and long sentences in general are confined at the penitentiary at Horsens, in Jutland.
Here most of the men work in association. Forestry and land reclamation
employ two groups of about 35 each, who are permitted outside the walls
for this purpose. They are the most trustworthy prisoners.

Fresh air, good food and plenty of sunlight are the rule in Danish
prisons. Prisoners are encouraged to decorate and paint their cells. Extreme
care is taken to prevent institutional odors, so prevalent in most American
prisons. Educational work is on a reasonably high level, since the Danes
well recognize its value in the process of rehabilitation.

(6) *ibid.*, p. 306.
(7) See Erik Kampmann, "Prisons and Punishment in Denmark," *Journal of Criminal
Law and Criminology*, vol. 25, (1934-35), pp. 115-117. Mr. Kampmann was director
General of the Danish Prison at that time.

The system of "parole" and aftercare of prisoners is notoriously weak. Measures have recently been taken to perfect such a system but the results are not at the moment obtainable. Mr. Lithgow Osborne, writing in *News Bulletin,* official publication of the Osborne Association, is enthusiastic about the Danish system of penal treatment. He makes the following point which explains to a degree the presence of a progressive system in that country:

> In a country having a homogeneous, naturally law-abiding population and a well-organized police system free from political influence, which makes the apprehension and punishment of criminals reasonably sure and speedy, the crime problem of Denmark does not present some of the difficulties which we face in the United States. Futhermore, the authorities have been left to work out their ideas unaffected by demands from an aroused but ill-informed public opinion, for greater severity rather than for more efficiency and the application of a spirit of scientific inquiry in dealing with the criminal.
>
> The Danish prison system is, like the American system, based on the theory that reform and rehabilitation are the primary objects to the secured—not punishment or retaliation. In operation I should say that this theory was far better lived up to in Denmark than in the United States.[8]

In conclusion, it can be noted that there is little to be found in the Scandinavian systems that would profit American prisons except cleanliness, labor and an air of conscientious official interest in the prisoner. With our adherence to mass treatment our prisons can accomplish little. However, if smaller units were developed, each housing no more than five hundred, there is reason to believe that the more personal relationship resulting would have real meaning for the inmates.

(8)   October, 1930, "The Danish Prison System."

CHAPTER V

THE PENAL LAW AND PRISONS OF GERMANY, AUSTRIA AND SWITZERLAND

GERMAN PENAL SYSTEM AND PENAL CODES

The Historical Development of the German Penal System

When one thinks of the prison system of a country a centralized concept is usually visualized. Prior to the Nazi régime this was hardly the case in Germany for this country was long characterized by a group of jealous and independent states, each guarding its sovereignty in political and religious matters. This was especially true before the unification under the iron rule of Bismarck. But, as Professor Hans von Hentig puts it, this rivalry between states continued to persist down to the ascendency to power of the Nazis. Writing in 1931, before the Nazis took over, he wrote:

> When we speak of the German development in the field of penal treatment, therefore, we are dealing with a generalization based on conditions in individual states. The strong religious and social differences of various German regions make it apparent that the tempo, purpose, and the means of reform must differ greatly.
>
> Germany is divided into a dozen and more states jealously watching over their independence and staunchly refusing interference by the Government of the Reich.[1]

Naturally, this overt rivalry no longer exists but it has left its mark on the habits and social thinking of the people.

In the days of John Howard the various states which now comprise Germany were energetic in establishing workhouses for vagrants and beggars. Felons were put to work on streets or fortifications or in the chalk quarries. At Nuremburg prisoners polished lenses; at Bayreuth they polished marble. At Mayence there was a design over the door of the prison which represented a wagon drawn by two stags, two lions, and two wild boars, with an inscription which stated that if "wild beasts can be tamed and induced to submit to the yoke, we must not despair of reclaiming the vicious and teaching them habits of industry."[2] Workhouses were established in Germany long before Howard's time. Following the example of London and Amsterdam, Bremen, in 1609, Lübeck, in 1613, and Hamburg, in 1622, opened such institutions.

The Pennsylvania System of separate confinement was adopted in Prussia and some other German states following 1834. It was in that year that Dr. Nicolaus Heinrich Julius came to America and spent two years studying penal philosophy as exemplified at Philadelphia and Auburn. He was enthusiastic about the philosophy of separation and was responsible for its adoption upon his return home. This system persisted down to

---

(1) "Germany's Prison System," *Annals of the American Academy of Political and Social Science*, September, 1931, pp. 174-179.

(2) F. H. Wines, *Punishment and Reformation*, Crowell, 1895, pp. 116-117.

recent times and no doubt it is still in operation under the Nazi régime. However, there have been modifications in the system through the years as is the case in all European countries.

Writing in 1937, Dr. Marie Munk, former judge of the civil court of Berlin, stated that Germany retained the old prison architecture with its central plant and cell system, with solitary confinement. The cells get direct light from the heavily barred windows. The minimum-security cottage type of architecture, and the dormitory, so familiar in America, are rare in Germany. As a rule, the prisoner is held in solitary confinement before trial and also during the early part of his sentence. Association of prisoners is permitted during work hours and separate cells are provided for sleep. But, as is often the case, overcrowding often prevents this being carried out.[3]

Germany provides two kinds of prisons for her convicted offenders: (1) *Zuchthaus,* comparable to our prisons with a mimimum sentence, one year, maximum, life; (2) *Gefaengnis,* comparable to our reformatory with a minimum, one day, and a maximum, five years. A *Zuchthaus* sentence carries much more stigma than *Gefaengnis;* in many cases it involves permanent or temporary incapacity to carry on special professions or to enjoy civil rights.

Prior to the rise of the Nazis, a new classification system had been developed in Germany. Prisoners were not only grouped according to their personality traits so that young offenders were kept in strict separation from repeaters, but a system of promotion was adopted with special privileges for good behavior. Each new prisoner started in the first class and could work up to the third, or highest. Privileges given the good inmate were: extra reading material, more letters, an increased number of visits, etc. Classification was carried on within institutions and between institutions.

Germany maintained many interesting judicial practices which were quite different from those in this country. It is significant that the same criminal law was in effect throughout Germany. There never did exist a grand jury in the American sense as an instrument for indicting an offender. There was a trial jury which originally was composed of 12 jurors but later was reduced to 6 in number. In 1924 the jury system was abolished except for serious felonies (murder, arson and perjury). However, even within these limits one cannot speak of anything comparable to the American jury system as there is no distinction between finding the accused person guilty and sentencing him; the trained judges and lay judges deliberate together on guilt as well as sentence.

Most criminals were tried before the *Schoeffengericht,* with one or two trained judges and two lay judges, one of whom might be a woman. The more serious cases, especially those involving murder, were tried before the *Schwurgericht,* a jury composed of three trained and six lay judges. The number varied with the states. These lay judges were chosen from a list of inhabitants of the city by a special administrative body. They served a few days or weeks each year and received a small fee.

(3) "The Philosophy of Criminal Justice in the United States and in Germany," *Prison Journal,* July, 1937, pp. 349-357.

The verdict was by two-thirds vote of the judges in the case, The defendant before the *Schoeffengericht* had the right to appeal to a higher court, the *Strafkammer*. If the prisoner could not afford an attorney, one was provided by the state. The procedure was quite informal. The presiding judge examined the witnesses, although the prosecutor and the defendant's lawyer might also ask questions. There was no cross-examination. The defendant could not take the witness stand and was not compelled to answer questions with regard to the alleged offense. In weighing the evidence, the court was not bound by rule, but used its own judgment. Often the law gave the court the choice between a fine or a sentence of from one to fifteen years, or both. Only the Board of Pardons might free the prisoner, although he could be released from prison after he had served three-fourths of his sentence.

Germany had no probation for adults as it is understood in America. There was a form of conditional pardon and social workers connected with the city welfare department made investigations upon the request of the court, for adults as well as juveniles. Neither was there parole connected with the penal institutions, but again the social workers were called upon to take charge of discharged prisoners.

In juvenile cases, Germany, at that time, took the position that children under 14 were not responsible for any kind of criminal act since they did not possess the mentality to understand the implications of their conduct. They were handled by a Court of Guardianship or Family Relations Court consisting of one trained judge. The procedure was quite informal. Parents were held responsible for their children's conduct so the onus of their children's acts rested upon them.

Between the ages of fourteen and eighteen, children were tried in juvenile courts, *Jugendgerichte,* special divisions of the Criminal Court. Before the hearing, the Judge determined whether the child should be held responsible.[4] If he was so held, he was tried in the Juvenile Court, sometimes before lay judges as well as trained judges; if not responsible, he was turned over to the Court of Guardianship. The same judge frequently served in both courts. Trials of children were always private and informal. If the child was guilty and the offense serious, he might receive a sentence to a juvenile Reformatory. If the offense was mild, he could be placed on probation or turned over to the Court of Guardianship for educational treatment.

Under the Nazis, reformatories and correctional institutions for the young offender, *Jugend-Gefangnisse,* are quite repressive. An atmosphere of confinement, discipline and repression is sensed at all times. Recreational activities in the German institutions differ widely from those found in American schools of similar nature. There are no radio programs, tournaments, leisure time hobbies or sports of any kind. The regulations applying to these establishments states that: "The young offender must be kept under strict discipline. If he shows good will, it may be valuable from the educational standpoint to give him rewards through privileges which con-

(4)　See Dr. Otto Reinemann, "The Youth Criminal Law in Germany," *Prison Journal,* January-April, 1935, pp. 150-154.

form with the object of the sentence and with the order and the security in the prison."[5]

The sentence, as well as its execution, reflected the idea of punishment and hardship which the offender should suffer in order to make good for his misbehavior. Life in prison was designed to be hard and unattractive. The cells were bare, clothing and food extremely simple, and work, hard. Quoting from the regulations again, we find:

> Each prisoner has to work during his whole sentence. Idleness is inconsistent with the execution of the sentence and endangers the order and security of the prison. The prisoner must learn the moral of workmanship and a trade so that he is able to earn a living when he comes out. He must learn to work constantly and properly. He must learn what labor and accomplishment mean for the life of the people as well as for himself. He must experience the satisfaction which comes from work and efficiency. Thus he will be trained to become a good citizen. His abilities shall be developed to efficiency and his efficiency shall be increased. Unskilled prisoners with longer sentences shall be trained to become semi-skilled or skilled workers, if possible, in handicraft work. Work in the open air, farming and gardening, shall be stressed. Prisoners shall not be kept busy by doing only unplanned and unconstructive labor.[6]

We in America will not quarrel with the concept of hard and constructive work, as the above regulations called for from German prisoners, youth and adult alike. Certainly this is one of the crying needs in our prisons today. However, the spirit of German prisons was one of repression and deterrence, rather than reformation as such. A constructive work program, with its basis firmly grounded on the concept of rehabilitation and individualization of treatment would go far in making prisons and reformatories truly effective rather than the liabilities they now are.

German prison labor made little use of the contract method. Prison goods were almost entirely absorbed by the State. Inmates were paid a small wage, the skilled worker receiving more than the unskilled. As is the custom in most countries, part of this compensation was sent home for family relief and part for the prisoner's own use.

Students of the problems of penal treatment, in writing on the conditions in German prisons, give great credit to the experimentation that was attempted there, but they also point out that there were many difficulties that had to be overcome. Professor von Hentig comments on these as follows: "Germany's difficulties are to be explained partly by its financial exhaustion, political confusion, and religious dualism."[7]

At the time von Hentig was writing, that is, during the days of the Weimar Republic, he described three types of prison treatment found in the German states. Briefly, we shall set down some of the features of these systems. First, there is Bavaria, dominantly a Catholic state, which experimented with the "progressive system" of penal treatment for many years. Through the efforts and work of Dr. Viernstein, director of the Mental Hospital division of the Straubing prison, emphasis was placed on the "crimino-biological" analysis of crime causation. We need not discuss that approach at this point.[8] Suffice it is to say that von Hentig feels such

---

(5)   Quoted by Dr. Munk, *loc. cit.*, p. 355.   Cf. Otto Kirchheimer, "Recent Trends in German Treatment of Juvenile Delinquency," *Journal of Criminal Law and Criminology*, September-October, 1938, pp. 363-370.

(6)   Quoted by Dr. Munk, p. 356.

(7)   *Annals*, September, 1931, p. 179.

(8)   See our section on Italy's penal philosophy, pp. 67-68.

an analysis is quite one sided. He states: "Commendable as may be the Bavarian experiment to discover the biological basis of the criminal, especially from the various manifestations of germ development, it has in the application of penal treatment, led to conclusions or practices which have a very weak foundation. . . . The Bavarian method must, therefore, be considered as valuable, but one sided."[9]

The second method was that practiced in Thuringia. In Bavaria the jurist and the physician were in control of prison and prisoner; in Thuringia, the teacher dominated. For example, on Sundays the wardens made excursions through the neighboring woods with selected prisoners, without armed guards. There were prison courts in which the prisoners acted as judges and imposed punishments for disciplinary offenses. Thuringia was the first state to introduce the useful division of the prisoners' treatment into three stages: observation, treatment and protection. However, there was no classification clinic for scientific observation and diagnosis. Consequently, the prison régime relied wholly on the initiative of the administrative officers as well as their personality. Environmental factors are emphasized rather than the biological. As von Hentig states: "The absence of the point of view of the natural sciences in Thuringia is no doubt a defect."[10] Nevertheless, there were many features of the prisons of this state that more than outweighed any such disadvantage. The scientific social worker (*Fürsorger*) was employed here with great effectiveness.

Prussia, after the last World War, presented an interesting spectacle, so far as penal philosophy was concerned. As von Hentig states: "Prisons were almost emptied during the War, and the first revolutionary amnesties continued this depopulation. Then 'humaneness' came into its own . . . but a purposeless and sentimental humaneness, sprung from no clear scientific conviction. A series of small improvements was made, but strong leadership was lacking, and Thuringia, Saxonia, and Hamburg surpassed the Prussian prison system by their accomplishments."[11] However, a change occurred in 1929 when an ordinance was passed which dealt with the subject of penal treatment. This called for a reorientation of the entire problem of the care of the criminal.

The reorganization plan called for: an entrance prison, a prison for advanced prisoners, and a discharge prison. The entrance prison was divided into various types, each dealing with a specific kind of offender, *e. g.,* the minor, the first offender, the short termer, the recidivist. In addition, institutions for the "least reformable" and one for the mentally diseased were also set up. Crimino-biological research bureaus were developed and a course of training for prison officials was also promulgated. Dr. Thorsten Sellin, in commenting on this course, describes it thus: "It was composed of ten lectures on the following topics: the 'progressive system' in Prussia, according to the decree of June 7, 1929; pedagogical practice; the study of the personality of the prisoner in the receiving prison; introduction to child welfare; juvenile court work; the 'progressive system' in Switzerland; introduction to public welfare; the psychology of evidence

(9)   *loc. cit.,* p. 177.
(10)   *ibid.* p. 177.
(11)   *idem.*

in sex crime, especially in regard to juveniles; social diagnosis; clinical psychiatric demonstrations and visits to the local asylum."[12]

In the beginning of the penal process, the fate of the prisoner in Prussia was not left in the hands of the judge but was decided by a sentencing board which prescribed "treatment" not only in accordance with the facts relating to the crime, but also with such data as could be obtained concerning the past history of the offender. The prisoner was considered an individual and throughout the penal process was given individual attention.

Upon entering the prison he was given a rigid examination by a body of specialists—physicians, psychologists and psychiatrists. He was then classified and reclassified until he finally reached the institution which offered the greatest benefit for him. While undergoing treatment, the prisoner was under the observation of a psychiatrist. His conduct was balanced against such findings as social specialists discovered in studying his previous history.

In the elaborate scheme set up by the authorities, sometimes referred to as the "grade system,"[13] provision was made whereby the inmates might progress from one stage to another. We have referred to this above in citing the provision of three different types of prisons. After a certain length of time, in no event less than six months, the prisoner was either promoted to the prison for the advanced, or transferred to an institution which cared for special problem cases. When half of his sentence was completed, he could be promoted, if the director of the institution thought it advisable, to the discharge prison.

Treatment necessarily varied in each of the three institutions provided. In the first grade, the prisoner was carefully supervised. At night he slept in a single cell, but during the day, there was group confinement. In the advance institution, the inmates were permitted to sleep in dormitories, and were allowed considerable freedom. Selfgovernment prevailed in this grade. Monitors were elected by the prisoners, and they had considerable voice in determining whether or not a prisoner was to be awarded additional privileges or demoted. The prison régime was gradually eased off so that there was not too great a break between the life within and without the prison.

Work was an essential part of the prison program. Those who had no trade prior to their entrance, were taught one, if possible. Those who proved themselves worthy of trust were paroled to employers for work outside of the institution. The prisoners in this class were permitted to keep a part of their earnings. They could walk outside the institution and even visit homefolks over week-ends. What amounted to parole was granted by the Director of the discharging institution with the approval of the Commissioner of Pardons.

Rudolf Ditzen (Hans Fallada) in his book *The World Outside*,[14] paints a depressing picture of the treatment afforded the discharged prisoner as he attempts to make a re-adjustment among a group of grasping and apathetic persons who made great pretense of "helping" him.

(12) "Europe Trains its Prison Personnel," *Prison Journal*, October, 1931, pp. 7-8.
(13) See James V. Bennett, "The Grade System in Prison Administration in Prussia," *News Bulletin*, The Osborne Association, New York City, February, 1931, pp. 1-2.
(14) Simon & Schuster, 1934; published in Germany under the title *Who Once Eats Out of the Tin Bowl*.

PENAL TREATMENT UNDER THE NAZIS

We shall now say a few words about Germany's prisons under the Nazi régime. Of necessity, our remarks will be brief since information is quite meagre. There is confusion regarding the treatment of criminals and that inflicted upon enemies and others sent to concentration camps. It is not the purpose here to discuss these camps since they do not belong to the penal system although some of the regular prisons are used for political enemies.

The horrors of these sadistically operated centers of human misery are well know to Americans since there has been a rich literature developed during the last few years. Methods of torture too barbarous to mention have been adopted by the bloodthirsty Nazis. Let us quote, however, from the account of one prisoner who was fortunate to escape from one prison which was turned into a concentration camp—the one located at Sachsenhausen.[15] He says: "At the beginning of November, 1935, there were in Sachsenhausen 300 criminals, 400 followers of the so-called Bible-scholars and 627 political prisoners—a total of 1,327 men. For these 1,327 prisoners who slept in three-story bunks, there were four toilets and twenty-eight water faucets. It took a full twenty-four hours for everyone to be served . . . If somebody in the camp falls seriously ill, he dies, for the so-called camp physician does not raise a finger for the prisoners. . . . Until November the rooms and dormitories were not heated; it was said the puddles outside had to freeze first." How many of Germany's real prisons have been turned into concentration camps, we do not know. But there is no doubt that much confusion reigns when an attempt is made to distinguish clearly between penal treatment and that accorded political "enemies of the state." We propose to deal with the penal philosophy of the Nazis rather than continue a discussion of their attitudes toward these political prisoners.

Dr. Hans von Hentig, writing in the *Annals* in 1931,[16] makes this remark, which has real meaning thirteen years after it was made: "We must wait until we see the outcome of this movement [the reform movement inaugurated in 1929]; and the next International Prison Congress, to be held in Berlin in 1935, will be able to judge with its own eyes if the wide approval which met the paper plan of the reform has been justified by real accomplishments." By 1935, the Nazi rule had been in operation for two years. We can best judge the results of those two years by quoting from a report of a member of the English delegation to that International Congress.

Writing in *The Penal Reformer,* Mr. Geoffrey Bing calls that assembly "A Congress in Chains."[17] He points out that the Nazi system of penal philosophy no longer places any credance in reformation, but rather "retribution for crime against the state." There were three main questions before the Congress. The first, and most important, was the fundamental issue of humane treatment of prisoners. Nazi philosophy repudiates this "sentimentalism" and, according to Mr. Bing, it was this question that brought on "the main fight . . .under the leadership of Mr. Alexander

(15)   Heinz Pol, "German Concentration Camps," *Living Age,* March, 1936, p. 30.
(16)   *loc. cit.,* p. 178.
(17)   *The Penal Reformer,* January, 1936.

Paterson—[18]a fight which had shown that the Western nations would never agree to abandoning."

The question of sterilization and castration of criminals brought forth more fight from the western nations. The Nazi delegates, voting unanimously on this issue as they did on all issues, claimed such measures expedient since they brought about a reduction of crime. Since the Nazi delegates outnumbered all others—they had 425—the measure passed. The third problem dealt with the rights of the accused in trial, where an attempt was made to justify the cutting down of appeals, the shortening of trials generally and the deprivation of the accused's rights to Counsel. Mr. Bing stated the position of the delegates from countries outside Germany when he said: "The lesson to be learnt was that nothing could be achieved by supporting, with a view to modifying, such a régime as the Nazi régime in Germany; the only way was to come out into the open and fight it."[19]

The outside delegates were naturally interested, and indeed concerned, regarding conditions in the concentration camps. Regulations regarding the victims in these camps were circulated at the Congress and we append some of them here, merely to show the strained relations which obviously resulted from the wide difference of opinion on this delicate issue:

Article 6. Eight days' strict arrest and 25 strokes is the punishment for anyone who makes derogatory or sarcastic remarks about an S. S. official (these men guard the inmates of the camps), or who intentionally omits to observe the prescribed salutes or who shows in another way that he will not submit to the force of discipline and order.

Article 8. Fourteen days' strict arrest and 25 strokes each is the punishment for anyone who expresses in letters or other reports derogatory remarks regarding the National Socialist leaders, the State and the Government institutions and administration, or who praises the Marxian or liberalistic leaders or November Parties or reports happenings in concentration camps or who proclaims his innocence in correspondence against his better knowledge and so leads to public unrest.

Article 11. Anyone who carries on political discussion in the camp, in the workshop, in the work barracks, in the kitchen or the lavatory or in the places of rest with the purpose of antagonistic atrocity propaganda regarding the concentration camps or who receives, hides or repeats to foreign visitors or other persons will be hanged according to revolutionary law as an agitator.

Mr. Bing, commenting on these drastic regulations, stated: "In the face of such regulations it was useless for the Minister of Justice to invite members of the Congress to go freely into concentration camps and ask the prisoners how they were being treated. Such regulations gave an air of artificiality to the whole Congress."[20]

We get some notion of the increase of crime in Germany from statements made by Miss Margery Fry, writing in the *Penal Reformer* in 1937. She records statistics that show the number of prisoners per 100,000 of the country's population which are not only interesting but revealing concerning the internal conditions of the country as well as penal philosophy at the time, which is 1937:

In Germany the figures . . .were, I think, not inclusive of the prisoners detained in concentration camps, yet even so the ratio of prisoners to 100,000 of the population for Germany runs up to nearly 157. Bulgaria had 152. Estonia, again a country with a good deal of political unrest, 275 in prison on one day of

(18)   Commissioner of British Prisons.
(19)   *ibid.*, p. 13.
(20)   *idem.*

the year for every 100,000 population . . .Then you have Finland, 231; Italy, 126; Latvia, 212; Lithuania, 161; Poland, 150. Lest anybody should be inclined to think that no country could be kept in order without some such proportion as that, let me give you some other countries. . . .Denmark, 43; Irish Free State, less than 20; England and Wales, 29.9; Scotland, 26.7; Northern Ireland, 30.9; . . .Sweden, 38.5.[21]

We are further informed of the Nazi philosophy of penal treatment from a communication which purports to quote various official statements relative to the treatment of the offender. They refer primarily to the youth of that country. In a German publication, *Gedanken ueber Strafvollzug an jungen Gefangenen,* is stated the fundamental premise of Nazi treat- of the young offender: "guilt requires expiation (*Suehne*), as the voice of our German conscience tells us and as our German feeling of cleanliness demands."[22] This article continues by condemning the pre-Nazi methods and describes present day treatment in some selected youth-prisons. While the publication contends that delinquency has dropped, it admits that length of sentence has increased tremendously, *e. g.,* for every 100 long sentences invoked in 1932, 1934 saw 245. Commenting on this article the spokesman for *The Penal Reformer* states:

> The pages of denunciation of what went before (i.e. the reforms prior to the Nazi regime) are perhaps intended to hide the poverty of the proposed "reforms." What is proposed is mostly a return to the good old idea of deter-rence by severity, and a long series of "Don'ts" is given. The idea that there ought to be rules for a kind of "fair play" between the offender and State is of course rejected, the rights given to the criminal by the maxim of "nulla poeno sine lege" are given up. "We have further turned away from the soft and decadent 'tout comprehende est tout pardonner.' from the kidglove method of handling the criminal and from the fear of hurting him." For "born criminals," "just severity" is considered the only fit treatment, but it is admitted that among selected young offenders, education and reform must play a part. But those worthy of special treatment must be carefully selected . . .This in practice means that reform is only to be tried on those easiest to manage, and that many cases which are difficult without being hopeless are left out in the cold. The percentage of "fail-ures" will thus no doubt go down in the future.[23]

Young offenders above eighteen, for the first several weeks, and, if necessary, for several months, are to be kept in solitary confinement, even at work, in order to induce reflection. "The maintenance of the strictest order, punctuality, discipline, and obedience must inexorably be demanded of every prisoner." Work is to be provided. It is argued by the authors of the publication that the penal character of treatment would be lost if prisons were to imitate camp life or youth hostels, reserved for free juve-niles. Privileges are to be extended at the Governor's hands when he thinks the case merits it. Some of these privileges are interesting: permission to make drawings or to keep a diary (both under the control of a teacher), to learn shorthand or, in exceptional cases, foreign languages, own choice books from the prison library, or permission to play "solitary" chess.

The chief aim of the education imposed in these youth prisons is to reclaim the youngster for the Third Reich and the Nation by propaganda. Education consists of from two to five lectures weekly. The theories of "blood and soil," racial teaching, the Nuremberg laws, the history of

(21) "Penal Reform at Geneva," January, 1937, p. 2.
(22) "The Young Offender in Germany: How the Nazis Treat the Problem," *The Penal Reformer,* April, 1937, pp. 15-16.
(23) *ibid.,* p. 15.

National Socialism, etc., play a large part in the curriculum. National holidays and festivals, important political speeches, and announcements are listened to on the radio. One Governor reports that the most read library book is *Mein Kampf* and another states that all undesirable books have been eliminated and the library is now based on books dealing with National Socialist principles. A third Governor states that such books are given the prisoners whether they wish them or not. The article closes by stating that guards practice with carbines and pistols at least once yearly.

Here we see a renunciation of progressive and scientific measures leading to reformation and a return to expiation and deterrence. Dr. Marie Munk, in the article quoted above, substantiates this by stating: "Germany, abandoning former efforts for a more individual and liberal approach, has reinstalled strict discipline. The segregation of first and repeated offenders is still in full operation in the correctional institutions for juvenile offenders from fourteen to eighteen years of age. Once committed they stay there until the end of their term or until they are twenty-five years old." She adds that there were at that time sixteen juvenile reformatories in Germany, ten for boys, six for girls. According to the new regulations, issued by the government on January 22, 1937, two of these institutions shall only be used for first offenders, two for repeated offenders and the girls' institutions for both groups. Where first and repeated offenders are in the same building, they shall be kept separate.[24]

PENAL PHILOSOPHY IN AUSTRIA

Austria today is merely a vassal state of the Nazi Reich. She was the first to meet the fate that has since been the lot of practically every country in Europe. Here we shall discuss the status of Austrian penology prior to Anschluss.

One of the most dramatic incidents in the life of John Howard was the summons he received from the enlightened despot, Emperor Joseph II, while visiting the prisons of Vienna. At first the great reformer declined the summons. When the Emperor gave him an option as to the time of the meeting, Howard consented. Here is an account of the interview:

Here Joseph received a man who never bent his knee to, nor kissed the hand of any monarch; here he heard truths that astonished him, and often did he seize hold of Howard's hand with expressible satisfaction and approbation. "You have prisoners," said Howard, "who have been confined in dungeons without seeing daylight for twenty months, who have not yet had a trial, and should they be found innocent, your Majesty has it not in your power to make a compensation for the violated rights of humanity."

(24)   For extra references on the Nazi criminal code, see the following: Clara Leiser, "A Director of a Nazi Prison Speaks Out," *Journal of Criminal Law and Criminology*, September-October, 1938, pp. 345-352; Edith Roper and Clara Leiser, *Skeleton of Justice*, Dutton, 1941; Robert M. W. Kempner, "Hitler's Criminal Code," *Free World*, January, 1942, pp. 395-397. Articles dealing with pre-Nazi criminal jurisprudence, not referred to above, are: Franz Exner, "Development of the Administration of Criminal Justice in Germany," *Journal of Criminal Law and Criminology*, May-June, 1933, pp. 248-259; also in the same publication, "The German Prevention of Crime Act," by Hermann Mannheim, November, 1935, pp. 517-537 and "Criminology in Germany," by Werner S. Landecker, January-February, 1941, pp. 551-575. For good descriptions of physical plants of the various German prisons, see *Proceedings, International Penal and Penitentiary Congress*, Berlin, 1935, pp. 592-615, (*passim*).

To the honor of this great Prince, let it be remembered that alterations were made in the prisons before Howard's departure.[1]

The Austrian code of Joseph II, drawn up in 1785, called for prisoners to be incarcerated alone in a light cell. However, it contained a clause forbidding the giving of food to any prisoner, at public expense, except bread and water. The purpose of the code was to suppress crime by severity.

The modern penal code of Austria dates back to 1852. Many of its basic principles go further back to 1803 and, indeed, show this influence. Many attempts were made to draw up a new code, but to no avail. Prior to the first World War, serious attempts were frustrated because of the onrush of that political and military upheaval. In 1927-28, a further attempt was made to collaborate with Germany in drafting similar codes for both countries. These also failed. Now that Austria is eclipsed for the duration of the present conflict, it is obvious that any independent effort along the lines of planning a penal code is out of the question. Austria suffered the dismemberment of its empire after the Peace Treaty in a way that few Americans can possibly visualize. However, some interesting and somewhat progressive measures were introduced after 1920. We shall review some of these.[2]

According to the archaic penal code, only children up to ten years of age were completely free from penal responsibility. Over fourteen, children were completely liable. However, the Juvenile Court Law of 1928 completely changed these provisions. This innovation is interesting, since it designates the period between the ages of fourteen and eighteen as that of "problematic maturity." The judge must investigate each individual case, and if he finds indications of illness, undernourishment, or neglect, the child is absolved of all blame for his crime. However, only about ten per cent of those apprehended are held irresponsible. The advances made in the psychiatric field in Austria were beginning to make inroads in the analysis and treatment of children's cases when the cataclysm that enveloped the country drew a curtain over what is now occurring in that state.

Children between the ages mentioned above, when sentenced, are kept apart from adult criminals. There are a few juvenile prisons, especially in Vienna, but, in most jurisdictions, children are kept in separate apartments of adult penal institutions. Here strict segregation is maintained. Education, gymnastics, sports, and agricultural work help make incarceration less irksome and more reformative. Sentences for minors of less than a month may be served in private institutions, some of which are county institutions for those in need of education. In general, the judge may choose from the following procedures in disposing of juvenile cases: educational supervision, placement in a family, a juvenile children's home, or assignment to a federal institution for those in need of education. Trades are taught in these schools if the children are adaptable for such apprenticeship.

(1)   From a portion of a letter sent to Dr. Benjamin Rush, of Philadelphia, by Dr. John Coakley Lettson of London, in 1787. The letter deals with Howard's visit to the Mediterranean countries. From the Minutes of the *Philadelphia Society for Alleviating the Miseries of Public Prisons,* October 8, 1787; reprinted in Teeters, *They Were in Prison,* Winston, 1937, pp. 38-39.

(2)   See W. Gleispach, "Twenty-Five Years of Criminology in Austria," *Journal of Criminal Law and Criminology,* vol. 23, May-June, 1933, pp. 176-197.

Austria is somewhat advanced in caring for its prostitutes. Here such activity is not specifically forbidden and therefore is not a crime as in some states in America. All prostitutes must register with the police and submit to periodic examinations. Brothels, *per se,* are forbidden in some communities. For example, they have been outlawed in Vienna since 1921. Vienna has twenty-five women police on its force. They handle all cases of children and females. The treatment of drunkards is not so modern. They are asked to sign the pledge and if they agree, are not imprisoned.

Vagrants are sent to the workhouses. County institutions of this type have been established by the central government. To these, in addition to beggars and vagrants, may also be sent criminals who show a disinclination for an orderly life. Five years is the maximum sentence to these institutions.

The laws of Austria are particularly severe for adult crimes but the provisions of the Penal Procedure Act of 1918 gave discretion to the judges in their mitigation of certain cases. Under this act a penalty of ten to twenty years may be reduced to as little as one year, if the judge sees fit. This provision was formulated in order to take cognizance between the "acute" and the "chronic" criminal. This act also stated that, where the penalty was five years or less, imprisonment might be avoided altogether, and detention substituted instead. This was an attempt to give a form of special treatment to the occasional offender, or in cases where extenuating circumstances were obvious.

The law of 1920 made conditional liberation an integral part of the Austrian penal philosophy. This is admissable in all cases in which the penalty is detention or a fine. The court, under this act, may even hold criminals for detention only, rather than imprisonment. Investigation on the part of the court is preliminary to the invocation of this act. He may then place the culprit on probation for a specified period, with certain injunctions relative to his subsequent behavior.

An interesting measure found in Austria is that which annuls the penal record of a person who has served a sentence of two years or over. The object of this is to make it easier for a discharged convict to become rehabilitated. After his release, and if he is extended the benefits of this law, passed in 1918, he is not required to acknowledge to question of either court or other authority that he has served sentence. When a sentence has been annulled, the police department acts as if the man's record were completely nonexistent. This is splendid theory but how it works out in practice is problematical. Another unusual innovation found in Austria is that which calls for the confiscation of the goods of a criminal if he cannot be apprehended, cannot be prosecuted, or by reason of penal exemption cannot be condemned, as for example, in cases of irresponsibility.

Convicts in Austrian prisons are divided into three grades. Upon entering the prison, they are put in the third category. Upon good behavior they pass on to the second and thence to the first. According to the law of 1920 which established conditional release, prisoners must serve two-thirds of their sentence, or at least eight months, before becoming eligible for release. In the case of life imprisonment, the term is at least fifteen years. They must during their imprisonment "repair the injury of which they are guilty to the best of their ability" and show that they will behave well after release.

The law of 1921 called for the appointement of three visitors to be attached to every court prison and to each state penitentiary. They are authorized to visit the prisoners and to receive requests and complaints from them. In addition, they report to the administrators of the courts and prisons on their findings. Prisons have libraries, schools, hospitals for the treatment of various ailments, musicals and lectures for the entertainment and cultural uplift of the inmates.

Austria, like every other European country, started out with strict separation of prisoners. This, however, has been modified in recent years. Writing in 1903, Professor Henderson stated that while convicts were given ample labor, they were not entitled to wages. They were obliged to pay for maintenance and, if diligent, a "gift" might be forthcoming upon release. However, they were not to expect any such gift. Usually, if the prisoner maintained good behavior and industry throughout his incarceration, he might return to his home community and find there awaiting him, a "gift" from the prison authorities, which consisted of a small sum of money. This phenomenon is an interesting and naive form of paternalism.[3]

The national penitentiaries, described by Professor Henderson, were located at Marburg and Korneuburg. There was a national reform school for neglected and delinquent children of both sexes located at Eggenburg.

In 1932, a school of criminological science and criminalistics was founded at the University of Vienna by Professor Gleispach. Briefly, this school sets up an interesting course of study for those going into the field of criminology and police work, as well as for law students who may wish to take advantage of the courses offered. The work of the Institute comes under three headings. They are: (1) Instruction of law students in the criminological sciences; (2) Advancement of research in these fields; and (3) Submission of expert opinion on criminological questions, when requested by the courts. Attendance to these lectures is not compulsory for law students, but there has been a movement on foot to make a certain number of such lectures an integral part of the law curriculum. The course for the first semester includes causes of crime, crime phenomena, criminalistic technology, statistics relating to crime, forensic medicine and forensic psychiatry. For the second semester: penology and a continuation of the courses of the previous semester. The third semester includes: Policies relating to penal legislation, laboratory work in criminalistic photography and psychology for criminal procedure. Fourth semester: presentation of criminal types, criminal psychology and criminalistic methodology.[4]

THE PRISONS OF SWITZERLAND

Just as John Howard found separation of prisoners in the workhouses of the Netherlands, so did he find that type of discipline in Switzerland. He stated that in every canton he visited he found felons possessing a room to themselves. The keepers stated in explanation of this: "that they

(3) See Henderson, *Modern Prison Systems*, pp. 71-94, for a description of Austria's prisons in the early part of this century.
(4) See Roland Grassberger, "The University Institute of the Criminologic Sciences and Criminalistics in Vienna," *Journal of Criminal Law and Criminology* vol. 23, September-October, 1932, pp. 395-403.

may not tutor one another." Howard adds that none was in irons, that their rooms were "more or less strong and lightsome, according to their crimes."

In the larger prisons at such places as Lausanne, Berne, Basel and Zurich, he found conditions somewhat different. In the Lausanne prison, there were many cells underground although at the time of his visit there were no prisoners in them. The tendency was to keep the less serious criminals in separate confinement supplied with inside work. The more dangerous convicts were chained to small wagons and forced to clean streets and remove rubbish. One amazing sight recorded by Howard was the presence of gallows erected along the road in the several bailiwicks. He found that each such judicial area not only had its own prison but had the power of trying and convicting those guilty of capital crimes.

The prisons of Switzerland still follow the cantonal decentralized pattern. Each canton possesses a penitentiary, one or more district prisons, depending on the population, usually a reformatory, and sometimes establishments for the "correction of the youth." There is no uniformity, although an attempt was made as early as 1855, to develop an intercantonal correctional institution. While each canton has its own system of prisons and correctional institutions, there is a tendency to unification under one penal code.[1] As a sample of the set-up in one of the larger cantons, let us look at Zurich. Here we find (1) the cantonal penitentiary; (2) a number of district prisons; (3) a correctional establishment at Ringweil for boys between 12 and 20 years; (4) a house of correction at Uitikon, chiefly for drunkards; (5) preventive or educational establishments, five in number.[2]

Switzerland has always been impressed with progressive ideas of penal treatment. As early as 1863, Jakob Dubs, later a Swiss senator, posed the question of separation of the young offender from the older and more hardened criminal.[3] It is well to point out that Switzerland is sandwiched between France and Germany and could scarcely have been kept in ignorance of the influences in penal philosophy that were coming from America. In the eighteen-thirties, de Beaumont's and de Tocqueville's analysis of the American Houses of Refuge and penitentiaries was studied in Switzerland as well as the reports of Dr. Heinrich Julius of Prussia, bearing on the philosophies of silence and separation of prisoners. Later, after the Reformatory was opened in Elmira, in 1876, news of this new departure from tradition became publicized in the little mountain country.

In 1893, Canton Aargau established a reformatory known as Aarburg. The previous year, Canton Berne opened a reformatory school called Trachselwald. Gillin describes the offenders sent to this latter institution, as (a) young people from sixteen to twenty whose imprisonment was desirable, and (b) those actually sentenced by the court between the same ages. He continues by stating that this was the first effort on the part of Switzerland to put into effect some of the new ideas coming from America.[4]

In general, the forms of penal treatment practiced in Switzerland are: (1) cellular confinement; (2) two stages of common imprisonment

(1) C. R. Henderson, *Modern Prison Systems*, 1903, p. 95.
(2) *idem.*
(3) Gillin, *Taming the Criminal*, Macmillan, 1931, p. 167.
(4) *ibid.*, p. 168.

by day (association), with cellular isolation at night. Only sick persons may be in congregate dormitories. Prisoners in cellular confinement work, eat, and sleep in their cells, but may attend church and school together. Those inmates who are in association may not talk with one another.

Prisoners who must serve one or more years are divided into three disciplinary classes. Prisoners in the first class must remain in separate confinement for three to six months. Advance to a higher class depends on good behavior. The usual disciplinary measures are in vogue in the Swiss prisons such as deprivation of privileges, simple confinement, and the dark cell. The most drastic penalty is known as "intensified arrest," which means the dark cell with a reduction of food, and usually follows attempts to escape, resisting an officer, repeated lying or simulating sickness and violating the rule of silence.

Working conditions are good in the prisons of Switzerland. All convicts who work "with industry and good behavior" receive wages, ranging from five to twelve per cent of the amount they have earned by their labor. Conditional release has been in existence in Switzerland since about 1868. Today, if a prisoner has passed through the three stages of penal life in a satisfactory manner, and can show that he has the means of supporting himself upon release, he may petition for probationary release (*probeweise Entlassung*). If his petition is acted upon favorably by the department of justice, he may be released with the requirement that he present himself monthly before a "communal officer" and report on his behavior. If he cannot find employment, a private society, *Schutzaussichtsverein,* organized for the purpose of aiding prisoners, will assist him. If he violates his "parole," he may be recalled to finish out his term of imprisonment.

Professor Gillin, in his work, *Taming the Criminal,* was much impressed with the penal colony of Witzwil, in Switzerland. Here is to be found an experiment which aims not only to reclaim men but large areas of land as well. According to Gillin, the plan was conceived as early as 1863, when the question was raised as to the possibility of separating young offenders from the older and more hardened criminals.

Two events made possible the creation of the Witzwil colony a few years later. One was the failure of a private company which had attempted to develop an agricultural colony on the shores of the Neuenburger Lake. Because of this Canton Bern bought up about 2,000 acres of lands belonging to this defunct company. The other reason for the colony was the desire to remove the canton's prison from the center of the city of Bern to some outside site. The magistrates, therefore, conceived the idea of a penal agricultural colony. So in 1895, Witzwil colony was opened.

The director at the time of Professor Gillin's visit was Herr Otto Kellerhals, who was assisted by his son Hans. Under his progressive and dynamic leadership much has been accomplished by means of this experiment. Some five hundred men annually have worked on a reclamation project of great service to the state and, in addition, of starting a new life work through preparation under the helpful supervision of the director and his sympathetic staff. They have been taught to work at constructive tasks. Their health has been improved. If they take naturally to agriculture and have the native ability, they are in a position to learn much valuable information concerning scientific farming. Since Switzerland is an agricultural state, there are few inmates who cannot profit from the activity carried on.

While Witzwil is frankly a project emphasizing agriculture and reclamation of land, most of the trades are those subsidiary to the main purpose. Perhaps this is a weakness. On the other hand, the time spent at a colony of this sort, where the discipline is not repressive and where the staff focuses its attention on remedial treatment rather than on pure custody, is apt to be profitable to the majority of petty offenders who need just such an experience.

The war has had its effect on the Witzwil colony. There is an average population of some 500 men in the colony, composed of a hetrogeneous group including many military internees. These latter are naturally uneasy concerning their status. Raw materials are scarce, a condition which has dislocated the labor situation to a serious degree. However, those discharged have no trouble in securing agricultural employment since the country is making every effort to be self-supporting. The management is still on the same high level that has been its chief characteristic since it was established.

Professor Gillin closes his description of the colony by asking the question: "Could not some of our states learn a lesson from Switzerland in the handling of prisoners? Most of our states have sufficient land, and good land. They have lands to reforest, bricks to be made for buildings needed. They have the prisoners, in many states lying in idleness in the prisons, and in most states, idle by the thousands in jails, degenerating physically and morally. Have we met the leadership of little Switzerland?"[5]

Since these words were written, many states in America have opened up and developed prison farms. The present war has stimulated an amazing growth in agricultural production throughout the states. Practically every state penal system now has at least one large prison farm and many have expanded their farm land by hundreds of acres. By January, 1944, prison farm products had increased by over six million dollars over the pre-war production. In fact, the percentage of increase was twice that of farm production for the country as a whole. Special progress was also made in the processing and preservation of foods. De-hydrating has also been introduced on a large scale.

There is no doubt that farming as a form of penal treatment will be gradually extended as time goes on. Such a development has many advantages but there are likewise objections to such penal philosophy. It is a healthy digression, there can be no doubt, but it fails to answer many of the knotty questions that one may raise in the field of reformation. This is is especially true in the industrial states.

(5) *ibid.*, p. 189.

CHAPTER VI

RUSSIAN PENOLOGY UNDER THE CZARS AND THE SOVIETS

Under the Czarist Regime

It is notoriously true that the Russian prisons under the régime of the Czars were foul places indeed. Major Arthur Griffiths, writing in 1894, stated: "Russian prisons and the penal system of Russia . . . have been so gravely censured and so weakly defended that they stand self-condemned. The most hostile criticism comes from the pens of eye-witnesses, who, at great personal risk and discomfort, have penetrated the inmost recesses of the Russian Prison-houses, and have brought back heart-rending accounts of what they have seen."[1]

In the time of John Howard, all Russian prisons were guarded by the military; there were no jailers, as such. There was no such thing as the reformation of convicts. We get a picture of conditions in those days from his writings. He stated that the governor of the police of St. Petersburg showed him the instruments commonly used for punishment: the axe and the block, the machine for breaking arms and legs, the instrument for slitting the nostrils, and that for marking the criminals, which was done by punctuating a part of the flesh and rubbing a black powder in the wounds. He further reports that he witnessed a man and a woman being flogged with the cruel Russian *knut,* a whip made of dried thongs of rawhide and wires woven together.

The great reformer also describes the conditions in the prisons of St. Petersburg, Moscow and Riga as very bad. Men were commonly in irons, they were overcrowded, and in general, miserable beyond description. Many were worked on the fortifications on the outskirts of St. Petersburg. In the great prison at Moscow, known as the Kaluska Ostrog, he saw men chained together in wooden cages. Liquor, called *quas,* and made of wild mint, was sold to the convicts inside the prison. The military prison at Butirki was especially bad. It consisted of a single room into which were crowded one hundred and thirty-six prisoners. The room measured twenty-nine by twenty-six feet. It was constructed of wood, surrounded by wooden palisades.

As stated above, there was no attempt made to reform prisoners. They were slaves, in reality, and treated worse than animals. It is ironical that the Russians would never tolerate capital punishment, except for political offenses, but experienced no qualms in torturing unfortunate peasants to death. Nothing resembling a parole system or any form of conditional release was so much as contemplated.

The first feeble gesture at penal reform followed the visits of Howard to Russia. The Empress Catherine, who had been deeply impressed by the work of Cesare Beccaria, *Essay on Crimes and Punishments* (1764), gave instructions for a new penal code calling for distinctions between convicts.

(1)   *Secrets of the Prison House,* London, 1894, vol. I. p. 397.

She said: "One ought not to confine in the same place; (1) an accused person, against whom there are only appearances; (2) a convict; (3) a criminal who is condemned to prison as a punishment. The accused is only detained; the two others are imprisoned: but with respect to the former of them, the prison is only a part of the punishment; with respect to the latter, it is the punishment itself."[2]

The prominent American penologist of the nineteenth century, Enoch C. Wines, dates Russia's penal code at 1845. In that year, the *knut* was legally abolished. Except for the legal abolition of the more vicious forms of corporal punishment, the code accomplished little else. A Commission was established in 1877 to study penal conditions and to inaugurate a new penitentiary system. It proposed three species of privation of liberty: (1) A term of 18 months to six years, with labor, exercise, school and church services in association, with the remainder of the time in individual cells; (2) A term of from two weeks to a year in strict seclusion; (3) In houses of arrest for a term not exceeding three months, strict cellular separation. At the same time, instruction for prison officers was contemplated. Investigators were sent to other countries to examine the various penal systems then in operation. As early as 1874, one of the professors in the University of St. Petersburg gave a course in penitentiary science."[3]

Major Griffiths, in describing the history of Russian penal institutions in 1894, states that there were no prisons for the reception of short term prisoners. Such persons were kept in ancient winevaults adapted for the purpose. A large and imposing prison was built in 1875 at St. Petersburg and known as the Central Prison. Griffiths thus describes it:

> The new "Central," as it is called, is an ambitious edifice, uniting all the newest ideas in prison construction. A good deal of money has been lavished upon its architecture, although it was built in a large measure by prison labor; convicts did the demolitions of the old prisons, and the excavations for the new; doors, windows, locks and fittings, bolts and bedsteads were constructed in the correctional prison of Litovski. These economies notwithstanding, the total cost of the St. Petersburg "Central" appears to be excessive, which amounts to about £180,000.[4]

Regardless of its excellent architecture, it was called by one witness "a soul extractor. It utterly destroys the human personality; and the customs, the personal characteristics, the traits that distinguish a man from other men are all annihilated after he has spent some time in the Central prison. Hence he becomes a mere thing, a number, he is not so much as a beast of burden, which is fed in order that it may work. In most cases he has no work to do . . . and this weight of idleness crushes him down more completely than the most grinding form of penal servitude. I saw many hardened criminals, who cared not a rush for their wives, weep like children when the latter refused to follow them to Siberia."[5]

The horrible dampness and solitude found at the time in the fortress of St. Peter and St. Paul were attested to by eye-witnesses and quoted by Major Griffiths. There seems to have been no conscious penal philosophy in operation during the long years of the Czarist régime. This is doubtless

(2) John Howard, *State of Prisons*, E. P. Dutton & Company, 1929 ed., p. 75.
(3) E. C. Wines, *State of Prisons*, Cambridge University Press, 1880, pp. 462-466.
(4) *op. cit.*, p. 403.
(5) Quoted by Griffiths, p. 404.

due to the influence of the vicious system of exile that had long since fastened itself on the political life of the country and which made it impossible for reforms to be inaugurated in the prisons.[6]

Work with delinquent children was begun in 1870, with the establishment of an agricultural penitentiary colony, semipublic in nature. The government furnished the site and granted an annual subsidy but the management was private. Since that time several such colonies were developed, for the most part without financial aid from the government. There were at the time, reformatories in the larger cities of St. Petersburg, Moscow and Kharkov. Wines also wrote of the beginnings of societies of patronage to care for discharged prisoners.

All that can be gathered regarding the prison system of Russia prior to the Revolution of 1917 leads one to the belief that it was unbelievably cruel as well as chaotic. There were a few progressive penologists during the czarist regime—Count Wladimir Sollohub, director of the Moscow Prison, and Mikhail N. Gálkine-Wraskoy, Director-General of all Russian prisons, for instance—but the vision and intelligent resourcefulness possessed by men of their type were stifled by the inertia and corruptness of the government. Further revisions of the penal code occurred in 1903, 1914 and again in 1916. We shall now turn to the penal philosophy under the Soviets.

THE SOVIET REGIME

It is somewhat of a paradox that under an authoritarian system such as exists in the Soviet Union there should be in operation such a redemptive penal system. Yet this is true, although as we view it today, together with its penal code, we find no little confusion. In the early days of the régime, Soviet Russia alone among the nations of the world, had realistically analyzed criminal behavior and put into execution a scientific system of "punishment," or as the Russians would prefer to call it, treatment. In doing so, they abolished the "prison," as such, by abandoning its very name, and called its substitute, "a place of withdrawn freedom," or a "closed colony."

We shall first discuss conditions as they existed in the early days of the Soviet's amazing experiment and later attempt to show what changes were made in the light of their experience with these new penal concepts. The Soviet judicial system is based on the theory, according to Sidney and Beatrice Webb, that:

> Crime, theft, robbery, murder — is the result of social and economic conditions . . . Remove the people from corrupting influences; give them the type of work which will make an appeal to them; offer them a means of subsistence—and they will not desire to lead a life of vagrancy in the streets.[7]

This theory of crime, held by the early Bolshevist leaders, subscribed to the broader concept that the criminal was made, not born. They repudiated the so-called criminal type. They insisted that most criminals came from the economically depressed classes. Hence, crime could be

(6) For one of the best accounts of the Siberian exile system, see George Kennan, *Siberia and the Exile System*, 2 vol., Century, 1891. This is briefly summarized in Barnes and Teeters, *New Horizons in Criminology*, 1943, pp. 451-454.

(7) *Soviet Communism: A New Civilization*, Scribner's, 1936, p. 586 n. See also J. L. Gillin, "Russia's Criminal Court and Penal System," *Journal of Criminal Law and Criminology*, vol. 24, (1933-34), pp. 290-312.

eliminated after the economic system set up by the Soviets could be put in operation.

Whether we agree entirely with this concept of the causes of crime or not, we must admit that the U. S. S. R. made sweeping reforms in attempting to solve the traditional penal problems that plague every civilized country on the face of the earth. These reforms were made in a highly intelligent and practical fashion. This they accomplished in the early days of their régime, by several sweeping reforms.

Long sentences, irrespective of the crime, have been abolished. The average sentence is three years, the shortest is not less than one year, the longest ten years, except in rare instances when it may run as high as twenty-five. The criminal is not permitted to be idle but is immediately given the kind of work he was trained to do, or, if untrained, is at once put through a course appropriate to his aptitudes. Probably the most striking of the innovations, and yet the most sensible, is that provision has been made for carrying on in the same fashion normal sex and family life. The prisoner is granted leaves of absence ranging from 14 to 30 days a year. On those days he may visit his family, whether they live in a nearby village or town, or at a distance. In some prison colonies, facilities are provided for the residence of whole families. The unmarried prisoner has a right to marry; and, indeed, men and women prisoners associate freely within the colony. Finally, the man who has committed an antisocial act does not lose his civil rights. Within two years after the expiration of his sentence, if he has not committed another crime, all record of his arrest and imprisonment is wiped off the books. In view of these reforms, quoting from Elias Tobenkin:

. . . a prison sentence in the Soviet Republic is the beginning of the state's interest in the offender. Imprisonment in Russia is for a twofold purpose. First . . . it is a measure of social defense . . . The second aim is to put the criminal in the way of such educational, cultural and economic advantages as will restore him to normal industrial society a changed, reformed man in as short a time as possible.[8]

Security for the masses was the keynote of the earlier Soviet Russia. As Sherwood Eddy has said: "If, so long as he usefully functions in society, he is provided for from birth to death, through unemployment, illness, accident and every contingency, what reason or excuse is there for the hoarding of fear or selfish acquisitiveness?"[9] Early official statistics show that crime decreased with the improvement in economic and other conditions, and that there were fewer crimes related to the destruction of property or theft of state property. However, later statistics did not bear this out. We shall discuss this interesting paradox below.

Especially notable in the Russian penal program is the provision of facilities for education. Libraries and schools are furnished in the institutions and colonies themselves, and in the urban institutions, certain selected groups of inmates are allowed to attend the university and technical schools, returning to their rooms in the institution after class hours. As Sanford Bates, former Director of Federal prisons in this country, observed in 1935:

(8) *Stalin's Ladder: War and Peace in the Soviet Union*, Putnam's, 1933, p. 211.

(9) "The Penal System of Russia," *News Bulletin*, June, 1932, p. 2.

In the summer of 1935 I visited the old prison of St. Peter and St. Paul at Leningrad, which for years has been a museum. The old dungeons are empty, and the guards are wax figures. . .

The modern method is to substitute for the all too prevalent jail-house chatter some more productive activities. This is why libraries are established, newspapers are permitted, and organized athletics are encouraged. The larger the number of wholesome engrossing activities that can be found to fill the minds and tire the bodies, the less opportunity there will be for hatching of plots or the rehearsing of exploits.[10]

The Russians have divided their institutions into four types, as follows:

1. *Agricultural colonies.* These are collectivized villages. They have their own machines, blacksmith shops, tractor stations, a corps of instructors and mechanics, and their own social, educational and recreational lives.

2. *Correctional Labor camps.* Here the men are collected into gangs and put to work of a rigidly manual nature, such as building the famous canal from the Baltic to the White Sea. These camps are also placed in the forests and among the collieries and peat bogs, wherever work of the roughest kind has to be performed.

3. *Factory prisons.* These come closest to the American prisons but are scarcely prisons in our sense of the word. The main difference between them and the industrial factory, as such, is that the men do not go home in the evening. They live within the factory, sleep in dormitories, and are granted periodic leave depending upon good behavior and diligence. They may even go home to help with the harvest if their conduct warrants it. Within this "prison," life approximates the normal as much as possible. Recreation, selfgovernment, and education for citizenship are intensively provided in these places of "withdrawn freedom." Each man is made to serve the state just as much as the man on the outside. Thus, the three thousand inmates of a factory prison on the outskirts of Moscow in a single summer produced thirty million bricks. Most of these factories, like all Soviet "prison" colonies, are economically selfsustaining. To quote again from Sanford Bates:

I was greatly impressed by a visit to the Bolshevo Commune near Moscow in the summer of 1935. There I found a colony of 9,000 people, only 3,500 of whom are convicted prisoners. They live in all of the freedom of a small village community. They labor at standard wages. They marry and raise families, they provide their own discipline. In other words, they work out their own reformation and salvation, which leaves them free to develop rather than restricts them abnormally. They do not have to worry about escapes — that is impossible under the Soviet passport system, and they have no incentive to do so, because they are just as well off where they are; at least they have steady work to do. They do not have to worry about their families, since they are permitted to carry on family relations in a normal way. As their time is fully taken up with productive labor, they are not idle enough to get into conduct difficulties.[11]

4. *Closed prisons.* These are the old prison buildings in the towns and are used both for detention and imprisonment.[12]

Discipline in the agricultural and industrial colonies is exceedingly mild. The régime, according to the Corrective Labor Code of the Soviet Union, must approximate the conditions of life and work of free men. Prisoners have an eight-hour day, receive wages and may even sue for

(10) *Prisons and Beyond,* 1936, pp. 220-221. By permission of The Macmillan Company, publishers.
(11) *ibid.,* p. 276. By permission of The Macmillan Company, publishers.
(12) Cf. Lenka von Koerber, *Soviet Russia Fights Crime,* Dutton, 1935.

such wages, and share in the benefits of insurance. They may smoke, receive periodicals and newspapers, move freely, go beyond prison bounds, and have private appointments. There are no fences, no locks on the buildings, and dormitories are kept open day and night.

We have a description of one of these industrial colonies presented by D. N. Pritt, writing in the *Howard Journal*,[13] He visited the place in 1932. He describes it as a pleasant colony in the pine woods about twenty miles from Moscow. It was built by the O. G. P. U. specifically for thrice-convicted criminals between the ages of 16 and 24. The establishment is indistinguishable from any other Russian community that has built itself about a factory. There is no wall, no fence, no guards, no boundaries. The factory buildings are built similar to those of a free community. Every person works and receives wages in colony "script" which he may spend at the canteen. Many of the prisoners have their wives and children with them. The population at the time included about 2,000, most of whom were convicted of thievery; about 500 women, most of whom were wives of the prisoners but many were also convicted thieves; and children numbering about 300.

In accordance with the almost universal practice in Soviet Russia, the management of the colony is in the hands of the men themselves. There is a "collective," or general meeting, which elects an executive committee every six months. All matters of administration and discipline are in the hands of this group. Breaches of discipline are punished by cutting off the weekly rest day, deduction of wages, or expulsion from the colony. Inmates are free to leave when they wish but few do as they stand better chances of regaining their citizenship, which they lost upon conviction, if they remain until properly discharged.

In the Bolshevo colony the men manufacture sports' goods. They chose this type of merchandise at first because of its wholesome psychological effect. All goods are sold on the "open market" which is a very easy matter in Russia, since there the limitations found in capitalist countries do not exist.

Staff officers are there merely to assist in educational work, and to care for the medical needs of the inmates. The usual recreational pursuits are followed with much enthusiasm in the colony. The radio, movies, sports of all kinds are in frequent demand. There are rules against card-playing, drink and drugs, since it is assumed that these were mainly responsible for the crimes the inmates committed.

This particular colony was originally started to care for the appalling problem of "homeless children" who roamed Russia in the early days after the Revolution. Gradually, however, it was turned into a labor colony for recidivist thieves. In order to belong to the colony, men committed to various other institutions (prisons) may make application. Usually those elected to membership have finished out most of their sentence in some institution previous to coming to Bolshevo.

This colony is no doubt the same one described by Sherwood Eddy. Here, he states, thieves and pickpockets are taught a trade; there are no armed guards, no fences nor walls. He describes it as follows:

(13) Vol. III, No. 4, 1933; "Bolshevo: A Russian Labour Colony for Criminals."

The colony near Moscow, which anyone may inspect, was begun a few years ago by a physician and a group of boys he sought to reclaim . . . Those on good behavior may be gone on a vacation during the summer. They may marry while in the colony; they may do almost anything that will serve to make them useful citizens.[14]

Contrary to the attitudes regarding the criminal in American prisons, where he must become a mere number, where he is forgotten by the state that put him away, where he is sent back into the world a marked man, wearing a ten dollar suit of clothes, ill prepared to meet life anew, a man coming from a "prison" in Russia, is in many ways in a more advantageous position than the average citizen. He has learned a trade and worked at it industriously. He is therefore in demand—not, as in this country, regarded as a social pariah by labor organizations and not permitted to utilize his newly-acquired skill—and by virtue of the social reeducation which he has undergone he is equipped to face his fellows as he never was when leading a subterranean life of crime. The new Russian prison system not only presents an attractive theoretical picture but produces practical results of a most satisfactory nature. The percentage of rehabilitation achieved by Soviet penology—properly discounting the overexuberance of its partisan supporters—is actually amazing. Since this enlightened and successful Soviet system of reformative prison administration is in no way directly related to communism or Marxian socialism and could just as readily be utilized by capitalistic countries, it is to be hoped that it will be widely adopted in other nations of the world in due season. As Sanford Bates says regarding its adoption in this country:

It will, of course, be recognized that we cannot at this time, at least, suggest duplicating such an experiment. But the Soviet Government claims complete success for this method of handling the ordinary type of criminal. It has substituted the idea of colonization for correction. We are obliged so to devise our correctional system that it will aid in the readaptation of the prisoner in normal life outside. The Soviet Union realizes the insuperable difficulty of such a process — restricting and reforming at one time. Perhaps the idea of rural resettlement can be expanded in this country to the extent of redistributing throughout the wide-open spaces some of the victims of our improper distribution of population, that enter our penal systems.

These prison colonies or communities may succeed where prisons have failed, on the theory that no man will escape unless there is an incentive to do so. He will go or stay where productive employment is possible, and he can prosper best under the operation of influences which assist in his reformation rather than impede it.[15]

It is interesting to note that if an offender is a poor worker, he is given a light sentence; if he is an intelligent citizen who "should have known better," or who has exploited a "weaker brother," he is given a heavier punishment; but if he is a member of the Communist Party, he is given the maximum sentence of the law. This is an interesting and new conception of class justice.

Penalties are measured less by personal guilt than by social consequences, for a crime against the state, or against society as a whole, will affect many people, and therefore is considered far more serious than a crime which involves one or two persons, such as murder. The only crimes in Russia that are punishable by death are counter-revolution, malfeasance

(14) *loc. cit.*, p. 2.
(15) *op. cit.*, p. 277. By permission of The Macmillan Company, publishers.

in public office, and exploiting the superstitions of the masses for the overthrow of the state.

This brings us to a discussion of the changes in concepts regarding crimes and criminals, based on the experience of the Soviets during the past ten years. As we stated above, those who were responsible for bringing the "new order" into being, were convinced that criminals were made by insecurity, economic exploitation, forced idleness caused by dislocation of industry in a capitalistic system, and other injustices flowing from the old order. Hence, it was believed that if these were cleared up, crime would disappear. Lenin, as early as 1919, believed in the greater use of the suspended sentence for offenders, of the "public reprimand," and the penalty of correctional labor without deprivation of liberty. The secret police were more vigilant in rounding up enemies of the state than in focusing their attention on the petty criminal, who, it was thought, would soon be rehabilitated by the enlightened system of correctional work camps, the suspended sentence, and public disapproval. With work provided to all who wished it, crime would disappear. But this did not happen. The younger students of the problem contend that those who commit crimes when work is available in abundance are those who "are too lazy to work." They are now regarded as parasites.[16] It is urged by these younger men that the new criminal code should take cognizance of this class by inserting a section dealing with "Crimes against the Principle of Toil in the U. S. S. R." However, we find:

> There are thoughtful middle-aged men who are also puzzled by the continuation of crime in a society in which there is no longer unemployment, but they do not jump to the conclusion that the majority of these criminals commit crimes merely because they do not want to work. Some of these men talk in terms of hangovers of bourgeois mentality. Others do not profess to know the answer, but they are telling each other that serious thinking must be done on this problem before a new policy can be enunciated. They continue to argue, as they have always done, for a more general application of the lighter, rehabilitating forms of penalty which remain the law as long as the present criminal codes are not superseded by the new All-Union code. These writers decry the tendency of the courts to apply the more severe penalties while the codes still provide a choice which includes lighter penalties.[17]

There seems to be a definite trend, however, in tightening up on offenders. It has been noted by certain Russian students that "correctional labor without deprivation of liberty" and "social censure" had little deterrent effect. These penalties truly represent a modest form of punishment and, it may be argued, that without the sort of supervision we understand in America, they merely represent "another chance." Even the suspended sentence is growing in disfavor, even though it was earlier advocated by Lenin.

During the past three or four years, the maximum prison sentence has been increased from ten to twenty-five years and the word "prison" is being revived, especially to those places where dangerous persons are incarcerated. Then, too, the attitude toward juveniles, over the age of 12, is becoming more severe. Hearings of older children are now held in regular criminal courts rather than, as heretofore, before children's tribunals, although there is an effort not to inflict adult penalties on minors.

(16)   John N. Hazard, "Trends in the Soviet Treatment of Crime," *American Sociological Review*, August, 1940, pp. 566-576.
(17)   *ibid.*, p. 569.

Figures presented by Mr. Hazard along this line are interesting: Criminal rowdyism is called hooliganism in Soviet terminology; of the young hooligans convicted in 1934, 16.9 per cent were sentenced to deprivation of freedom; in 1935, this figure rose to 42.4 per cent; and in the first half of 1937 to 65.3 per cent, and in 1938, first half of the year, to 66.2 per cent.

Conflicting stories regarding Russia's experimentation have been coming out of that country for the past twenty years. This is equally true regarding her penal reform. For years we were told of "forced labor" camps where prisoners, especially political prisoners, were treated abominably. No doubt such stories may have been substantiated. We hold no brief for Russia. We are merely reporting what many observers and students of Russian institutions have recorded. It would not be fair if we did not include herewith something that will give a picture which nullifies, to a degree, what has gone heretofore. It is reprinted by the *Howard Journal*[18] from Olavi Veltheim, *A Foreigner in the U. S. S. R*:

> . . . The journey from Sverdlovsk to the penal camp in Siberia appears to me like one continuous night.
> We had to travel in cattle trucks with one narrow chink for a window covered on both sides with a thick layer of ice. It was dark both by day and by night. In the day time the darkness was relieved by a faint glimmering of light through the cracks between the boards, and at night by the red glow from the burning-hot stove. Twice during the day the train stopped at empty derelict stations buried in snow drifts almost up to their low-pitched roofs; a bucket of hot water and a sack with slices of black bread were pushed in at the truck door. Wild with misery, the whole mass of prisoners rushed to the narrow opening of the sliding door, but in the crush no one had a chance of seeing anything or even of enjoying a whiff of fresh air; with a screeching, clanking sound the door was shoved to, the heavy iron bolt was placed across it and the key rattled in the frozen iron lock.

The author proceeds by saying no one knew their destination but they were kept in such close quarters—in a cattle train—for a fortnight. He describes the bath given the prisoners during that nightmare journey:

> Judging by the inscription the town was Omsk. In the railway bath-house everyone was given a piece of soap the size of a lump of sugar and allowed ten minutes for washing. The place was packed and the crush indescribable. It was only when we saw one another in the well-lighted bath-house that we fully grasped what that fortnight of cold, darkness, hunger and lice had done to us. All were black with smoke and grime which covered our eyes, noses, ears; all had swollen faces, hands and feet; everyone's eyes had a wild, feverish look. That visit to the bath-house was a perfect nightmare. One almost felt that it would have been better not to leave the darkness of the cattle truck or discover how thoroughly we had lost human semblance. And there were trains and trains behind us carrying the same kind of load.

The load of human misery had still another week of nightmarish travel. They finally landed at Kusnetsk. "There are lots of penal camps around Kusnetsk," said one old-time criminal, a convicted thief. "I know these parts. Camps were started as soon as they found iron ore here. . . . And there's coal at Kusnetsk. They're building a railway to carry it, and there are roads, too. They're also making a railway from Kusnetsk to the Mongolian frontier; that's in case of war."

Upon their arrival at the prison-camp, they were unloaded, herded together and marched to the barracks. The description continues:

(18)   Spring, 1940, pp. 257-262.

The convoy was drawn up in line; many of the soldiers had typical Mongol faces—high cheek bones, flat noses, narrow slanting eyes, dark and expressionless.

As we tumbled out of the trucks the first thing we caught sight of were the contemptuous ill-natured faces of the G.P.U. officials, sick to death of meeting and counting the dirty, ragged and lousy crowds of prisoners. . . A cold, piercing wind was blowing clouds of black icy dust; we were growing numb with cold; some stamped with their feet, others huddled themselves together, their teeth chattering.

At the distance of about a mile from the train we saw a tower, sentries, barbed wire, and unconsciously slowed down.

"The 9th section of the *Siblag,* Osinovsky Camp-Centre," was written on the gates. Beyond it could be seen a well-trodden piece of ground, a three-storied building for the overseers and twenty barracks for housing 12,000 prisoners. Our four hundred were swallowed up without a trace. During the winter the death rate in the mines had been so terrific that there was a continual shortage of workers; we were immediately sorted out and told to begin work the following morning.

The above description sounds much like the old days of the Czarist régime instead of the days of enlightened penal policy of the Soviets. The recency of the book referred to leads to the disquieting realization that in times of danger to the state the authorities feel compelled to inaugurate a system of terrorism in order to cope with its enemies, real and imaginary.

Women prisoners in Russia are apparently not so well handled, at least at the time Lenka von Koerber wrote in 1935. This writer stated that there were few female criminals in the Soviet Union, scarcely eight per cent of the total. The women arrested in the Moscow district were remanded as well as imprisoned after conviction in three dormitories of the huge Taganka prison. Their lot was not an easy one since they were overcrowded and not separated as to types.

There is a women's prison at Perm but at the time there were also employed here many men convicts who were used to train women inmates in the various trades. In the vast Ukraine there were no closed prisons for women. Both men and women were housed in the same institutions and enjoyed recreation and labor in association with few restrictions. Miss von Koerber thought this situation was a splendid idea which hardly squares with thought in the United States, for example.

Most of the females sentenced to imprisonment had led "licentious lives" and apparently were unable to get along in close association with women in general. It is probable that by now the women prisoners in Russia fare somewhat better.[19]

CRIMINAL PROCEDURE IN SOVIET RUSSIA

The lower courts in the Soviet Union are known as People's Courts. They are presided over by a professional judge who is assisted by two lay juror-judges who have equal powers of decision in law and fact with the professional judge. The professional judge is elected for a term of three years and is supposed to have training in the law. The lay judges, who may be either men or women, are elected by local groups for a period not to exceed ten days per year. While, as a rule, a defendant usually pleads his own case before this court, he may choose an attorney. He may also call his own witnesses.

(19)   Von Koerber, *op. cit.,* pp. 154-155.

The next step in the judicial hierarchy is the Regional Court. This serves as a review court and for serious crimes, a court of original jurisdiction. The judges of these courts are elected by the Regional Soviets for a term of five years. When this court serves as an appellate court, all judges are professionals. In cases of original jurisdiction, there is one professional judge and lay juror-judges, the same as in the People's Courts.

The next higher court in each Republic is the Supreme Court. Each Supreme Court is divided into different tribunals to hear cases of civil or criminal nature. Judges of these courts are elected by the Supreme Soviets of the respective republics for a term of five years.

At the top of the judicial system is the Supreme Court of the U. S. S. R. which is composed of various branches, including the Military Section and the Transport Section. It is almost entirely an appellate court with original jurisdiction in only the most serious of cases.[20]

Since the German invasion the jurisdiction of the criminal courts has been largely supplanted by military tribunals. This change has intensified the vigorous application of punishment.

With the eventual coming of peace and the return to normalcy it is to be hoped that in Soviet Russia an extension of the enlightened judicial philosophy and progressive penal treatment that had been marked by so intelligent a beginning will be realized.

(20) For a discussion of the court system of Soviet Russia, see Mary S. Callcott, *Russian Justice,* Macmillan, 1935 ; see also, John N. Hazard, "The Legal Framework of Russia," *The New Republic,* November 17, 1941, pp. 660-663.

CHAPTER VII

THE PRISONS OF EASTERN EUROPE

THE PRISONS OF POLAND

After Poland was granted her independence in 1918, great strides were taken in centralizing all prisons inherited by Russia, Austria and Germany, which dominated the country prior to the last war. Three types of prison administration were to be found in these institutions, so it took the new state some time to bring all three groups into a common system of penal discipline. Those of Upper Silesia were the last to come into the centralized group, in the year 1922.

These three groups of institutions consisted of 33 large prisons, 70 still larger establishments, 35 small prisons and 262 "arrest" prisons—400 in all. These were narrowed down to 300, which are still maintained in Poland.*

Poland has tried courageously to adapt its penitentiary system to the principles of modern penology. Throughout the entire system a note of honesty and sincerity is maintained. Due to the confusion existing in the years after the last war, with three different systems prevailing, the country had no little trouble in centralizing its institutions and inaugurating a consistent policy in regard to them all. However, she has succeeded admirably and consequently deserves a great deal of credit.

In 1928 a new law dealing with penal institutions of all kinds was promulgated. It consists of 72 different articles and deals with: I. Prisons and Reformatories; II. Control and Supervision; III. Enforcement of the Sentence and Transport of Prisoners; IV. Labor of Prisoners; V. Religious Help and Education; VI. Food and Clothing; VII. Communications with the Outside; VIII. Special Prescriptions; IX. Disciplinary Prescriptions; X. Use of Arms and Convocation of Armed Force; XI. Associations of Patronage; XII. Temporary and Final Regulations. It will be seen that the new penal law was comprehensive in scope.

All prisons are under the jurisdiction of the Ministry of Justice and are divided into three classes:

Class I Prisons: all prisons which can contain more than 450 convicts and prisons for criminals serving longer than three years' sentences.

Class II Prisons: all prisons which contain 150-450 convicts and prisons for criminals serving sentences of from 1 to 3 years' duration.

Class III Prisons: all prisons which contain 150 convicts and prisons for criminals serving sentences of one year duration, as well as prisons attached to the Justice of Peace offices.

Women's prisons and places for the detention of minors are separate.

Poland has adopted the "progressive stages" system familiar in the English system. Within the prison, inmates are divided into classes and pass

(*) The material for this section of Poland's prisons is from Edouard Neymark, "The Prisons of Poland," *Howard Journal*, June, 1929, pp: 321-327. See also article on the same subject by this author in *Journal of Criminal Law and Criminology*, vol. 19, November, 1928, pp. 399-407. No doubt there have been changes since that time.

from one stage to the other with regard to their individuality, the nature of their offenses, their behavior while in prison, their progress in studies and in work, as well as their moral regeneration. All ablebodied prisoners work since Polish authorities are convinced of the moral efficacy of steady occupation. The type of work pursued by each prisoner depends first upon his own personal desire. Special care is exercised that nothing connected with the labor system will contribute to the ill health or danger of the prison inmate. Prisoners are insured against accidents or illness caused by industrial machines. The Polish system of prison discipline recognizes the importance of outside agencies and selected individuals in assisting in the moral regeneration of criminals. The law suggests that agencies or committees be formed by citizens to cooperate with prison authorities concerning the moral training and to venture their opinions relative to "remission of sentence and pardon of prisoners." This is unquestionably a progressive step in modern penology but how far this arrangement has gone, we do not know.

The prisons are well stocked with books and reading is encouraged by the authorities. The educational system apparently is quite well developed with regular teachers employed in effecting a generous and broad-gauged academic program. In addition, lectures, dramatic plays and radio programs are encouraged. However, subjects of a controversial political nature are forbidden.

The physical comforts of all prisoners are scrupulously cared for; the law requires that each prisoner receive 3,000 calories of food per day, if working, and 2,400 calories for nonworking inmates. Extra calories of the proper nature are given the sick. The only disciplinary measures are those which deal with deprivation of privileges or a curtailment of food for short periods. No corporal punishment is allowed. There are definite limits placed on the number of hours in a dark cell or days in solitary confinement. For good behavior or progress in work, prisoners are tendered rewards in the shape of little special privileges, such as permission to smoke, prolonged exercise, permission to receive visitors or more books, etc. Remission of sentence may also follow in some cases.

The aftercare of prisoners and their relations with their families are under the "Association of Patronage." This Patronage works under a statute and is in charge of the President of the Court of Appeal in Warsaw. Branches are to be found in several of the larger towns of the country, the members being known as prison curators. They are privileged to visit prisoners while in the institution and do all within their power to work out a satisfactory plan upon release from prison. As we have stated in reference to Italy, where this system undoubtedly is even more advanced, little satisfaction can be gained from the use of volunteers without training. It is more and more accepted in penology that trained, full time men and women are needed for this delicate assignment.

The Juvenile Court was established in Poland in 1919 but owing to the lack of funds only three were realized. These are at Warsaw, Lódz and Lublin.

Women play a large part in the procedure of the Juvenile Court. The first judges of the Warsaw court were women. Children are handled exclusively by women recruited primarily from the intellectual classes and many of them are college graduates. Educational institutions work closely with the courts in carrying out investigations.

Reformatory institutions are quite plentiful in Poland and in most cases they are modern in every respect. In 1930 a special organization known as the "Special Children's Care Society" was founded in Warsaw. It functions under the Juvenile Court with the court judge as president. Its object is to furnish proper nourishment and clothing to poor and destitute children as well as necessary medical assistance. It also provides evening classes for children, excursions into the country, free swimming facilities and moving picture shows.**

In general, then, Poland's prison system is on a reasonably high level. It is hoped that this ill fated country may pick up the threads of penal reform after the present hostilities cease and carry on from where she was so rudely interrupted by the brutal invasion of the Nazis.

CZECHOSLOVAKIAN PRISONS

Prior to the occupation of the Czech state and the control exercised over Slovakia by the Nazis, the former free state had worked out a reasonably progressive system of penal treatment, according to Professor J. S. Roucek who visited the country's penal institutions a few years ago.[1]

The prison system is unified with the rudiments of classification provided for. Employees are selected by civil service after they have completed a three months' special course. After appointment they must serve a year's probationary period. The entire staff looks upon their profession as one of permanent tenure and promotions are determined in terms of "continuous in-service" training.

All prisoners, with the exception of those incarcerated for political reasons, work every day and are paid each according to his industry and capacity. Part of the wages accrue to the State as a partial repayment of the cost of maintenance. The remainder is set aside for him until his release. Skilled workers are provided employment compatible with their training; unskilled workers are taught a trade. Products of the prisons are disposed of through the state-use system. Most of the prisons have their own farms so that agriculture is a part of the work and training program. In some cases prisoners are permitted to work for private persons in return for real wages.

Every convict and county prison in Czechoslovakia has a special fund out of which released prisoners are assisted, each according to his needs and behavior. In addition there exist some eighteen associations throughout the country whose objective is to aid released prisoners. Enrolled in these societies are about 8,000 members

There are two reformatories for boys under the ages of twenty-one in which there is an excellent educational system. In fact, Professor Roucek was much impressed with the educational system in Czechoslovakian prisons, rating it even higher than the best in this country. Regular classes are

** The material on the juvenile courts is from Georges de Fiedorowicz, "Children's Courts in Poland," *Howard Journal*, 1936, pp. 295-298.

(1)   See his article, "The Educational Aspects of the Prison System in Czechoslovakia," *School and Society*, vol. 47, pp. 513-514 (April, 1938). See also, "The Prison System in the Czechoslovak Republic," Prague, 1930, published by the Ministry of Justice.

conducted by the regular teacher, physician and priest attached to each prison. Teachers from outside the prison are also employed to direct classes who also arrange special lectures for Sundays and holidays. Each prison also has its own library and musical organization which are well patronized by the inmates. All prisoners receive a special weekly periodical, *Noving* (News), which contains a review of all current events and items of cultural interest. All inmates under twenty-one must participate in religious courses and services. Every recognized sect has the privilege of conducting services, any expense for same being borne by the State. The physician in each prison supervises institutional hygiene and gives periodical lectures in his field. Regular hours are set aside for physical education.

One interesting prison in old Slovakia is that located at Leopoldov. The oldest part of the structure was built by the Emperor Leopold in 1669 as a fortress against the Turks. Later it was used as a military establishment. The form of the high outer walls, or earthworks, is unique as it assumes the shape of a six-pointed star. Few guards are needed to police the walls. It has been a prison for over a century and today it is used as a hard labor institution for some 800 long term convicts. The buildings are within the walled enclosure as well as gardens, orchards and the private dwellings of the officials.

There are three separate stages through which the convicts must pass. If their conduct is good, they may be obliged to spend only a third of their sentence in each stage. The first stage, or department, is strict separate confinement. Not only must they be alone, but the more "dangerous" are weighted down with a heavy chain around their ankles which is supported by leather straps attached to the wrists. From this state they move on to the second department where they enjoy "association" in a large room which they share with some 18 to 20 other companions. These rooms are something like "men's clubs," since they are permitted to play games or read. They work in small groups in the shops located in other parts of the great prison. The trades are the conventional types found in most prisons, carpentry, locksmith, carpet weaving, bookmaking, etc. The well-behaved prisoners receive red stripes for their arms of which they are quite proud.

The third department is for those prisoners serving the last third of their sentences. It is located outside the prison proper in a large building containing several rooms adjoining the farmyard and farm buildings. Only one guard is on watch. The men here give up their prison garb and wear neat blue suits, with an opportunity of wearing their own clothes on Sundays. They live as in a family or social group and the spirit is reported as being exceptionally fine. It is not unusual for some of these men to be released on a sort of "ticket-of-leave" and return to their homes, the only supervision being the local police authorities. All of the conventional features of prison life are on a high plane at Leopoldov—education, work, compensation, recreation and food. Hospital facilities are especially efficient and modern. This prison and its progressive régime existed as it is now even under the former Hungarian administration. Czechoslovakia very wisely continued it as it was found after the expiration of the first World

War. The same officials who locally administered the prison are still in charge, although some of them are Hungarians. From reports, it would seem that this is one of the better prisons on the European Continent, in spite of the first department of separate confinement.[2]

Probation was established shortly after the country was created, that is, in 1919. Its provisions compare favorably with those of the more progressive countries, providing supervision by special officers for those granted this form of treatment. Volunteer supervisors are also employed.[3]

This, in brief form, is the penal set-up in one of the most literate countries in the world, that of Czechoslovakia, created by the Peace of Versailles, but eclipsed temporarily by the Nazi Juggernaut. At the expiration of the current war, there is no doubt that this small and enlightened democracy will go forward with a progressive penal philosophy worthy of her high intellectual and cultural background.

THE CZECHOSLOVAK PENAL SYSTEM

1. Six convict prisons for offenders serving sentences of over one year up to life:

  (a) Two prisons for first offenders and for other nonincorrigibles: Plzeň and Leopoldov.

  (b) Two prisons for incorrigibles: Kartouzy and Ilava.

  (c) One prison for offenders who are chronically ill or invalid: Mirov.

  (d) One prison for females with a special section for youthful offenders: Řepy, near Prague.

2. Two reformatories for boys:

  (a) The Reformatory and Penal Institute at Mikulov for offenders under 21 years of age serving a sentence of more than six months.

  (b) The Komeský Institute at Košice, a State Reformatory, with criminal section for youths who have been sentenced by the Courts to a term at a reformatory, and with a social welfare section for youths who have been neglected, are morally menaced or defective.

Neither of these institutions retains its inmates longer than the age of 21.

3. The Provisional Penal Institute at Leopoldov—for offenders sentenced to long terms who have served two-thirds of their sentence but who, in spite of good conduct, cannot be released as "good conduct" men owing to the fact that some further legal conditions have not been fulfilled.

4. Thirty-seven prisons attached to the courts of the counties for persons under remand (detention) and for prisoners serving sentences up to one year. These prisons contain separate department for males and females, for persons under remand and actual prisoners, for young and adult offenders (the maximum is six months). The largest of these prisons

(2)   This material is taken from Frederick Hankinson's description appearing in the *Howard Journal*, June, 1929, pp. 315-318.

(3)   See Timasheff, *op. cit.*, p. 54.

is that of the Prague Criminal Court which can accommodate more than 800 inmates.

5. Three hundred seventy-nine prisons attached to the District Police Courts for persons under remand and for offenders sentenced by the District Police Courts—from 12 hours to one month.

In addition to the above, all of which are operated by the State, there are several so-called Provincial penal settlements and reformatories in Bohemia, Moravia and Silesia which are conducted by the provincial authorities. These were designed mainly for vagrants, for those convicted of offenses against property, malicious negligence and "gross avarice." These are:

In Bohemia

For men: Prague and Pardubice; for women and girls, Kostomlaty; for boys, Králiky and Opatovice-on-the-Elbe.

In Moravia and Silesia

For men: Brno, Šumperk and Znojmo, the latter also accommodating women; reformatories for boys, Uherské Hrad, Albrechtice, and Nový Jičín; for girls, Boskovice and Mohelnice.

PRISONS AND PENAL REFORM IN HUNGARY

This impoverished country of central Europe presents a number of amazing contrasts in her treatment of the offender. Her adult prisons are repressive and reactionary but her reformatories compare favorably with those of other lands. Prison administration is on a low plane, yet Hungary has no imprisonment for debt, no capital punishment for persons under twenty-one and no corporal punishment at all.

Still rankling over what she considers unjust treatment at the peace conference of the last war, in which she lost much of her territory, she finds herself not only impoverished but obliged to care for thousands of refugees who have come to her large cities from much of the surrounding territory which she lost.

The large penal institution at Vác has many innovations of modern design which even outstrip many to be found in America and England. For example, there is a large theater inside the walls, quartz lamps, laboratories for tests and an up-to-date dental clinic. The hospital facilities are remarkable. This is perhaps the most outstanding feature of the institution and presents a marked contrast to the repressive methods of penal treatment in operation in the institution. Tuberculosis is quite prevalent in Hungary so that an unusually large number of men suffering from this disease is to be found in the prisons. As one writer describes the tuberculosis ward at Vác: "It was a sad sight to see long rows of men lying out in caged balconies, gazing it is true at a wonderful view across the Danube, but none of them was reading or occupied in any way."[1]

Hungary's prisons are operated on the principle of separate confinement. One writer, in describing the system as it operates there, says:

Solitary confinement in Hungary means, according to law, confinement in a cell never exceeding eighteen cubic meters in size, where even in summer not a ray

(1) Clara D. Rackham, "The Hungarian Prison System," *The Penal Reformer*, (published quarterly by the Howard League for Penal Reform, London), January, 1938, p. 10.

of sunlight ever enters. The damp walls of the cell are white and yellow from salt-peter, and the prisoner must wear winter clothing even in summer owing to the cold. With the exception of the guard, conversation with whom is forbidden, the prisoner never sees anybody. Food, in any case scanty, is reduced by a third. Better food at one's own expense, visits by relatives, books, paper, and writing materials are not allowed.

According to law, solitary confinement can extend only for one-third of the sentence, not exceeding one year for sentences up to five years, two years for sentences up to ten years, and three years as the absolute limit in case of higher sentences. In addition, the law provides that strict solitary confinement may be carried out only where the health of the prisoner permits.[2]

No book or occupation is given the prisoner for the first ten days. He may then avail himself of a prayer book only, until the end of three weeks when a secular book is permitted.

However repressive the system, everybody works. The penal system is operated on the philosophy that prisons and criminals must pay for themselves. This concept permeates the entire system, even to the establishments for young boys and girls. The labor system is on the contract basis, frankly and openly, so that prison made goods run unfair competition with private goods outside. This is done in spite of the fact that Hungary usually has large numbers of unemployed. The practice also encourages the prisons to be factories rather than institutions designed to "cure" or "reform" offenders. The prisoners who work get a small wage which they may spend at the "canteen." It was noticed by one of the visitors that the men spent their money for bread, which led to the conclusion that they were not well fed. Meat is served only once a week with the main diet being vegetables and bread.

The chief women's prison is in the country and has a large farm worked primarily by women. Many women serve as high as twenty years' sentences at this prison. It is in charge of nuns, and the atmosphere, though "strangely cold and dead," is kindly, with few punishments. There is no form of relaxation yet the women apparently prefer the farm work to indoor factory pursuits. Male guards patrol the place in full uniform and a few men do the heavier work on the farm.

Another prison is located at Budapest and known as the Law Courts Prison. In the suburbs of that city is located an institution for adolescent girls. The punishment cells in this reformatory are quite forbidding. They are completely bare except at night when a straw mattress is thrown in by the attendant. It is not unusual for girls to be incarcerated in such places for fourteen days. Suicides are frequent. However, there are some good features of this institution. There are gardens in which the girls are employed and morale seems good. One unique occupation found here is that of combing the hair of a large stock of Angora rabbits.

In spite of obvious repressive characteristics of the reformatories of Hungary, it is the purpose of the penal law to think of such treatment in terms of "individualization and family life." An interesting description of the technique used in the Hungarian Reformatories for boys is presented by Dr. Stephen Schäfer, a Budapest lawyer, which bears quoting:

There is little doubt that education in the Reformatories is an education-by-force, and inmates entering such institutions are obsessed by the exasperating word "force." When the inmate faces his master for the first time he will regard him as an enemy, and as the first movement toward friendliness will not come from the

(2)   Lettau Santo, in the *Nation*, vol. 142, March 4, 1936, p. 295.

inmate, the master has to show a cordial interest, and by so doing is able to disarm him. Inmates must be made to feel and appreciate the atmosphere of a family circle and to understand that good friends save future trouble. Our institutions carry out their work to further this end.[3]

After a strict medical examination, the boy puts on the regulation clothes and is "inducted" into the "experimental family" class. After a few weeks of observation in this preliminary family group, he is designated to a "regular family" group. It is in the regular family groups that the process of real education begins. The routine is not severe. All boys work at trades or go to classes if found necessary. As Dr. Schäfer describes these institutions: "Reformatory buildings are well constructed with large windows, sunny rooms, lovely gardens and everything is kept spotlessly clean." He feels that while the Reformatories are doing a splendid piece of work for young delinquents, they are given too much work, and, as we have seen in other European countries, little thought is given to aftercare. This is due in Hungary to lack of finances. However, the Minister of Justice is alert to the needs of discharged prisoners, and is "doing everything possible to effect beneficial changes in the interests of juvenile offenders" particularly.

In spite of the enthusiastic comments that may be recorded concerning the progressive "family system" practiced in the Reformatories, the following description more than belies such utterances:

It was, however, at the Boys' Reformatories that the absence of women on the staff was most severely felt. Boys as young as 12 and looking much younger are entirely in the charge of men and it only needed a glance at their listless faces, the dreary rooms, and the fare and ill-equipped kitchen, to see how much the whole place needed a woman's care. No doubt it was also the fact that the boys ate, slept and washed in the same room that added to this unattractive impression.[4]

Then, too, the work provided the boys is dull and monotonous and has no practical value so far as providing training for release. They are engaged in making toys of papier maché or pasting small pieces of molds in which the Reformatories of Hungary maintain a monopoly.

In contrast to the treatment afforded the older boy, Hungary is apparently trying hard to handle the problems of the real juvenile delinquent in a sympathetic manner. The age of criminal responsibility is 14 in that country and no child under that age is considered capable of criminality. The onus is placed on the parent or the child's circumstances. Hence, no child under 14 can theoretically be sent to prison and no record is made of any such cases. The work of the Juvenile Court is on a reasonably high level. This children's court takes advantage of a Voluntary Home and Works School where children may be sent under relative freedom. They may spend their nights at home, and during the day, mingle with children who have left school permanantly—the children in Hungary may leave school after they have completed four years of primary school, which usually means at 12 years, although they cannot work at profitable employment until they are 14. The interim time is usually spent in a Works School where they are taught various trades. This is a definite attempt to bring supervision to those children who must, for one reason or another, leave school at an early age, or who are what we in America might call predelinquent.

(3)   "Reformatories in Hungary," *Howard Journal*, Spring, 1940, pp. 252-254.
(4)   Clara D. Rackham, *loc. cit.*, p. 11.

The Juvenile Courts are in charge of professional judges and, on the whole, quite informal. Children placed on probation are assisted by "officials of patronage" who not only assist in the court proceedings but help the child in his adjustment. There is an employment bureau established as an adjunct of the Court where probationers can be advised concerning employment. Probation in Hungary dates from a law drafted July 30, 1908 which provided for such treatment for adults according to the Franco-Belgian pattern (suspension of the execution of the sentence) and for juveniles according to the American system.[5]

Hungary, it may be seen, has a long way to go before she can rank with those few nations that are attempting to utilize some of the concepts and ideals that characterize modern penal treatment. However, it can be stated that she leads that block of countries usually designated as south-eastern Europe. While her treatment of juveniles makes no use of child-guidance clinics and diagnostic centers, her methods are far from being unsound or unimaginative.

(5) For details, see Timasheff, *op. cit.*, p. 33.

CHAPTER VIII

PRISONS IN THE BALKANS AND THE NEAR EAST

THE BALKAN STATES

There is little doubt that penal conditions are worse in the Balkans than in any other country in Europe. By the Balkans, we refer here to the countries of Rumania, Yugoslavia and Bulgaria.

Aside from the attitude of hostility on the part of officials toward any investigation of the prisons, a conspicuous feature of the régimes is the total lack of any recognition of the physical and mental needs of the normal human being once he is incarcerated. In general, there is naturally no system of prison visiting; there are no educational classes and no libraries and rarely is there a lecture provided. What meagre education is pursued is in the hands of priests and then only to illiterates.

In some places work hours are so long that they almost approximate a form of slavery. Working conditions are unwholesome and the shops crowded. In other places, no work is available—nothing but dismal idleness. One visitor describes the obvious arrangements made prior to her visit—a sort of "window-dressing" indulged in so cannily in some American prisons. She writes:

> Yet the accustomed observer sees a little more than he is meant to. Rows of suspiciously clean towels, carpets precariouly balanced on stairways, little mountains of filth in corners still showing the sweep of the brush, colored paper pinned and tucked round ineradicable dirt (the newly opened quires still littering the storeroom), parades of plants in unlikely places, flower-pots whose freshly turned earth showed their occupants to be newly moved in, prisoners hastily pushed aside and doors shut, cells a little too obviously selected for display, dripping passages smelling too freshly of soap, naive enthusiasm of a sick woman over a radiator warm for the first time — all these give hints that a good face has been put upon things for the visitor. Perhaps, like wary old birds, we cocked a too suspicious eye at the chaff which had been prepared for our catching. After all, it is only natural to aim at a good impression, and to a large extent the really tragic side of the prisons was not altogether in the control of the officials.[1]

The writer of the above article, however, stated that the best impressions were made by those officials who showed their worst with their "pathetic best"—crowded workshops, unsanitary conditions, dark punishment cells, with a courageous attempt made to conduct a half-respectable hospital or maintain a well tilled garden. She adds: "There were some officials who roused sympathy and admiration by their struggle against insufficiency of staff, of salary and of funds."[2] She mentions one story which contended that some of the governors of certain prisons in one country threatened to release their prisoners and close the institutions if they could not get more money to feed their charges.

(1) Margery Fry, "Prisoners in the Balkans," *Living Age*, vol. 354, pp. 121-126, (1938).
(2) *ibid.*, p. 122.

We learn further that in Bulgaria, it is impossible for the prisons to be heated unless the inmates themselves pay for the fuel; in Rumania, budgets for maintenance of prisons dropped drastically from 66,000,000 lei in 1930 to 22,000,000 in 1934. Judged by our money, prison administrators were forced to feed prisoners on less than six cents per day per man. Prison salaries are disgraceful. A governor (warden) of a large prison may get no more than £ 12 per month (Less than $60).

Separate confinement is scrupulously maintained in all the Balkan countries. The solitary life prisoners lead there is nearly unbearable. The idea still persists that the prisoner needs much solitude to think over the enormity of his crime. No privileges are extended him in connection with this benighted practice. It is not unusual for prisoners to emerge from these cells with eyes seriously impaired by the constant blackness of their cells.

One does not get this impression regarding Bulgarian prisons from one who writes from the standpoint of a native of that country. N. Dolaptchieff, dean of the Law School of the University of Sofia, states that while conditions in the prisons were deplorable while Bulgaria was under Turkish rule—up to 1878—they are now quite modern. Commenting on this, he says:

> Imprisonment is the principle kind of punishment in the kingdom. A short time after the liberation of Bulgaria, the prisons were very poorly organized. . . Old buildings of former Turkish barracks were used as prisons. The whole prison system was very primitive. One decade later reforms were under way and now Bulgaria has very modern penal institutions. The grade or progressive system has been introduced in the reformatories. Schools, workhouses, agricultural colonies have also been organized.[3]

He further states that the system of labor pursued follows the plan that all convicts, except political prisoners, must work; that the type of labor indulged in must be expedient and productive, and prisoners must be paid. He continues by stating that the income from prison labor is "so large that it is sufficient to cover all of the expenses for the maintenance of prisons and prisoners, with a sufficient balance for improvements and for the construction of new penal institutions."[4] This is undoubtedly an amazing state of affairs, if true, since few systems of reformative and productive prison labor could ever approach this excellent objective. We can scarcely avoid wondering what the status of the prisoners of Bulgaria could be under such an economic system.

Continuing with this glowing tribute to Bulgaria's penal system, we find that "the Bulgarian law knows also the conditional sentence, probation, and parole. Besides punishment, there are some measures of social defense for the irresponsible adult criminals and for the juvenile delinquents. Two educational institutions, especially for juvenile delinquents have been erected; one in Sofia and the other in Plovdiv." But, this writer adds: "there are not yet special juvenile courts, this being the next problem which the Bulgarian lawmaker has to solve in the near future."

In Yugoslavia there may be found a grade system of a sort. After the initial period of solitude, the prisoner is given ordinary "within-the-walls" treatment. After two-fifths of the sentence is served, a freer régime

(3) "The Criminal Law in Bulgaria," *Journal of Criminal Law and Criminology,* vol. 23, March-April, 1933, pp. 1012-1019.
(4) *ibid.,* p. 1019.

is allowed. Conditional release is possible after one-half of the sentence is served but this does not hold for political prisoners, of which there are many. Most of these are of a religious sect known as Nazarenes who are religious pacifists. They represent Yugoslavia's "whipping-boys" just as the Jews do in other European countries. Their lot is especially hard.

Buildings serving as prisons are usually low and vary from excellent to unspeakable. They are all cold which, together with the miserable food served, make the prisoners' lot one of constant misery. Some of the women's prisons are adaptations of monasteries or chateaux of considerable beauty, but—all cold. Even the hospitals in most prisons are made up of sordid quarters with dirty bedding with nightshirts and sheets often lacking. However, some hospitals are reasonably well equipped and comfortable, but none modern in our sense of the word.

There seems to be no physical or corporal punishment practiced in Balkan prisons, the only real suffering coming from the day by day deprivation of physical comforts. The old story, so often heard in America and England, is reiterated here, that even with such discomforts "it is like heaven to get into a real prison after the police detention" which certainly does not augur well for the methods of these gentlemen. What we call "third degree" methods are the rule rather than the exception in southeastern Europe. Many are the harrowing tales related by prisoners of the hounding and brutality inflicted on them prior to entering prison. We quote from Miss Fry's article concerning such practices:

> One . . . man suffered agonies from having the intestines inflated by a pump thrust up his anus. A lad accused of theft was actually killed by a police officer who jabbed at his temple with a fork to force an admission of guilt. The case was interpreted as suicide. . . It is said that in a large number of arrests (we have heard it put as high as 25 per cent of the total number) the accused are beaten, either to make them confess or to procure evidence against supposed accomplices.[5]

Probation is none too well advanced in the Balkans. Bulgaria adopted it through a poorly-drawn law in 1904 which invoked many complaints from the press. Rumania attempted it in 1897 but, due to the poor state of criminal statistics, rejected it. Years later, in 1936, juvenile courts were established and with them, "supervised freedom" for children and "conditional condemnation" for adults. Yugoslavia, after much groping, enacted a penal code in 1929 establishing juvenile courts and with them a form of probation which has not proved very satisfactory.[6]

This description of conditions in the Balkans leaves one with the firm conviction that it will be many years before this section of the world can even approach a reasonable understanding of what modern penology means to the cultural life of the entire social group. The philosophy, or lack of such, as expressed in these unhappy countries, is symptomatic of the unrest and national insecurity which we have seen in recent years.

PENAL INSTITUTIONS IN GREECE

Information regarding the penal system of Greece is fragmentary at best. Professor Olof Kinberg of Sweden visited some of the prisons of the country in 1937 and from his impressions we record the following data.

(5)   *loc. cit.*, p. 126..
(6)   Timasheff, *op. cit.*, pp. 22, 53-54, 55.

An amazing phenomenon occurs in Greece. Not only are philanthropic institutions often donated by wealthy and socially-minded citizens, but prisons as well. Some of the large prisons of Athens are of such origin.

Greece has found it difficult to give much thought or attention to penal philosophy or practice due, primarily, to the fact that the counrty has been in the throes of war, revolution and dictatorship for so long a period.

Idleness and overcrowding are rampant in the prisons. Separate confinement does not exist but only because it is impracticable, rather than because it is undesirable. Only the bare necessities of life are provided the prisoners. There is little air space, no recreation, inadequate food and no work to amount to anything. In fact there is not enough convict clothing to go around so many prisoners wear their own suits. This may be desirable since the regulation convict garb is quite coarse and is conspicuous by its broad yellow stripes which makes the wearer look like a tiger.

What labor is available is on the contract basis and those fortunate enough to be employed may earn one-fourth remission of their sentence.

The institutions visited by Professor Kinberg were: the Sypgrou prison for adult males in Athens; the Averoff prison for young offenders, also in Athens; the Averoff prison for females; the foundling home for fatherless children whoes mothers are in prison; the Ameleíon Orphanotropiíon, an orphanage for girls founded by Queen Amaleía and well supported, housing over 300 girls; the Ephivíon institution for vagabond boys, very poorly managed due to lack of funds; and the Sanatorium for tuberculars which is maintained on a high professional level.

There is a lively interest in criminology in Greece regardless of the poor status of its prisons. There is a chair of Criminology in the Law Faculty of the University of Athens and there is a psychologist operating in the penitentiary. In addition, there is maintained a Quarterly Penitentiary and Statistical Review carrying material on the movements of the prison population and criminology. In 1937 there were ten thousand prisoners in Greece.*

THE TURKISH PENAL SYSTEM

In discussing the prison system of Turkey we must not lose sight of the fact that as we go farther East, prevailing mores differ widely from those of western Europe or America. This is especially true in countries which have only recently felt the impact of ideas crystallized in western lands. While India and Egypt have had the experience of Great Britain to draw from, and have accordingly fallen under her spell, such is not true of Turkey. This is an important fact to be considered when reviewing the penal system of this country.

Since the creation of the Turkish Republic in 1923, it has achieved a revolution in political, economic and social fields. These almost cataclysmic changes were effected through the dynamic leadership of the late President Kemal Ataturk. Through his enlightened administration the country turned its attention to prison reform.

* Olof Kinberg, "Impressions of Penal Policy in Greece," *Howard Journal*, 1938, pp. 34-38.

Turkey, with an area somewhat larger than the state of Texas and a population of sixteen million, has 362 prisons, with an inmate population in 1935 of around 35,000. However, this figure includes persons arrested and awaiting trial, women, juvenile offenders, tax evaders and persons unable to pay fines.

The small prison is characteristic of the Turkish penal system. Of the 362 prisons, 271 have fewer than 50 inmates and only six have between 551 and 750. Three prisons are reasonably modern in plan and construction and some fifty were originally built for prison purposes. The rest have served as fortresses, barracks, schools and warehouses. As a rule, little has been done to fit them to accomodate prisoners; they are often in a bad state of repair and afford no opportunity for anything beyond the most elementary custodial régime. In Istanbul there is a modern jail separate from the prison, the purpose of which is to hold persons awaiting trial. Elsewhere, such persons are kept in the local jails. In the Istanbul jail, separate quarters are provided for women, whether awaiting trial or sentenced, and a separate department for juvenile offenders. However, in case of the latter, the separation is more theoretical than real.

Classification, as it is understood in England and other more progressive countries of Europe, does not exist in Turkey. There are rooms, for example, in some Turkish prisons which hold up to 200 inmates. In these rooms, which are typical of the prisons, may be found murderers serving twelve to eighteen years, tax evaders, and persons sentenced for a few days or weeks for breaking some municipal ordinance, not to mention persons awaiting trial of an appeal to the Court of Cassation. Short term prisoners constitute a large element in the population. Sentences for life and the death penalty are extremely rare.

The prisoners of Turkey enjoy a great deal of freedom. There is no fixed program. Inmates may smoke, talk, eat and play backgammon or cards as they see fit. They may purchase or receive food from relatives, as well as extra clothing and other articles which they may wish. Only the most unfortunate prisoners must subsist on the official ration of 900 grams of bread per day. In a few of the larger prisons, some work is provided. However, few participate, since it has been traditional for prisoners to live in idleness—and sometimes unhygienic idleness at that.

Turkey is an agricultural country and the majority of its people are peasants living under the simplest conditions in small villages. The prison population reflects this. The average prisoner is from 22 to 39 years of age and his crime is more than often murder superinduced by jealousy or revenge or in connection with a quarrel over property boundaries. Of the 19,931 prisoners serving sentences on December 1, 1936, 8,580 (8,247 men, 186 women and 147 juveniles) were sentenced for murder. Abduction is another characteristic crime. Among certain groups in Turkey, abduction has in the past been treated with social approval or at least, indifference. However, under the new Penal Code, it is punishable. The stealing of live-stock and highway robbery bring a certain number to prison every year. The former crime is being checked by a recent law which provides "transportation" for second offenders in addition to imprisonment. The latter crime, thanks to better police methods, especially in rural areas, is tending to disappear. Stricter laws, inaugurated under the Republic, have been applied to the crime of smuggling so that now more persons are being sent to prison for this offense than formerly.

Turkey has few gangster criminals or racketeers, even in the metropolitan centers. And if there are mental defectives with delinquent tendencies, the relative simplicity of the environment and the responsibility for the care and protection of such persons, are undoubtedly the reasons why they are so insignificant in numbers in the prison population. Women and juvenile offenders are also relatively few. Between 1934 and 1936, only 431 to 642 women were sent to prison; the number of juveniles during that time ranged between 353 and 484. Recidivism is quite low, although standards of identification are unsystematic and necessarily crude.

The Turkish Penal Code, adopted in 1926, was patterned after the Italian Penal Code in operation in that country at that time. It called for the solitary type of confinement, but, in order to put this into operation, a tremendous outlay of money would have been necessary. Fortunately, because of more pressing tasks and budgetary limitations, serious consideration of prison reform was adjourned until fuller information had become available and wiser ideas prevailed.

In 1929, there was some discussion in Turkey regarding juvenile courts and special juvenile institutions, but up to date, nothing has developed along these lines. Prison reform actually began with the adult offender. In 1933, the Prime Minister, General Ismet Inonu, appointed Bay Sukru Saracoglu as Minister of Justice. Saracoglu is a graduate of the School of Government Administration; he has studied in Switzerland, has been a director of a college and has filled with conspicuous success the posts of Minister of Public Instruction and Minister of Finance. It so chanced that about a year after he had become Minister of Justice, a certain Mutahhar Serif Basoglu graduated at the head of his class from the Law School of Istanbul University. While practicing law, Basoglu became vitally concerned with the lot of the Turkish peasant and also interested in penal reform. Subsequently he was appointed by the Minister of Justice to make a survey of Turkish prisons and penal methods.

Drawing largely from the experiences of America, through the *Handbooks* issued by the Osborne Association of New York, and actually serving voluntarily in the prison at Istanbul, Basoglu turned in a report to the Minister which was startlingly different from the official statements heretofore submitted to that administrator. The Minister became thoroughly convinced that a complete reform of penal conditions was necessary. But before he decided to act, he sent his young investigator to Switzerland, Belgium and some of the Balkan countries to study penal reforms in those countries. At that time, Basoglu was only twenty-six years of age. Upon his return to Turkey he was made Acting General of Prisons.

Prison reform in Turkey was inspired by three principles. First, that Turkish penal methods must be based upon the Turkish prisoner and Turkish social conditions, rather than merely copying conditions suitable elsewhere; second, the reforms to be considered must be experimental and pragmatic; and third, penetrated with the idea that the personality of personnel is of greater importance than buildings and programs.

The first step in penal reform was the establishment of an agricultural penal colony on the island of Imrali. This island is a small one, lying about thirty-eight miles from Istanbul, and seven miles from the nearest point on the mainland. The soil is fertile and the climate moderate. At one time it had been inhabited, but in 1936, when Basoglu took his first fifty prisoners there, no one lived there; only a few ruins remained that gave evidence of previous habitation. These fifty prisoners had committed serious crimes for which they had already served part of their sentences in the Istanbul Central and other old prisons. They had been selected on the basis of their records while in prison and also, because they possessed the skills needed in the new colony. Most of the convicts were young.

In this island colony, each day counts for two days of the sentence. A strict régime of work and modification of the honor system were set up by the young director. The men work hard and wages are paid. The sums earned are placed in a fund which the prisoners receive upon their release. A school is also maintained, instruction being in charge of the more intelligent inmates. Within a year, much progress had been made on the island. About 250 acres are under cultivation, the proceeds of the products raised going far to pay for the expense of the colony.

A second agricultural colony was started soon after, in May, 1936. This is at Edirne. A nucleus of the colonists from Imrali was transferred to the new colony and housed in a barracks which had previously served as a prison. There are about 100 prisoners at the Edirne colony and about 165 at Imrali at this time.

A third venture was the next to be undertaken by the energetic Basoglu. A carefully selected group of prisoners was assigned to a private coal mine at Zonguldak. A carefully worked out contract was made with the mine owners, the conditions drawn up designed to safeguard the prisoners' health. Barracks were built and an educational and recreational program formulated. About seventy prisoners are employed in this project.

Other projects under consideration by Basoglu deal primarily with the care of juvenile delinquents. It is hoped to take all minors out of the adult prisons and create special institutions for them. What has been done in the last few years in this direction is not known. In 1927, the old rigid solitary system was modified in favor of a system of "progressive stages," so characteristic of European penal systems. A new dispensation which has for its purpose the training of an efficient and intelligent personnel has been contemplated. Included in this are plans to materially increase the compensation paid to guards who have been notoriously underpaid in the past.

This is what prison reform in Turkey has so far accomplished and what it proposed to accomplish before the present cataclysm in Europe engulfed that continent. No great number of prisoners has been affected; no great and modern buildings have been erected to catch the eye. But when it comes to the manner in which the prison problem is thought of, to the principles which inspire the effort to find a solution and to the quality of the persons who exemplify these principles in action—to those convictions which cannot be expressed in figures or in steel and concrete—then there is a quite different story to tell and one the significance of which deserves thoughtful consideration.*

* This material somewhat abridged, is taken from an article written for *Correction*, October, 1937, by Mr. G. Howland Shaw, and used with his permission. Another source, from which information regarding the Imrali colony was drawn is that of E. Gueron, "Turkey Plans Better Prisons," *Christian Century*, vol. 53, 1936, p. 1508.

EGYPT'S PRISON SYSTEM

The prison system of Egypt is in the Prison Department of the Ministry of Social Affairs. It has jurisdiction over both the prisons and the children's reformatories.

The prisons are divided as follows: (1) *Penal Servitude* or convict prisons of which there are two, designed for males sentenced to hard labor. There is a farm of 600 acres for those charged with criminal negligence and a reformatory, treated as a convict prison, for habitual offenders and recidivists; (2) *General Prisons* for males sentenced to detention for more than three months, nine in number; (3) *Secondary Prisons,* for males sentenced to less than a year, six; and (4) *District Prisons,* for confinement not exceeding three months. There are also two reformatories for vagrant male minors from 7 to 21.

Though Egyptian prisons are fulfilling their mission to the best of their ability, it has been deemed necessary to introduce certain reforms embracing prison buildings, management, treatment of prisoners, medical care and education so that the system may truly become an instrument of reform.

Prison punishment includes isolation, corporal punishment and hard labor when needed. The system of privileges is too widely diversified for comment due to lack of space.*

THE NEW PENOLOGY IN IRAN

In 1925 Reza Shah Pahlavi was chosen the ruler of Iran by the parliament of his country. One of his first acts was the promulgation, in February of 1926, of a new penal code based on European models. A serious attempt was made to modernize all phases of jurisprudence by enlisting scientific methods.

The execution of penalties was also modernized and the treatment of prisoners improved. Protection of society within the framework of humanitarianism has since been the keynote of the newer concept developed in this country. At Teheran, the capital city of Iran, a large penitentiary of European style was erected, including a modern hospital. Special efforts were made to provide a maximum of air and light with spacious yards and gardens for exercise and mental relaxation..

Much has also been accomplished in preparing the men for release. In large and bright rooms the inmates of the prison learn skills that will serve them later in earning a living honestly. Handicraft and mechanical trades are taught and, in addition, art and sculpture are practiced.

Habitual and professional criminals are kept apart from other offenders and are subjected to preventive detention. Minors from fifteen to eighteen years of age are also segregated from adults. Iran has also adopted a form of probation.*

* In an interview with Mohamed El Sherif, Director, Department of Technical Research, Egyptian Ministry of Social Affairs, Cairo. Mr. El Sherif was in attendance at the meetings of the International Labor Conference held at Temple University in May, 1944. This material was inserted after the book went to press so that its brevity was compulsory.

* In remarks by M. Matine-Daftary, Secretary of State of Iran, to the delegates of the *Eleventh International Penal and Penitentiary Congress,* Berlin, 1935, pp. 513-516.

CHAPTER IX

PENOLOGY IN THE FAR EAST

JAPAN EXPERIMENTS WITH WESTERN IDEAS IN PENOLOGY

Before discussing Japan's penal system, it is interesting to record how the initial reforms were set in motion in the island Empire. There has recently been published an account of a man who apparently loomed most important in prevailing on the Japanese authorities to launch forth upon a program of humane treatment of prisoners.[1]

In 1873, Dr. John C. Berry was called to one of the prisons in Japan where there was raging an epidemic of beriberi. While there ,he was shocked at what he saw. Prisoners were treated in the most barbaric manner. The filth, the stench, the lack of proper food, and the brutality were beyond imagination. He saw convicts spread out on the ground, face down, their arms and legs extended in "spread eagle" fashion, in which position they were flogged with bamboo flails. There was no classification whatsoever. Prisoners awaiting trial were treated in the same manner as sentenced convicts. He determined to do something to improve such distressing conditions.

He wrote a long report of what he saw to Governor Kanda. Here is what he included in his remarks:

> He pointed out that the institution was a breeding place for both disease and crime, and suggested many changes. He gave a detailed outline of reforms, including better hygienic requirements, drainage, disinfection, proper care of the sick; the introduction of manual labor and industrial employment, with the purpose of teaching the prisoner some trade; the appointment of a prison chaplain, starting of a prison library, abolition of corporal punishment, classification of prisoners, separation of sexes, ventilation, suitable quarters. He even turned architect and drew up plans for new prison buildings. He advocated shortening of the prison term for good conduct, return a portion of the proceeds of the prisoner's labor on his release as a help toward his self-support till he could find employment, the training of prison officers for their position, organization of societies to aid prisoners after release, and the establishment of schools for the criminal class.

The Governor was much impressed with Dr. Berry's pleas and saw to it that conditions were vastly improved. Encouraged by this action, the American crusader resolved to extend his efforts throughout the whole of Japan. At his own expense he visited several of the larger prisons of the country and found the same brutality and neglect. Accordingly, he sat down and wrote to both Japanese and American officials. Here he ran into difficulties, diplomatic in their nature. While waiting for his hoped for results, he wrote to Dr. Enoch Wines, distinguished penologist of New York, asking for his reports on penal conditions. We quote:

> With these reports in hand, he formulated a detailed program for the reformation of Japan's entire penal system, the first ever attempted. This was rendered into official Japanese by young Liyoji Ito. . . The final reports of the Doctor outlining a comprehensive plan based on scientific knowledge of prison reform he could obtain were compiled into a pamphlet and then read throughout the penal

(1) Katherine Fiske Berry, "A Pioneer Doctor in Old Japan," the story of Dr. John C. Berry, Revell, 1940, see pages 54-57.

institutions of the Empire. These reforms . . . became the foundation of Japan's present penal system.

We shall now discuss the penal system of Japan, many features of which show a similarity to American and European philosophy, the result, no doubt of the pioneer work of this intrepid medical reformer of seventy years ago.

Japan has copied extensively from British methods of dealing with criminals which go back, in some features, to the old Pennsylvania system of separate confinement. Wherever we go in the world, not only in European countries but in Asia and Latin America as well, we find this ubiquitous separate system, however diluted it may be.

In the Japanese system there are four types of prisons: (1) the prison for those who, under the law, are sentenced to "penal servitude" as was practiced in English prisons; (2) the prisons for imprisonment—for those guilty of less serious offenses; (3) houses of detention—for those sentenced to "detention" for still less serious offenses; and (4) prisons of confinement—for those suspected and awaiting trial as well as for those sentenced to death. In addition to the above establishments, special institutions are provided for young offenders under eighteen years of age and sentenced to penal servitude for a period of two months or more. In some districts where such institutions have not been provided, these latter offenders may be placed in adult prisons but carefully segregated from older persons. In every prison there must be complete separation of males and females.[2]

An offender committed to prison for the first time is placed in solitary confinement for a period of three days, the purpose being observation and questioning by the officials of the institution. Whether prisoners are to continue in a state of "separate confinement" depends upon the law and the discretion of the governor (warden) of the prison. In general, the following are given this special form of treatment: (1) prisoners sentenced to two months or less; (2) prisoners under twenty-five years of age and over eighteen; (3) first offenders; and (4) those who have not yet served the first two months of their sentence. In addition, those who commit some infraction of prison rules may be placed in separate confinement. While the law permits "associations," especially for medical examination and religious services, it suggests that different times be allocated for different classes of prisoners, and prisons are required to provide box seats for each man in assembly halls so that communication between the inmates is difficult, even if not impossible. Except in special cases, no prisoner may be kept in separate confinement for a period exceeding two years. For prisoners under eighteen, six months is the limit at any one time. According to Professor Gillin, Japan is making every possible effort to carry out this system so popular in many European countries, but long since abandoned in America.

In spite of the adherence to this archaic system, Japan, just as other countries, does provide for congregate assembly of certain types of prisoners and it is not uncommon to find cells which house three or more prisoners. Japan has erected many institutions in a courageous attempt to

(2) The material for this section is largely from J. L. Gillin, *Taming the Criminal*, MacMillan, 1931, pp. 1-34.

classify. There are prisons scattered all over the Empire, each for a different type of prisoner. It is interesting to note that when the urge to classify prisoners approaches that of a fetish, measures are taken that look almost ludicrous. This is simply because no two prisoners are exactly alike and so long as we recognize this, classification will be a tremendously expensive system to operate and maintain. As Professor Gillin succinctly states: "In spite of a hundred years of experimentation in the classification of delinquents it is still a moot question whether classification is worth all the money it costs to carry it out properly. One wonders whether better returns for the money would not be obtained by putting in superior officers and teachers of prisoners."[3]

Careful consideration has been given the system of prison labor in Japan. The industrial prison is a characteristic of the system, rather than farm colonies. In pursuing a policy of labor, sanitation and the general economy of the particular prison are carefully considered. The type and amount of work imposed on the convict depends upon the offense, the length of the sentence, the prisoner's health, ability, former occupation and future prospects. For youthful offenders, his education must also be considered. Prison labor is halted on the many Japanese holidays, and if a prisoner's father or mother dies, he need not work for three days! Wages are paid in accordance with the amount he has produced, his conduct, and his general economy in producing his "stint" or task. Such compensation is retained by the governor until release unless it is needed for the support of the inmate's family. There is also a form of social insurance. If the prisoner is ill, or if he dies while in prison, adequate compensation is provided in each specific case.

One interesting feature of the Japanese prisons is the garb worn by various classes of inmates. Prisoners under sentence must wear dark red clothing; all others, including the indigent, workhouse inmates and those under eighteen, wear blue clothing. Prisoners undergoing detention may furnish their own clothing and bedding. Prisons in Japan are very poorly heated. Consequently, the garments worn by the prisoners are heavily padded. Upon the front of the prisoner's clothing is sewed an insignia depicting the crime for which he has been sentenced, the time he must serve, whether he is a first offender or a recidivist as well as other information. relative to his prison status. The hair of all prisoners is closely clipped.

The disciplinary measures found in Japanese prisons are interesting as they represent an older method found seldom in modern prisons in America, but quite prevalent a hundred years ago. The devices used to subdue recalcitrant prisoners are: the strait jacket, completely abandoned in American prisons now, fetters, handcuffs, chains and ropes. The strait jacket cannot be used for more than six hours at a time. Fetters are anklets fastened together with a short chain with another chain running through them, then wound around the waist and locked under the girdle. This device was used frequently in colonial times in America and was found in early English prisons. For instance, the "chain-room" at old Millbank prison in London was one of its great show places. Prisoners working outside the prison walls in Japan are usually chained together to prevent escape. In order to ensure protection of the guards, they are

(3) op. cit., p. 11.

required by law to carry either a sword or a gun.

Due to the frequency of earthquakes in Japan, a provision has been made, in case such a calamity occurs, for prisoners to be transferred to safer places or released, with specific understanding that they must report to a police station within twenty-four hours and give themselves up. If they fail to do this, they are caught and severly punished.

Probably the most hopeful feature of Japan's penal system is its personnel. As Professor Gillin remarks: "Japan stands out as the one country . . . which devotes itself seriously to the training of prison officials. The two sets of courses which she assiduously pursues and which she forces all of her prison officials to take, are of the very greatest significance. In this matter she has set an example for the entire world."[4]

As early as 1888, an organization was set up, known as the Japanese Prison Association and having the status of "a corporate and judicial body." It has an endowment of $100,000 and a membership of 12,000 divided into four classes. These are an honorary class, supporting class, sustaining class and ordinary class, designated on the basis of the amounts of their contributions. The majority of the ordinary members are prison officials. The purposes of this organization are: (1) conducting a training school for prison officials; (2) censoring educational materials; and (3) operating a kind of pension system for prison officials. The first of these is of particular interest in this connection. Two training courses are carried on, one for the higher officials, and the other for the rank and file of the guards, continuing six months annually. The former course was inaugurated in 1925, whereas the latter was conceived as early as 1908. It is probably true that this particular course constitutes the first training school for prison personnel ever given. The courses are thorough and include a wide variety of subject matter. In short, it might be said they include a general knowledge of penology, welfare work, factory management, as well as technical knowledge in such things as bacteriology, labor hygiene, fingerprinting, surgery, etc.[5] In addition, all officials are taught *judo* (jujitsu) and *kendo* (fencing). The Association provides a number of scholarships for students of criminal science which enables them to continue their studies in criminal law, criminal sociology, psychology, etc. It is indeed a very comprehensive curriculum and no doubt makes a signal contribution in the selection of prison personnel.

The Japanese prison system is scrupulous in matters dealing with moral instruction, education and medical treatment. Regular bathing by prisoners is required as well as frequent shaving. Compulsory exercises of thirty minutes at least each day is carried on, although there seems to be a total absence of organized recreation such as may be found in most American prisons. Food, while ample, is coarse and somewhat monotonous so far as variety is concerned. No smoking is permitted nor are newspapers allowed. However, books are provided and the prisoners are allowed to look at pictures and maps. It would seem that libraries are nonexistent, or at best, very meagre. Visits are permitted but always in the presence of an officer. There seems to be no system of lay visiting, that is, visits by

(4) *ibid.*, p. 305.
(5) See Professor Gillin's description of these courses, *op. cit.*, pp. 30-31.

others than relatives of the inmates. However, lawyers are permitted to consult with their prison clients.

In order to be released on what we in America call parole, the discharged prisoner must have employment and must submit to police supervision. Just prior to release, he is instructed by the governor of the prison. He is placed in solitary confinement three days prior to his release for this instruction which includes advice and the governor's opinion of him, gained by knowledge of his actions while incarcerated. In general, however, the after treatment is quite superficial. Japan, like many other countries, is woefully weak in its care for the discharged prisoner.

Much as we may be impressed with some features of the Japanese penal system, we are told by one student of that country that the legal procedure and police system do not measure up to standards we might reasonably expect. While western concepts such as the jury system, a more liberalized penal code, the creation of labor unions, and the extension of suffrage have been introduced in Japan in the past quarter century, they find traditional philosophy resisting them at every point.

The police in Japan are particularly reactionary. Their methods are autocratic and high-handed. Due to the interesting tradition in Japanese legal practice, by which no punishment may be inflicted until the suspected prisoner is found guilty, the police harrass him by "third degree" methods until a confession is extracted. Every opportunity is afforded the police to get this confession. Prisoners are detained without the benefit of a lawyer for weeks, in strict seclusion, until they "talk." Mr. Harry Emerson Wildes, writing of this practice, tells of a case in which a pyromaniac was arrested and, in the process of procuring his confession, he "admitted" he was guilty of firing 536 houses. It turned out that these cases happened to be the exact ones for which no one had been previously arrested.[6]

The author continues by stating that the police system is honeycombed with spies and stoolpigeons. So-called "frame-ups" are the general rule since spies, in order to earn their hire, must turn in victims, guilty or not. Contrary to Occidental penal theory, the suspected culprit must prove his innocence. Laws relative to suppressing crime news, admirable in themselves, in reality protect the police in their grilling habits. Writes Professor Wildes: "By invariably assuming that the prisoner is culpable, an attitude which is . . . in conformity with legal principles accepted in Japan, the papers aid in building up hostile public sentiment."[7] He adds: "Police theories, supplied with the connivance of the authorities, are printed as proved facts, and additional details may be invented to corroborate the theory. All this is against the law, but seldom is it prevented and seldom punished."[8]

After the confession is obtained, and every possible loophole closed by which the accused might conceivably escape the penalty attached to the crime for which he has been detected, he is brought to trial. Then, for the first time, he may consult a lawyer. Both judge and jury look upon the signed confession as *prima facie* evidence of guilt. Consequently one finds a very low percentage of acquittals before juries. It is interesting

(6)   See his article, "The Japanese Police," *Journal of Criminal Law and Criminology,* vol. 19, November, 1928, pp. 390-398.

(7)   *ibid.,* p. 394.

(8)   *idem.*

to note, that since so few are found "innocent" of their crimes, it is of some moment when such a situation does occur. This has resulted in a movement in Japan to compensate those "subjected to false arrest." The amount mentioned is very small, and, in addition, no provision has even been suggested to repay the thousands who have been arrested and detained for weeks and then later dismissed for lack of evidence. This proposal had not been passed when Professor Wildes discussed this practice in his article already referred to above.

The conclusion of Mr. Wildes is one with which we might well conclude this entire section concerning Japan and her people. He states: "Autocratic government, operating through a despotic police force is once more brought to grips with a weak but slowly strengthening democracy. Past history throws a revealing light on what may be expected in Japan."[9]

This statement was made in 1928. Events of the past three years have made prediction even more sure in the case of this autocratic country. Western ideas were more vigorously resisted, especially if they bore the imprimature of democracy. The strengthening process has collapsed. When Professor Gillin visited Japan, it was no doubt evident that she was trying hard to develop a sane and rational penal program within the framework of deterrence, expiation and reformation. But one could see that the old shackles of tradition were present. The one great advance worthy of mentioning once again is the interest in preparing her prison officials for the great responsibilities placed upon them. This, in itself, is worthy of unrestrained praise from occidentals.

PENAL TREATMENT IN THAILAND

Thailand, known to most Americans as Siam, has an area about the size of Texas—200,000 square miles—with a population of about fifteen million. Bangkok, the capital, is its largest city, with a million people. In this small country there are about 31,000 prisoners. About 5,000 of these are incarcerated in national prisons and the remainder, 26,000, in the various provincial institutions.

According to the statistics on Thailand's prisons, most of the crimes are committed against property rather than against persons; a greater number for defamation of character or reputation than for crimes against the interests of public safety of persons and property. It is also interesting that more imprisonments are made for reasons of morality than for overt acts against public administration.

Criminals are incarcerated in provincial prisons located where the crime is committed unless the penalty is more than ten years. In such cases they are sent to the Mahantatote prison at Bangkok. Petty offenders in Bangkok are sent to a prison in that city and known as Lahutote prison. There is also a reformatory and an apprentice school for young offenders. In each of the seventy provinces there is one prison which, as stated above, handles most of the cases in the specific jurisdictions. There are few capital crimes and only rarely is a person sent to death, which is by shooting.

As there are few women criminals in Siam, they are housed in wings of the various male prisons. There are also six prison camps scattered

(9) *loc. cit.*, p. 398.

throughout the country each of which specializes on one particular form of work. Here well behaved prisoners from the prisons mentioned above, are sent. In one camp, road building is featured; in another, cattle raising; others engage in agriculture, forestry, fishing and mining. In these camps there is a great deal of freedom and few escapes are recorded. It is reported that the morale in these camps is especially high and the relationships between inmates and administrative officers are extremely healthful. Cooperation is stressed and much constructive work is accomplished for the state. The labor program in the two national prisons is varied. In both Mahantatote and Lahutote there may be found a clothing factory, mattress factory, broom and brush shop, and laundries. Products are used by the government and also by the general public. A prison store is in operation in Bangkok and it is reputed to do a good business. The profits are divided into two parts. One part, amounting to five per cent, is given to the inmates as their bonus upon release and the remainder is taken by the state. There seems to be no antipathy to prison labor or to prison made goods in the country.

There is to be found in the prison program the rudiments of a rehabilitative program, although the standards are none too high. Education is divided into academic and vocational. Illiterates are taught to read and write and a school is maintained through the high school level. Correspondence courses are also available for those who can assimilate them. Standardized educational achievement and diagnostic tests have not as yet been employed. Provision for religious instruction is made. Most of the inmates are Buddists, as is the case with all of Siam. Basket ball, soccer and other forms of sports, together with music, are not only permitted but recommended by the officials who feel that recreation is vitally necessary in prison programs.

There is little, if any classification as understood in America. Neither is there probation, parole or conditional release of any kind.[1] There is no juvenile court system, although it has been discussed for some time. It has been argued that these functions may not prove suitable in Siam. The results that might flow from these typically Western innovations might prove inimical to the mores of this country.

Discipline is not severe in the prisons of Siam. Corporal punishment is absolutely prohibited. The only disciplinary measures permitted are reprimand, restriction of privileges, solitary confinement and restricted diet. In the Mahantatote prison some inmates are disciplined by wearing shackles or handcuffs to restrain them from violence to themselves or to others.

What steps will be taken in the future to place the prison system of Thailand on a par with those of this country, we do not know. One may gather that the officials are in a receptive mood to welcome suggestions from America, especially in the field of classification and in the appraisal of professionally trained services such as that performed by social workers, psychologists and even psychiatrists. On the whole, their system is not extremely repressive although they subscribe to the general dictum of the

(1) However, Professor Timasheff, *op. cit.,* p. 67, describes a form of probation to first offenders where the offense does not exceed one year.

International Penal and Penitentiary Commission of the League of Nations, which states: "Prisons and reformatories should not be conducted in the interest of the prisoner solely, but with the thought in mind of protecting the communities."*

THE CHINESE PENAL SYSTEM

THE BEGINNINGS OF MODERN PENOLOGY

The year 1902 marks the beginning of the movement to improve and modernize China's prisons. It was then that it was decreed that workshops should be established for all prisoners sentenced to "exile and imprisonment" for the purpose of teaching trades.

In 1909 a model prison was erected in Peking with the hope that similar ones would be established throughout the provinces. The Revolution came before this could be fully realized although prisons were established in the provinces of Fengtien, Hupeh, Kiangsu and Anhui.

Since the founding of the Republic the construction of penal establishments took on real significance so that by 1918 there were more than thirty modern prisons. In 1921 all Russian prisons in the Chinese Eastern Railway Zone were taken over by the Chinese government, their officers and wardens, however, being retained.

The system of one cell for each prisoner, day and night, was introduced in the first Peking prison in 1922. Since 1922 reformatory schools for juvenile convicts, as well as "Associations for Rendering Assistance to the Reformed" and "Associations for Helping Russian Ex-convicts," have been established. By 1925 there were seventy-four modern prisons in China built after the "European Model." All prisons are under the Department of Ministry.

There are three large prisons in Peking and at least one in each provincial capital. In addition, each district where the magistrate has concurrent judicial functions there is one small prison. This makes a grand total of some 1,700 prisons throughout the country.

By 1925 there were large and "complete" prisons in the following provinces: 3 in Peking, Chihli, Fengtien, Kirin, Shantung, Shansi, Kiangsu, Anhui, Kiangsi, Chekiang and 2 in Hypeh. In addition there were about forty partially completed prisons.

Prison labor is considered of paramount importance in Chinese prisons. In the men's institutions one finds brick making, blanket and straw hat weaving, the making and canning of bean sauce, the manufacture of hair nets, varnished articles and a great deal of printing. Agriculture is engaged in on a large scale as is also work on public buildings. The building of the Ministry of Justice, for example, was erected by convicts. In the separate prisons for women the occupations are sewing, weaving and braiding. Compensation depends on the type of work done and one-third goes to the family of the prisoner.

The training of prison officials is considered very important. All officials must take courses in jurisprudence, constitutional law, criminal law,

---

* The foregoing information has been taken, by permission from a paper prepared in 1941 by Dr. Seng Tancharoensukh who studied recently at Harvard University under Dr. Sheldon Glueck. This was prepared prior to the occupation of Thailand by the Japanese.

study of prison rules and administration, methods of identification, police systems, social psychology, hygiene, statistics and prison construction. Such training follows the line set up in 1926 when all judges were appointed from the list of successful candidates of governmental examinations. By 1941 hundreds of judges and court officials throughout China had been chosen purely on merit.

Conditional release is exercised in a very primitive manner in China. In the Peking prisons, a prisoner who has conducted himself well may be released on application to the authorities and turned over to an organization known as "The Peking Society for the Aid of the Reformed Citizen." Little is known regarding the mechanics of this makeshift type of release. There is no parole as understood in the United States.

There is an elaborate system of rewards and punishments in the prisons of China. The rewards include: more frequent visits and letters, use of personal underwear and stationery, permission to read one's own books, extra compensation for work, and allowances of extra food. Strange as it may seem, a Chinese prisoner may gain extra privileges by "revealing privately circumstances in connection with another's plan of escape," by "assisting in the capture of an escaped convict" and by showing merit at the time of a calamity.

Punishments take the nature of deprivations. There are no corporal punishments listed but the dark cell is employed up to seven days at the most.

Children under twelve possess the "inability to commit crimes" and are turned over to their own families for control. There are no juvenile courts. Between the ages of 12 and 20 such youths are imprisoned separately. In recent years a few reformatories have been erected. All persons awaiting trial are detained in separate houses of detention with their own administrators.*

THE SITUATION SINCE 1935

The Penal Code under which present day China operates was prepared and set in motion in 1935. It consists of 195 different articles and is quite comprehensive. One of its purposes was to provide more rational treatment for offenders. According to Paul S. Chiang, a number of provisions were made for special types of offenders all of which are familiar to occidentals. They include:

(1) Special Treatment for Young Offenders: Youths who have not passed their eighteenth birthday are separated from adults and placed in a prison for minors. The aim, according to Mr Chiang, is "to keep young offenders, with their plastic minds, in a place where the personal influence and examples of trained leaders can create a corporate spirit and teach standards of social behavior more easily than in a mixed institution, where different kinds of criminals are gathered together."

(2) Classification of Adult Prisoners: China has adopted the "grade system" and has divided the convicts into five grades. At the time of admission, the prisoner is listed in the first grade. By good conduct he ad-

* The above material is taken from *Chinese Prisons* and published in 1925 by the Extraterritorial Commission. This pamphlet describes in great detail and with appended ground plans, each of the great provincial prisons. On the Chinese court system reference may be made to "China At War," published by the Chinese News Service, 30 Rockefeller Plaza, New York City in March, 1943.

vances to the higher grades. In the case of bad conduct, he is degraded. When he reaches the fifth grade, he is recommended for conditional release, which is granted by the Superintendent of Prisons. This functionary must state that, in his judgment, the prisoner "has abstained from the habit of vice and is working to be a useful and industrious" citizen.

(3) Prison Labor: This subject has caused more discussion in China than any other phase of the penal program. There were those who felt that prisons are a tremendous drain on the taxpayers, hence no wages should be paid; that every effort should be made to make the prison program selfsupporting. The other group strongly urged the payment of wages for rehabilitative purposes. The Penal Code finally disposed of the knotty problem in its own way. It decreed that the bulk of the money derived from the labor of prisoners would go to the state; that the diligent prisoner would be granted a sum of money as a gratuity, providing he made restitution to the parties he may have injured in the commission of his crime. Out of the remainder, if any, he is called upon to help support his dependents. The rest is kept for him to defray his traveling and working expenses upon his release. One would gather from this provision that the Chinese prisoner sees little, if any, real money while incarcerated. Nothing is said about his own petty needs such as tobacco or extra food, as is the case in most prisons.

(4) Education, recreational and medical attention: The Penal Code tries hard to mitigate the "awful isolation" of prisoners by allowing them the privileges of reading, writing letters, visitation, etc. For those serving longer periods of time: "music and educational pictures may be introduced for the sole purpose of mental stimulus." The publication of a prison paper is permissable to keep the inmates in touch with the outside world. All prisoners are given periodic medical examinations. Infectious diseases are strictly controlled by placing those in this condition in isolation. Vaccination and injections are given all prisoners upon entrance. Chinese authorities realize that many delinquencies are the direct result of physical imbalance so a good medical program is thought quite necessary.[1]

We get a view of the so-called Model prisons in China from the following description of the prison in Peiping by A. R. Caton, writing in the *Howard Journal*. This article was written in 1928:

> In Peking, I visited one of the Model prisons of China. It is Western in structure, built on radiating lines, and almost entirely cellular, though the cells often contain two or more prisoners. The cells are furnished with a wooden plank-bed, mattress, blanket and hard Chinese pillow. Different types of offenders, e.g., robbers, murderers, etc. are said to be classified to some degree. Eight hours are spent in industrial work, printing, blindmaking, weaving, carpentry, cooking and laundry. There is also a kitchen garden. Habituals are given harder and more deterrent work. Two hours are spent compulsorily in classes in the evening and the thousand character system is taught. Lectures are given and one on Christianity by a Chinese member of the Y.M.C.A. It is largely attended. There were at the time of my visit a number of Russian Communist prisoners, who have slightly easier treatment for the reason that they are of a more educated class. They have heated cells and three meals daily instead of two. There is a wing in the prison for women prisoners; no cellular confinement there, but dormitories holding from twelve to twenty. Such offenses as procuring children are looked upon lightly in China. The prison "guards" are of rough coolie class. Their salaries are paid only irregularly. Chinese prisoners are said to be docile.

(1)   This material is from Paul T. S. Chiang, "Progress of China's Prison Legislation," *China Weekly Review*, June 13, 1936, vol. 77, pp. 73-74.

In spite of the up-to-date structure and the system of this prison, I gather that medieval methods, such as executions without trial, are not unknown in Peking. Opportunities for research, however, were being freely given to a Chinese student of Yenching University. The information gleaned in this prison by means of an interpreter from a polite "chief guard" over many cups of tea was obtained under difficulties, and absolute accuracy is not guaranteed.[2]

EFFECTS OF THE WAR ON THE PENAL PROGRAM

Just prior to the war the Judicial Yuan directed the control of several new prisons, six for the city of Shanghai and five for other cities. This plan had to be abandoned because of hostilities. Many convicts had to be evacuated and transferred to temporary prisons. At the end of 1942 there were 83 prisons, 15 branch prisons and 4 juvenile prisons. In the districts having no prisons, convicts serve out their terms in makeshift prisons attached to the jails. In 1937 the National Military Council promulgated a set of regulations governing the release of prisoners for military service. These were revised in 1940. Life convicts having served more than five years and others who have served one-fifth of their sentence come within the scope of the new regulations. Their days in the armed services are counted off their unexpired term of imprisonment. In case of distinction in battle, or disablement, their sentences are rescinded. Approximately 15,000 convicts have served in the armed forces. Many of them have served with distinction and not a few have become battalion commanders.

THE PRISON SYSTEM IN THE PHILIPPINES

A few words about the prison system of our erstwhile possessions, the Philippines, should be of interest. Professor J. L. Gillin, in his work, *Taming the Criminal,* was much impressed with some of the features of the penal system in operation there, especially those connected with the penal farm of Iwhig.

There are three large convict institutions and fifty-two provincial jails under the supervision of the Insular Director of Prisons. The former are; (1) Bilibid, a great industrial prison in Manila, accommodating over two thousand convicts; (2) Iwhig penal colony with a capacity of 1,500; and (3) San Ramón Prison Farm, set aside primarily for the incarceration of native Moros who are sentenced for crimes committed by them. The total prison population on the island, counting those awaiting trial and insane prisoners is around 6,500.

The industrial prison of Bilibid was built by the Spaniards in 1865. It is surrounded by a wall and comprises about seventeen acres. Inside the enclosure, the ground is divided into two separate parts by a wall running through the center. In the center is a watchtower where is stationed the guards who operate the prison gates by electric mechanism. They are adequately protected from any attempts to rush them or the gates so that we find few prison breaks. There are also guards armed with machine

(2) From the October, 1928, issue of the *Howard Journal*. The student from Yenching University, referred to, is Ching-Yueh Yen, who has made penology his life work. He came to America where he received his doctorate and later, visited the countries of Europe, especially Russia, in order to study progressive ideas in penology. He is at present warden of a prison in Shanghai.

* This material, naturally, alludes to the Philippines prior to their occupation by the Japanese. What the future penal system will be like on the islands would be pure conjecture.

guns at the corner of the walls. In fact, this great prison is a penitentiary in the American sense of the word.

Inside the walls and on either side of the dividing wall, are the various buildings arranged like spokes of a wheel with the guard tower representing the hub. Each of the spaces between the spokes is a dormitory for the inmates as well as supplying rooms for certain classes.

Women are housed in one of the "spokes." They are shut off completely from the male prisoners, working and sleeping in their own quarters at all times. Another "spoke" houses the prisoners condemned to die and here also is the electric chair. One feature of this prison is that there are no individual cells, except a few for punishment purposes; all inmates sleep in dormitories.

All convicts work. There is a wide variety of industries at Bilibid such as automobile repair shops, the manufacture of bullock carts, rattan furniture, hammock weaving, carriage making, as well as the conventional crafts such as carpentering, tinsmithing, etc. Women make embroidery and lace and do domestic work. Much of the work is sold on the open market, there being a great demand for their products from the outside. The motive of prison labor in the Philippines is to teach the convicts a trade, if possible, so they can make a living upon release. The inmate, where possible, is assigned to a job "for which he is best fitted by nature, ability or past experience."[1] Every prisoner works industrially. To quote Professor Gillin:

> Yet it must be said of Bilibid, what cannot be said of many prisons in the United States, every prisoner is kept busy, from the unruly fellow, who in stripes and chains pulls monotonously back and forth the giant fan over the workers to keep them cool, or those others whom I saw industriously mauling a tough knot of Philippine hard wood . . . to the artistic woodcarver and rattan weaver or the 450,000 peso bank embezzler who kept the prison accounts.[2]

Inmates are in four grades at Bilibid. Upon entering convicts are placed in the second grade. They are clothed in blue denim and have a small variety of ordinary privileges. Third grade prisoners are those demoted for misconduct or lack of industry. They are clothed in the convict stripes so familiar to the American movie goers. They have few privileges. The first grade is composed of those promoted from second grade for good conduct over a certain period. They enjoy many privileges and receive a larger wage. The fourth class is made up "trusties" and are given extensive privileges and receive still larger wages. The prisoners receiving wages for their work may use half of them for the support of their dependent families; the other half is withheld until their release.

The discipline at Bilibid is semimilitary. Discipline in cases of a breach of the regulations consists of the deprivation of privileges, demotion in grade and being assigned to hard and disagreeable labor. Only the most recalcitrant are placed in solitary cells. Some critics feel that the discipline at Bilibid prison is too lax. Sarcastic remarks, similar to those heard in the United States, refer to the place as a "vacation resort," while others contend that the institution is quite repressive and point to the showy display of machine guns on the walls. On the whole, however, it is a reasonably well administered prison, judged by Professor Gillin's re-

(1)   Gillin, *op. cit.*, p. 39.
(2)   *ibid.*, p. 42.

port. There is a school which illiterates must attend. Since most of the inmates belong in that class, the attendance is unusually large. The director is a civilian and the teachers are inmates, the usual practice found in American prisons. The prison has a band, a system of self government, of a sort, and a splendid hospital. In short, all of the traditional services known to penology may be found in Bilibid. It is the conventional industrial prison not unlike dozens to be found in our own country, with few differences.

The penal colony at Iwahig, which is a unique feature of the penal system of the islands, is located on the island of Palawan, which, during the Spanish régime, was the place of banishment for criminals and political prisoners. After the United States took over the Philippines, this place of exile was abolished. However, in 1904 a movement was undertaken to establish the place into a colony for first offenders who have proved their good conduct and industry at the Bilibid institution. There are over 100,000 acres in the colony and an average of 1,500 to 2,000 prisoners. These are divided into two groups, colonists and settlers. The latter are those who are permitted to bring their families to live there. These family groups live in separate dwellings near the administration station, so that the children may attend the schools provided for the children of the officials.

The colonists are scattered in some forty districts in groups ranging from 30 to 60, each carrying on different forms of labor. These are: animal husbandry, maintenance and repair, farming, forestry, horticulture, bridge and road construction and similar pursuits. The principal and gratifying feature of the colony is the apparent contentment of the prisoners. They are all busy at appointed tasks and receive wages for either their own use or for that of family support, the same as at Bilibid.

In the Philippines, however, we find that same weakness so prevalent in many other systems we have examined—poor machinery for conditional release. There is no parole, as such, nor is there a system of probation. Prisoners may be released only through good behavior, with a consequent shortening of sentence, or pardon. This latter practice encourages political collusion which is the bane of many systems of penal administration outside the Philippines. Commenting on this weakness of the system, Professor Gillin says:

> The chief menace threatening the prison system of the Philippines is politics . . . I am told the director constantly has to resist the pressure of politicians to have him recommend the pardon of some of their friends. . . Graft and influence are felt everywhere. That is the trouble with most of the provincial prisons, and that creates practically all the difficulties for the officials in the Bureau of Prisons. The declared purposes of the law and of the Bureau of Prisons are in accord with the best penological principles. But what demons of political demagoguery and graft they have constantly to fight![3]

Nevertheless, the penal system in the islands is humanely and efficiently operated and, in most particulars, measures up fairly well to the standards set by modern penologists. Aside from the backward state of probation and parole, it compares favorably to most of the systems found in several states of our own country.

(3) *ibid.*, p. 63.

CHAPTER X

THE LATIN AMERICAN COUNTRIES AND PENOLOGY

THE PENAL SYSTEM AND PENITENTIARY ADMINISTRATION OF LATIN AMERICA

*Clara González de Behringer and Sr. Guillermo Zurita**

A GENERAL STATEMENT

While it is somewhat true of Latin American countries today that reform, involving both the progressive treatment of the convicted criminal and the insurance of social defense, is not felt with force, one cannot help but note a sincere desire to incorporate into penal legislation and penitentiary administration some of the more advanced concepts employed in some of the other countries throughout the world. Proof of this is the relatively recent interest manifested in most of the Latin American countries to improve or to revise their penal codes, many of which have remained untouched for more than a century.

The fact that already two Congresses of Latin American criminologists and penologists have met to discuss such important propositions as prison classification, social work in penal institutions, conditional release, as well as the suppression of short term (privative) punishments for which will be substituted more effective measures, less humiliating to the victim,—indicates a serious interest in implanting in Latin America a scientific system of penal discipline.

It is the ardent hope that in the next Penal Congress, to be held at Rio de Janeiro in the autumn of 1944, to which naturally the leading penologists and criminologists of the United States have been invited, even more beneficial and effective action will be consummated.

THE SYSTEMS OF PENAL CODES. In all Latin American countries there exists a system of penal codes dealing with all forms of penal legislation. The precedents settled by the highest tribunals of justice have value as a doctrine but lack the power of legal enforcement. Thus the system of penal legislation is contained in the respective penal codes. We have in Argentina the Code of 1922 which replaced that of 1887; in Brazil, that of 1940; in Chile, that of 1874 with some modifications in the Law No. 4,447 of 1928; in Bolivia, that of 1834 (a project for a new code is now being studied); in Cuba, that of 1938 which replaced the one of 1870; in Colombia, that of 1936 replacing the one of 1890; in Peru, that of 1924, a substitute for the one of 1862; in Mexico, that of 1931, a substitute for one of 1929; in Uruguay, that of 1934, reforming the one

---

* Commissioner and Deputy Commissioner of the *Institute of Vigilance and Protection of the Child* for the Republic of Panama. Naturally they are not responsible for the errors in translation or misinterpretation of fact. Parts of their material have been inserted in the proper places in the ensuing discussion of penology of the various Latin American countries.

** The two Congresses were: Buenos Aires, 1938; Santiago, Chile, 1941.

of 1889; and in Panama, that of 1922, next to be replaced by a new code already formulated but not yet approved.

CLASSIFICATION OF INFRACTIONS OF PENAL LAW. In the majority of the Latin American countries there is a bipartite classification of all violations of the penal law. This consists generally of dividing them into felonies and misdemeanors (*delitos y contravenciones*), the former being the more serious and whose disposition falls to the judicial authorities; the latter being the less serious offenses and dealt with by the administrative authorities and judges of police. In Chile, however, there is a tripartite division which comprises serious crimes, simple crimes and misdemeanors (*los crímenes, los simples delitos y las faltas*), assigning to serious crimes the greatest severity. (Franco-German System).

PUNISHMENTS. Punishments vary in number and grade, classified in most of the countries as serious and disciplinary (*principales y accesorias*). In some countries there still exists the death penalty, as in Cuba, Brazil and Chile, as well as in some of the Mexican states. However, the Federal government of Mexico has abolished the death penalty. Life imprisonment is common in the various countries, such as in Chile, Cuba, Brazil, etc. Panama has neither capital punishment nor life imprisonment. The Chilean code still permits the use of the lash.

In relation to punishments, the tendency manifested by the penologists attending the Congresses mentioned above is that of abolishing gradually the short term punishments and replacing them by fines to be imposed on the basis of the individual's capacity to pay, or by the subjection to supervision by the authorities, or by the suspension of sentence, or by the compulsory performance of certain duties for the benefit of the state. Students of the matter maintain that these short term punishments constitute a danger to the state rather than serve as a measure of social defense. Besides being costly, they are degrading since they familiarize the offender with the common jail and, in addition, place him in the category of known delinquents. These short term punishments do not deter but rather tend to contaminate the novice or first offender by subjecting him to the companionship of the dangerous criminal.

CRIMES. The number of commissions and omissions punished by the law varies also in the different countries. Aside from ordinary crimes, the act of sensationally publishing a crime committed by a minor under 18 is, in Ecuador, a serious offense. Aiding or abetting a criminal by approving of his acts (*apología del delito*) is, in Colombia, a grave offense. In Brazil usury is one of the most serious crimes just as any other crime which might undermine the economy of the state. For this reason the application of the strongest sanctions (such as the death penalty) is invoked by a special tribunal (Tribunal of National Security).

PENAL RESPONSIBILITY. The majority of the codes follow the Neo-Classical criterion of the responsibility of the agent of the crime, admitting extenuating circumstances, the mental state of the accused who may be disturbed by abnormal situations such as great fear or anger, and by a pathological or toxic conditions. Partial responsibility is also admitted for minors, depending on the country. In Panama and Cuba, the age of complete irresponsibility is 12; in Argentina and Colombia, 14; in Chile, 16; and in Mexico, 18. In Argentina and Colombia, recidivism of minors under 18 is not taken into account, even though they may have violated the law on several occasions. This unusual procedure is due to the fact that is is believed that these minors have a great possibility for rehabilitation.

In many countries it is already recognized that minors should be subject to a special legal code (Code for Minors) and that judgment and treatment should be handled by special departments such as Tribunals for Minors (juvenile courts), training schools and other such institutions for the protection of children. This is especially true of Uruguay, Argentina, Chile, Brazil, Ecuador, Colombia, Mexico, Peru and the Dominican Republic.

In Panama there is no juvenile court nor a code for juveniles but the *Institute for Vigilance and Protection of the Child,* governed by Decree No. 467 of 1942, is an indeterminate institution between the regular courts and the juvenile court. It has jurisdiction over cases of delinquent, abandoned, neglected and defective children up to the age of 16. In Costa Rica, the *National Patronage of Infancy* assumes legal representation for minors before the regular tribunals and sometimes serves as an agency of social assistance for them.

PENAL LAW REGULATING INDIANS (*Indigenas*). In some of the Latin American countries where the Indian population is especially large, there exists a tutelar, or guardianship legislation which applies preferentially to it even in civilized life.

In the Peruvian Code, it is provided that in the treatment of crimes perpetrated by semicivilized Indians or by those degraded by slavery or alcohol, the judge shall take into account their mental development, the grade of their culture or their customs, and shall proceed to reprimand them with prudence as well as to reduce the punishment to the legal minimum. He shall also be able to substitute for a penitentiary sentence or *relegación,** an indeterminate sentence in an agricultural colony, the length of time to be served not to exceed the gravity of the offense.

PENITENTIARY MANAGEMENT. In some of the Latin American countries there exists a central agency which governs the administration of the prisons. For example, in Chile we find the General Administration of Prisons; in Panama, the Department of Corrections; in Brazil, the Penitentiary Council; in Cuba, the Superior Council of Social Defense; in Argentina, the General Administration of Penal Institutions; in Colombia, the General Administration of Prisons; in Mexico, the Department for Social Prevention.

Almost all of the Latin American countries have established some form of conditional release (parole) as well as suspension of the execution of the sentence for slight offenses such as may be found in Cuba, Panama, Argentina, etc.

So far as conditional release is concerned, there is no uniformity regarding the authority which governs it. In some countries it is still a judicial function as in Colombia, Argentina, Uruguay, Cuba, Peru, Ecuador and Bolivia. In others it is an administrative function in charge of the central penitentiary administration, as in Panama, Mexico and Chile.

* A form of "exile" usually, however, within the country and without the loss of citizenship.

The growing tendency regarding conditional release is that of not considering it as a grace, or privilege, but as a right, which the offender has as soon as he has demonstrated that he can live at liberty without constituting a social danger, that is, when he can prove that he is a good risk.

The treatment of the liberated offender is not so well developed in Latin American countries, especially so far as supervision is concerned. In very few countries does there exist any organization which assumes charge of liberated offenders and to assist them in the process of readaptation to community life. The Patronship of the Liberated, (*Los Patronatos de Liberados*), either public or private, which deals with aftercare, exists in Argentina, Chile, Cuba, Brazil and Mexico, but it is difficult to ascertain whether they accomplish the purpose for which they were created.

What is really understood as probation in the United States is not well developed in Latin America. In Cuba and Colombia, *Libertad Vigilada* (probation) is spoken of in the codes of laws and corresponds to the suspension of the execution of the sentence.*

Social work, usually associated with the penitentiary administration, has not been sufficiently felt. In some countries social investigation has been introduced, especially in Chile, Argentina, Mexico, and in Panama, applied to minors up to 16.

In the prisons, convict labor is obligatory but it is exercised more in the manner of exploitation than as education. There are shops in the majority of the penitentiaries and the penal colonies carry on agriculture. In productive work the prisoner receives a wage and the remainder of the profits is used to reduce the expense of the prison.

The state of the prisons, in general, is lamentable and especially in disciplinary management there is to be noted much of the repressive and of the spirit of exploitation.

Women and children are segregated in special institutions but treatment in the direction of social rehabilitation is none too progressive.

PRISON REFORM IN ARGENTINA

In a rather conspicuous manner, Argentina is taking an outstanding place in the front rank in penal reform, especially since 1937. Probably the most significant feature of that country's penal law is that it forbids not only capital punishment, but corporal punishment as well. In addition, the sentence, "hard labor" is not used, yet all prisoners are supplied work on the state-use, or as it is called there, government plan.

For many years, the capital, Buenos Aires, has long employed all of the above progressive features but it has been only within the past few years that real reform has been carried to the provinces. The great National Penitentiary in the capital has long been a model prison in many respects. Although it was erected over sixty years ago, on the star-shaped plan, with eight wings extending out from the central hall, it is still a remarkable institution for its spacious gardens and sunlit corridors, its scrupulous cleanliness and its many large cells.

---

* Probation in Latin America is in the form of suspension of the execution of the sentence which follows the Franco-Belgian concept. For details the reader is referred to N. S. Timasheff, *One Hundred Years of Probation*, Part II, Fordham University Press, 1943, pp. 62-65. (Editor).

Up until 1925, the only quality that was expected in the local district jails was security. There were thirteen of these local establishments. In 1934, a law was passed creating the office of Director General de Institutos Penales de la Nación and these were placed under central control. An outstanding Argentinian, with Irish blood in his veins, Dr. Juan José O'Connor visited these local prisons and indicted them as "centers of corruption and vengeance." He has been in the process of renovating these places since taking office, in spite of local opposition so often found in most countries.

By the use of convict labor and with the aid of small grants, he is slowly replacing them with modern and model prisons operated similarly to the National institution at the capital. The country has long had a system for the treatment of young offenders run on lines similar to the Borstals of England where every boy and girl is trained to perfect himself with a trade. They are surrounded by healthy conditions, are well fed, paid for their work and, in general, enjoy a progressive system of treatment.

One interesting feature of the National penitentiary is the large number of murals and paintings on the walls of the corridors and cells, placed there by convicts. This is encouraged by the management and stimulates a real interest in the arts. As one writer describes these paintings:

And the pictures! The oil paintings which decorate the walls! Everyone is the work of a convict. There was no unrecognized master among them, no sentenced Gauguin or Van Gogh, but the intention and gusto were astonishing. Rustic comedy of a *paisano* being thrown from a lively Creole horse; gaunt portrait of San Martin, the national liberator, staring from his equestrian heights toward a shrunken version of the Andes-rural and patriotic motives nearly all. But the fact that these men should have bothered to paint pictures here, should have cared to decorate the background to their constrained lives, is indication enough that they keep their self-respect.[1]

The Argentine convict must make some restitution in the form of compensation for the damage done his victims. Part of the money he makes goes for that purpose, part for his and his family's maintenance, while the small remainder he may spend as he sees fit. He has the privilege of brewing his own tea or cocoa in his cell, which, in Argentina, must have special significance for the immured criminal.

Argentina has also achieved much success with and recognition abroad for her system of criminal identification, fingerprinting, crime detection and other phases of what is known as criminalistics.

The present penal code of Argentina was established in 1922, having succeeded that of 1887. More recently a new project has been developed which is known as the *Project Coll-Gómez*.

This new code provides the following types of punishments: imprisonment, fines, and the deprivation of political rights. Children, as well as women, must serve their sentences in special establishments. Respectable women may serve their sentences in their own homes, providing the term does not exceed six months.

Relative to conditional release, there seems to be no provision for probation (*libertad vigilada*) nor for parole (*libertad bajo palabra*). However, the following rules do deal with these concepts in penology:

(1) Rupert Croft--Cooke, "Prison Reform in Argentina," *Pan American Bulletin*, vol. 71, pp. 695-697, (1937).

CONDITIONAL RELEASE (*parole*)

ARTICLE 13.   The prisoner condemned to life imprisonment who has served 20 years; the prisoner with a sentence of more than 3 years who has served two-thirds of his sentence; and the prisoner with a sentence of three years or less who has served eight months in prison, conforming with regularity to the prison rules, can obtain his freedom by a judicial ruling, if previous information has been given by the head of the establishment, under the following conditions:

1. that he shall live in the place determined by the judicial regulation which frees him;
2. that he shall observe the rules of inspection determined by the regulation, especially the obligation to abstain from alcoholic beverages;
3. that he shall adopt during the time determined by the regulation, a trade or occupation of some sort if he does not have means of subsistence of his own;
4. that he shall not commit new crimes;
5. that he shall place himself under the care of some patronage, indicated by competent authorities.

(These conditions shall exist until the end of this temporary punishment, and in the life sentences until five years after beginning of the day that the conditional release is granted).

ARTICLE 14.   Conditional release will not be granted ex-convicts who commit a new crime.

ARTICLE 15.   Conditional release will be nullified when the convict commits a new crime or violates his obligations to live or reside in a specified area. In such cases the time spent in conditional release will not be counted as numbers 2, 3, and 5 of Article 13, the tribunal will be able to judge or decide whether the time spent in conditional release shall be counted as part of the sentence.

ARTICLE 16.   If the term of the sentence has been completed, or the term of five years, as pointed out in Article 13, without conditional release being abrogated, the punishment will be considered ended.

ARTICLE 17.   No convict whose conditional release has been nullified will be able to obtain it again.

SUSPENDED SENTENCE (*probation*)

The Argentine system is contemplating the suspended sentence which is in reality the suspension of the execution of the sentence according to the following circumstances:

ARTICLE 26.   In cases of first offense or imprisonment which does not exceed two years, or of fines, the tribunals will order at the same time that the serving of the sentence is to be suspended. This declaration will be founded on the moral personality of the convict, the nature of the crime and the circumstances surrounding it in so far as they may be able to assist in understanding said personalities. The tribunal will require the information which it deems pertinent in forming an opinion. In the cases of reoccurrence of crimes, conditional serving will proceed if the sentence imposed does not exceed two years of imprisonment, or fine.

ARTICLE 27.   The sentence will be held as not having been pronounced if within the term of the prescription of the punishment the convict does not commit a new crime. If he does commit a new crime he will suffer the punishment imposed in the first sentence and that which is imposed on him by the second crime according to the laws of the accumulation of punishments.

JUVENILE DELINQUENCY.   Regarding the treatment of juvenile delinquents, children under fourteen years of age are not punishable. When they are not dangerous they may be placed under the care of their parents. Otherwise, they will be interned in a correctional institution until they are eighteen. Children under twenty-one, but over fourteen, who commit crimes can also be placed under jurisdiction of parents or guardians according to circumstances, but if they are dangerous, or it is inconvenient to allow them freedom, they will be interned in a correctional institution.

Minors not over eighteen cannot be sent to prison. Also there are no preventive prisons for minors under 18. When they have been accused of a crime, or when victims of a crime, they may be disposed of temporarily, if they are materially or morally abandoned (neglected or destitute), by turning them over to some reliable person, relative or otherwise, or to an institution of private or public welfare, or to a public reformatory for minors.

For the segregation of abandoned minors who commit crimes, Argentina has institutions of the cottage type (Colonias-Hogares), among which is the Colony of Ricardo Gutiérrez, possibly the best of its kind in South America. In addition, Argentina has various types of institutions for the mentally deficient, for the mentally ill and for the treatment of tuberculars.

PENITENTIARY MANAGEMENT.   The penitentiary system is under the direction of the General Director of Penal Institutions which is composed of an Assessor Council and of the Technical and Administrative Personnel. In addition, it has under its jurisdiction a Classification Institute which is in charge of the psychophysical diagnosis of the convicts. This institute has a psychiatric branch (*Anexo Psiquiátrico*).

In spite of the fact that the granting of conditional release is given to the judicial authorities who know the case, the General Directory of Penal Institutions is called upon to make the necessary recommendations concerning the health of the convict, his behavior, the amount of instruction acquired in prison, and also his aptitude for work demonstrated while in prison.

PRISON LABOR.   All prison inmates are required to work and their product is dedicated to indemnity, for the maintenance of their dependents, to paying for their own maintenance in prison and to form a savings' fund which will be given to them upon release.

There are no industries, as such, in the prisons, although there seems to be some work within the prison establishments. Most prisoners are employed on public works.

There is a Patronage of ex-convicts (*Patronato de Liberados*) in charge of lending moral support or any other kind of assistance to released convicts who have been placed on conditional release.

THE PRISON SYSTEM OF BRAZIL

Little, if anything, appears in English regarding the prison system of Brazil, yet it is known that this great country has made amazing strides in social reform during the past decade. The writer has attempted to secure recent information regarding penal philosophy and administration from various sources but with little success. What appears in the first few paragraphs below may be of practically no value in visualizing the status of penal thought and practice in this largest of South American countries but at the time it was written it apparently was an accurate account. Since prisons and penal philosophy change so slowly it may well be not too far afield.

The well known penologist, Enoch C. Wines, described Brazil's penal system in 1879 in his *State of Prisons*. He pointed out that there were twenty provinces in the country which made up a total of 480 jurisdictions corresponding to the same number of municipal judges. The cost of erecting the various prisons was borne by the provinces.

At that time Brazil had only one central prison, at Fernando de Noronha, an island two hundred and ninety miles northeast of Recife, the capital of the province of Pernambuco. Convicts sent to this prison were subjected to a regimen of hard labor including several of the trades. They received, in addition to a share in the product of their labor, moral and religious instruction.

The other prisons were not central or state controlled but rather were designed to imprison criminals in the various provinces. Among these were the prisons at Rio de Janeiro and São Paulo ;[1] the workhouse at Bahia and the detention prison of Recife. At the time, all inmates were under strict silence with separation at night and association during the day. Dr. Wines stated that when he visited the country there was not one cellular prison to be found.

In 1874 a Commission proposed the adoption of a modified plan of progressive stages patterned after the Irish System. Convicts were divided into grades according to their conduct. There were visiting privileges and an educational program. The prison labor system was similar to the state-use system in operation in the United States. Quarrying, stonecutting and agriculture comprised the occupations and the prisoner received a portion of the product of his labor. There were no Patronage societies at that time but it is understood that they are now in operation.

(1) Over the main door of the administration building appears this inscription which translated states : "Here, work, discipline and kindness mend the error committed and restore the offender to his status in the social community."

Capital punishment was abolished in Brazil in 1891 but it was reinstated in 1938 for "cases of extreme perversity only." These crimes are determined by the Tribunal of National Security and include those which interfere with the national economy such as usury and excessive speculation in price-fixing of necessary consumer goods. It is reported on good authority that there have been no executions since the death penalty was restored.

When Dr. Wines visited Brazil the penal code then in operation decreed that minors under fourteen years of age were not responsible for crimes; however, if they committed delinquencies with knowledge they were sent to correctional establishments until they were eighteen. These institutions were privately operated. One such was founded in 1875 at the Villa Izabel in Rio de Janeiro where children could learn trades and receive moral instruction. Another was in the province of Pernambuco known as the Colony Izabel. In São Paulo was the asylum of Doña Anna Rosa and at Petropolis was a school for girls.

The penal code now in operation provides for children through a section known as a Code for Minors. There are juvenile courts with social workers attached to them.

In 1940 a new penal code was adopted for Brazil. Previously, in 1934, Decree No. 16,665 was set up which established the Penitentiary Council. This is composed of the Attorney General of the Republic, a representative of the local Public Ministry and five other officials, three of whom are professors of law, and two physicians. The Council handles all matters dealing with conditional release, pardons and penal discipline of all types of prisoners. The penitentiary at São Paulo is considered one of the best in Latin America.

Brazil maintains probation, following the traditional pattern of the Franco-Belgian system, modified to some degree by the so-called American system. In fact, Brazil was the first country in Latin America to consider probation in a rudimentary form. This was in 1893. But it was not until 1924 that it was actually put into practical operation. Probation is limited to first offenders and is further denied to those whose crimes violate "the honor of families."

There is probation of minors in the juvenile courts which were established in 1927. Children placed on probation are either returned to their parents with a supervisory guardian in charge appointed by the court, or placed in a welfare institution. The time limit of juvenile probation is limited to twelve months.[2]

PENAL PHILOSOPHY IN CHILE

In the year 1930, the Country of Chile passed a new and somewhat spectacular penal code which, in many important respects, broke with the concepts of traditional penology and criminology. In the magazine, *Chile*, Sr. A. R. González, describes its various provisions.[*]

First and foremost, the new code abolished the death penalty. This in itself shows the length to which the government was willing to go in setting up a rational and progressive penal philosophy. Unfortunately, however, capital punishment was reinstated in 1937. The method used is by

(2) Timasheff, *op. cit.*, vol II, pp. 63, 65.
 * July, 1930, pp. 19 f.

shooting. But the 1930 code envisaged some interesting concepts which bear close scrutiny by American jurists and students of criminal philosophy. For example, the code reflected an unwillingness to enter into the controversy between free will and determinism. As Sr. González writes: "Crime is no longer defined. For the old interpretation, 'a voluntary action or failure to act punishable by law,' leads to confusing controversies on 'free will' and 'determinism.' The new code recognizes that from the standpoint of the individual and his relation to the community it matters not whether his will is free or predestined; crazy or sane, master of his fate or slave of circumstance, he is a member of society, and if he becomes a menace to that society, it must be protected against him."

Consequently the personal factor is the principal consideration in fixing his responsibility and reformability. Analysis is made of the motives impelling him to commit the crime, his physical condition, his economic necessities. Accordingly, social rehabilitation becomes the primary objective in treatment.

Emphasis is now placed on the criminal instead of the offense. It naturally follows, therefore, that treatment must be individualized. This is done through the indeterminate sentence. The judge does not fix a definite duration for the prison term to be served. It is interesting that the penal code of Chile insists that a person who has attempted to commit a crime is treated as if he had actually accomplished the crime. As Sr. González remarks: "A frustrated crime is no longer classed separately, but included in the category of attempted crimes; the penalty for an attempted crime is now identical with that of the accomplished crime, and the accomplice is held to be as guilty as the actual doer of the deed. Naturally, whether a crime succeeds or whether it fails, whether a person takes a tacit or an active part in its perpetration, the danger to the community represented by that criminal plan and by its germinators remains the same."

Not only are sentences individualized, but so are fines. It is the duty of the court to see that the fines exacted are based on the ability to pay. Installment fines are provided for by the code. But even more significant is the fact that fines are made relative: "fines are imposed according to the income and financial obligations of the subject, and their standardization is one of units rather than of amounts." If two persons, for example, have committed the same crime and have each been fined thirty units, the judge may interpret a unit in one case as ten pesos, and in another as thirty pesos, the one consequently paying a fine of 300 pesos and the other, one of 900 pesos.

The penal code calls for higher qualifications for judges than formerly. Magistrates of civil tribunals must know law but magistrates in criminal courts must be acquainted also with psychology and sociology. In addition, the code insists that judges must possess general culture; specialized knowledge in juridical sciences; knowledge of criminal anthropology, history of crime and punishment, prevention of crime, crime, criminal sociology, comparative penal legislation, and penitentiary procedure.

Following are the salient points of the penal code of Chile:

1. The fundamental purpose is prevention of crime; not vengeance.

2. The criminal is to be reformed, not punished.

3. Prison sentences are indeterminate, depending on the refomability of the subject.

4. The death penalty and life sentences are abolished.

5. Fines are imposed according to the prisoner's ability to pay.

6. Adultery is no longer a crime for the woman and not for the man.

7. Psychological, sociological, biological causes of crime are to be considered determining factors in every case, and reform is based on modern scientific knowledge in these fields.

In connection with the establishment of Chile's progressive penal code, a number of developments were projected in revamping institutional treatment. The code called for the erection of a new penitentiary at Santiago; a prison-sanitarium at Maipo for tubercular prisoners; a jail at Santiago with capacity for a thousand inmates, annexed to which would be the courts of criminal justice and separate quarters for prisoners enjoying conditional liberty and those not at work, and also for those released from prison and for whom no employment has been found. Provision was also made for forty additional jails with annexes of various types. The code also called for the enlargement of the penitentiary at Antofagasta as well as the prisons at Los Andes, Rengo, San Fernando and Chilean. This work was to be finished by 1933.

Other provisions of the code include the following: special treatment for those with venereal diseases, better nutrition for prisoners, the recognition of "ignorance" as an extenuating circumstance in the commission of crime, and more flexibility in judicial proceedings.

From what we have been able to gather, it would seem that Chile has gone far in developing a rational system of criminal jurisprudence. The abolition of the death penalty and the forthright adoption of the complete indeterminate sentence are enough to indicate the vision of those who are determined to place Chile among the front rank countries in progressive criminal and penal procedure.

Most of the prisoners are compelled to do work of some sort while in prison, for which they are paid. The work is always of a vocational nature and is very simple, consisting of such things as the manufacture of license plates and small pieces of electrical and carpentry equipment. The rate of pay is small, however.

In addition, prisoners are required to attend classes of instruction under the direction of a service known as the School for Prisoners. This school undertakes instruction at the primary level of such subjects as reading, writing, and simple calculation. In addition there are special courses in music, drawing, modeling and physical culture. There are libraries in each institution.

Most of the buildings are old but they are kept in very good condition and the general opinion is that the penal system of the country is progressive and well operated.

THE PRISON SYSTEM OF PERU

Very soon after her emancipation from Spain, Peru began to think of establishing a penitentiary system in harmony with her new constitution. As early as 1825, the idea of a workhouse was considered for the city of Lima. However, this idea lay dormant until 1853.

In that year, Sr. Felipe Paz-Soldan visited the United States with a view of surveying penal systems then in operation. He returned to Peru and reported his findings and recommendations to President Ramón Castillo. Immediately, the president gave orders to erect a penitentiary. The edifice was completed and inaugurated with much solemity in July, 1862. One month later, the first prisoners were committed to the establishment. Sr. Paz-Soldan was the first director. In 1867, he was succeeded by Dr. Thomas Lama.

Dr. Lama must have been a man of real vision. Upon taking over his duties he immediately contended that in his opinion, the larger part of the prisoners were more unfortunate than criminal, and that their offenses against society were to be ascribed to bad education rather than to any deep corruption or vicious instincts. Accordingly, he recommended use of mild discipline toward them believing that it would be more efficacious than more rigorous measures.

In 1879, when Mr. E. C. Wines described Peru's system of penal discipline, he spoke highly of the construction of its prison. He considered it as being one of the best of its kind to be found anywhere. The system of associated labor by day and cellular separation at night was put into practice. Labor was provided the prisoners and they were paid wages in accordance with their ability. In 1876, M. Aurelio Villaran was appointed director of the prison and he is said to have carried out the work of his predecessor since he entertained practically the same ideas of prison discipline.

THE PENAL CODE. The present penal code of Peru dates from 1924 (Law 4,868) having replaced the earlier code of 1862. The principles of this code are judicially precise. Running counter to the Franco-Germanic tri-partite classification of offenses, the Peruvian code follows the bi-partite classification and recognizes felonies and misdemeanors (*delitos y faltas*).

PUNISHMENTS. The measures of security in Peru are internment, the penitentiary, *relegación,* prison, expatriation, fines and the deprivation of civil rights. Peru does not have an absolute fixed sentence as is so customary in most countries. There exists a wide range between the legal minimum and maximum by which the judge may fix the sentence according to the circumstances of each case as well as the potential danger of the offender.

The sentence of internment refers to twenty-five years or over and constitutes the most serious of all forms of punishment. The sentence is served in the central penitentiary and calls for hard labor in isolation for the first year. The next year the inmate may work in association with other offenders who have been committed to the same type of punishment.

Penitentiary punishment ranges from one to twenty years. It may be served either in the central penitentiary or in an agricultural colony or in a penal colony. Isolation ranges from one week to six months with work included. Following this, association is permitted.

CONDITIONAL RELEASE. All those committed to prison may be conditionally released with the principle of revocation explicit. It may be granted only after two-thirds of the sentence is served in case the sentence is over one year in the penitentiary or eight months of *relegación* or prison. Evidence of rehabilitation together with a good conduct record are necessary for possible conditional release. It can be granted only by the sentencing judge who imposes the terms of the release.

SUSPENSION OF THE SENTENCE. The Peruvian code, like other Latin American countries, has adopted the Franco-Belgian system of the suspended sentence which refers only to the suspension of the execution of the sentence. It applies to those offenders who are sentenced to less than six months or a fine and who have not been previously sentenced for a deliberate crime.

THE PENITENTIARY SYSTEM. All penal establishments are under the authority of an official called the General Inspector of Prisons, who is appointed by the Executive Branch. The inspection of the prisons is in charge of the technical director of institutions and integrated by an inspector and a secretary, both of whom must be lawyers, a physician specialized in legal medicine and psychiatry, and an administrative staff.

In connection with the penitentiary system of Peru, it is cogent to recall the words of the distinguished Spanish penologist, Sr. Luis Jiménez de Asúa, who, in a lecture at the National University of Cuba, said:

In every penal reform it is necessary to consider three essential aspects, as follows: first, the penal code; second, the judges who are to apply it; and third, the penitentiary system where sentences are to be executed. In order for a penal code to function it is not enough to have a perfect code in so far as the technicalities are concerned. It is just as necessary to have the judges well trained and possessing a knowledge of how to apply this perfect code and, in addition, a *modern and reformative penitentiary system.*

Referring to penal reform in Peru, Sr. de Asúa stated:

What is the use of a good penal code as you have in Peru if all the penitentaries that exist in Lima are deplorable? The penal code exists to be applied and the science of penitentiary treatment makes this possible.

WORK OF THE PRISONERS. Work is obligatory for all inmates of penal institutions. An attempt is made to have all work in the open air and it is organized not only for purposes of education and hygiene but also for technical training and for purposes of economic restitution. Religious and moral training is also obligatory. There is segregation of males and females in the prisons. All prisoners are in isolation at night.

There is a classification system based on physical and mental potentialities, previous background and aptitude for work.

PATRONAGE FOR THOSE RELEASED. Patronage (aftercare) is composed of a member of the Tribunal, a representative of the Attorney General, a member of the Department of Welfare, a director of the penal establishment, a professor of penal law, a lawyer, a physician connected with the Department of Health, and a representative of the labor unions. Their functions are to supervise and to help inmates while they are in prison as well as after they are released.

JUVENILE DELINQUENTS. In the cases of minor delinquents from 13 to 18 years of age, or of neglected and dependent children, or children in moral danger, the government official in charge can provide for their care by placing them with a reliable family or in a private or public educational institution until the age of eighteen. Children and adolescents are subjected to a special juvenile jurisdiction in order to protect them by educational means. For this purpose a juvenile court has been established and staffed by technical personnel.

Special provisions for Indians are a part of the Peruvian code. These have been discussed in our general analysis of Latin American penal law.

Children's courts were provided for the first time in Peru by the new penal code passed in 1924. As little was known in that country about the more scientific treatment of juvenile delinquents, a group of women, known as the National Council of Women, was formed to cooperate with the newly established court and to provide friendly advice and service to the children falling under its jurisdiction.

Accordingly, the first act of this group was to ask for help from the United States Children's Bureau, the National Committee on Mental Hygiene, the Bureau of Child Guidance and the National Probation Association. It was their determination to place the treatment of delinquent children on as firm a basis as possible, in the light of the most recent scientific findings. The Peruvian government gave the group a small subsidy and official sanction under the name of *Sociadad Especial de Patronato de Menores*.

There are three correctional institutions in the city of Lima, one for girls and two for boys. The girls' building is merely an annex of the women's prison of Santo Tomás. Both the prison and the annex are operated in a "rough and ready," though efficient fashion, by a congregation of sisters known as the Third Order of Saint Francis of Assisi, founded for the expressed purpose of carrying on penal work. The régime is described as "understanding and humane, and the women are kept constantly employed in light work of various kinds." Many of the women have babies with them. These are cared for properly and the atmosphere is described as "cheerful and soothing." The percentage of criminality among Peruvian women is quite low, the most serious offenses being those of passion. The girls' reformatory is run by the sisters, but it is described as overcrowded.

The two reformatories for boys are run by "lay officials." The reformatory at Surco is located in the open country amidst pleasant surroundings. However, its farming land was taken over by the president of Peru for a flying field. The new penal code created a detention home for boys to be operated in conjunction with the children's court, but the housing facilities are not adequate for the purpose. There is a large floating population of children in the country because of the "improvidence of the half-breed working classes and the irregularity and promiscuity of marital relations among them." This is described as "perhaps the gravest social problem confronting Peru and other Latin American countries."

The women criminals are described as "harassed and generally a hard driven, devoted class"; whereas their mates "seem to be about evenly divided between two extreme types—the sober and industrious family man and the unprincipled and self indulgent irresponsible, whose amorous

exploits leave a long and tragic trail of misery and squalor behind them."
The latter type seems to be in the majority.

The work of the *Patronato de Menores* consists of semiofficial
duties of inspection of the reformatories and friendly cooperation with
them, and also of the proper disposal of those children whom the judge
does not see fit to send to the reform institutions. Most of such children
are homeless or come from depraved homes and must be placed in more
wholesome surroundings. The *Patronato,* in 1931, was studying a plan
to send groups of boys to an agricultural colony in the wild and fertile
tracts of the Montaña, the huge inland region watered by the tributaries
of the Amazon, to learn farming and to carve out a future for themselves
under the direction of the Franciscan missionary fathers.*

BRIEF NOTES ON THE ECUADOREAN PENAL SYSTEM

Dr. Emilio Uzcátegui*

Up until shortly after the various Latin American countries had gained
their independence, Spanish law, composed of the so-called Laws of the
Indies and the Royal Decrees, had complete jurisdiction over all civil and
penal matters. This was, therefore, true of the country of Ecuador.

Justice was administered in the first place by the Supreme Court of
the Indies which functioned throughout the peninsula and then later by
the *Audiencia* (a court of oyer and terminer), and the magistrates and
the mayors.

The seat of the *Audiencia* was Quito. This Tribunal was composed
of a president, four lawyers and an attorney general, in addition to a
reporter and a notary public. Its judgments were called mandates and were
handed down after the attorney general was heard.

The mayors of each city and town exercised their jurisdiction in all
civil and criminal matters but appeal could be made from their judgments
to the *Audiencia.*

Punishments were fines, prison, whippings and other severe penalties
such as mutilation of organs or other parts of the body, confiscation of
goods, exile or the gallows.

The jails were of two classes: for the poor, dirty cells even deprived
of fresh air; for the rich, all existing conveniences.

Similar to the police was the *Institución de la Santa Hermandad*
charged with enforcing public order.

The first penal code of Ecuador dates from 1872. It was taken almost
literally from the Belgian Code of 1870 which in turn was inspired by the
French Code of 1810. Since that time there have been many modifications,
more in detail than in substances or doctrine, such as isolated reforms and
re-editions of the Code, the principal ones being those of 1889, 1906 and
the most fundamental, of 1938.

The reform of 1906, being adapted to the Constitution of the same
year, which introduced liberalism to Ecuador, suppressed crimes and offenses

* This material is from an article in the Pan-American Union Bulletin, vol. 65, November, 1931, pp. 1134-1139.   It was written by Mercedes Gallagher de Parks, and entitled "Children's Court Work and Reformatories in Peru."

* The author of this review is a prominent lawyer and author living in Quito.

against religion since no official religion was recognized. This reform guaranteed freedom of worship.

The penal code that actually governs Ecuador dates from March, 1938, and was established by the government of General Enríquez. While it is modern in many respects, since it notably shows the influence of the Positive school, it still clings to much of the Classical spirit of the older codes.

The political constitution of the State, in Article 26, sets up two standards on which rests the penal system: the right to be considered innocent until proven guilty, and the guarantee of not being compelled to testify against wife or husband, offspring, ancestors or relations to the fourth civil grade of consanguinity or to the second grade of affinity, or compelled by oath or other pressure to declare against the same, or to assume any penal responsibility for same, or to be secluded for more than twenty-four hours, or be subject to any form of torture.

The disposition of misdemeanors (*contravenciones*) falls to the Chief of Police; that of crimes (*delitos*) to judges and to the Tribunals of Crime and to *Juardos de Imprenta,* according to the type of cases. Sentences are in general possible of appeal through to the Supreme Court.

There are two classes of establishments for the punishment of the delinquent: the penitentiary and the jails. Criminals guilty of the more serious crimes are sent to the penitentiary, that is, those whom the law has condemned to *reclusión.* These are divided into four classes according to the gravity of the offense.

The most severe type of imprisonment (*reclusión mayor*) calls for forced labor and cellular confinement, the ordinary term being from four to eight years and the extraordinary term for sixteen. In the less severe imprisonment (*reclusión menor*) the ordinary term is from three to six years and the extraordinary for twelve. These latter delinquents are also subject to forced labor but this is carried on in communal factories or outside the penal establishments in agricultural colonies. In these cases isolation is only used as a punishment for infractions against the penitentiary management and then only for eight days.

There exists for this type of imprisonment only one such penitentiary, the so-called Panopticon or *Penal García Moreno,* named in memory of the president who erected it in 1870 and which was constructed as an exact reproduction of the best penitentiary in the United States at that time. Its maintenance is under the direction of the state. At the time it was erected it was one of the largest prisons in the Americas. At present it has been suggested that, for the most efficient accommodation of prisoners as well as for local needs, a penitentiary be constructed for the coastal regions.

Correctional prison, which handles cases with sentences from eight days to five years as well as misdemeanants whose punishments vary from seven days spent in jail, are under the direction of the municipalities of which there exists one in each district.

For prison work, the inmates are paid but in the amount proportionately less than the wages of free workmen. From the prisoner's remuneration one-third may be retained for his credit and received by him upon release; one-third serves to pay his expenses in the institution (maintenance), and the remaining third is claimed by the court to take care of his civil obligation incidental to his crime.

Since 1936 there has existed a penal colony (*Colonia Penal de Mera*) situated in the *Región Oriental* on the banks of the Pastaza River where may be found fifty carefully selected prisoners. This venture has produced satisfactory results and although the laborers have been submitted to a regimen of productive work there have been no escapes or serious infractions. As the majority of these prisoners come from the rural sections of the country they can carry on the agricultural work there without difficulty. Even today they devote themselves to the cultivation of sugar cane, corn, bananas, yucca, and the breeding of birds and hogs. In earlier times, the system of penal colonies was carried out, under very inadequate conditions, in the Galápagos Islands and the archepelago of Colón.

The administration of the National Penitentiary, which in all matters of discipline is exactly like that at the colony of Mera, dates from 1915 and requires a complete renovaton because of its archaism and extreme severity.

In addition to a prison sentence, the penal code of Ecuador establishes punishments of fines, confiscation, loss of the exercise of the professions, arts and offices, subjection to the supervision of the authorities and the suspension of political and civil rights.

Among the fundamental reforms introduced in the peanl code now in force is the institution of probation (*condena condicional*). This is applied only in the cases of first offenders and for infractions whose punishment does not exceed six months although there may be a concurrence of infractions, or also in a case where the penalty is only a fine. In these two circumstances, provided the offender does not commit new crimes during the probationary period and two years thereafter, the punishment is as if it had not been pronounced.

There has also been introduced in Ecuador the system of special vigilance of the authorities in view of which the judge can prohibit the offender from appearing in certain places even after he has completed his sentence. Such a person must obtain permission from the police to move to another place. Those sentenced to strict imprisonment (*reclusión*) can be subjected to the vigilance of the police for five to ten years, or a vigilance lasting all their lives if they commit more crimes of the same or greater gravity.

Conditional release (*parole*) has been instituted for those delinquents who have completed three-fourths of their sentence in a correctional prison and provided they do not lack more than three years to complete their sentence. In all cases certain requisites are needed, the principal ones being: residence in a determined place, that the applicant is accredited as having a profession, office or sufficient means to live honorably, and that he has satisfied all civil obligations imposed.

Of exceptional importance is the creation in Ecuador of the Institute of Criminology as a scientific aid to justice, created in September 1936 by the engineer, Federico Páez. Since its establishment this organization has been lending valuable services especially in regard to the exercise of pardon (*La Ley de Gracia*). Its Director is the Director General of Prisons.

Among the principal functions of the Institute are: the study of the bio-physical-social aspects of the delinquent prior to the imposition of sentence, the study of the prisoners for their reclassification and treatment, rendering opinions in cases of commutation, deduction and remission of punishment or for the concession or cessation of conditional release, study of crime and its causes in Ecuador, and the fixing of norms for the treatment, education and management of work for all prisoners.

For the realization of its labors it depends on laboratories of anthropology, psychology and medical biology and on the identification files of those who have studied minutely thousands of criminals whose records are classified and preserved. Since its founding the Institute has published an excellent magazine called *Archivos de Criminología, Neuropsiquiatría y disciplinas conexas.*

There has also been functioning for a short time in Ecuador the *Institute of Legal Medicine* which supplements the scientific work on criminology.

Also the administration of Federico Páez decreed in 1937 the aftercare of prisoners (*Patronato Post Carcelario y Post Asilados*) among whose functions is the securing of work for ex-prisoners, to provide educational opportunities, to foster institutions and crime prevention measures and practices. Unfortunately, perhaps because of the complex and numerous composition of the *Junta* (council), it has been in session very few times and it can be said that up to the present, nothing has been done to fulfill any of its objectives.

As a general observation it can be said, fortunately, that in Ecuador, relatively few crimes are committed. In the coastal zones, sex crimes and crimes against the person predominate while in the interior, thefts of cattle, robbery and, on a lesser scale, crimes against the person, are committed.

It can be affirmed that among the principal causes of crime in Ecuador are alcoholism, social degeneration, sickness and poverty, and lack of education.

Along the line of juvenile delinquency there exists a special legislation which dates from 1938. The Code for Minors established a special form of treatment for those who have not yet reached the age of eighteen and who, according to prescribed conditions, cannot be detained more than twenty-four hours without being handed over to the courts for minors (*Tribunales de Menores*) on whom their judgment falls. These divest themselves of their legal aspect and make a psycho-pedagogical, anthropological and biological examination.

The Tribunals for Minors function in every provincial capital and are headed by an educator, a physician and a lawyer who examine each case of juvenile delinquency on the basis of the information given them by the *Policlínicos* after the studies have been made in the House of Observation. The Tribunals are also assisted by the social visitors (social workers) who make a study of the home and social conditions in general. These visitors are also charged with the duty of supervising minor delinquents even in the cases where they are reinstated in their homes.

Although the above-mentioned Code for Minors seriously considers the establishment of a series of institutions designed to prevent juvenile delinquency, in reality little has been done except the founding of some child shelters and work schools. A special effort worthy of mention is the formation of Children's Clubs established by the Institute of the Brethern in cooperation with several national societies of beneficence, culture and work.

Finally we shall give a few paragraphs to female delinquency, a field in which the penal law of Ecuador has progressed the least. In very few places are there special establishments for women prisoners. Usually there are sections, to a degree independent, inside the penitentiary and the ordinary jails.

Also, there are few exceptional modifications in consideration to sex in the legislation as, for example, that established in Article 61 of the penal code which says: "a pregnant woman may be notified of a prison sentence only after seventy days after the birth of her baby." This ruling attempts at least to protect the interests of the new-born child.

In proportion to the number of male criminals, there are few female delinquents. Crimes against the person are the most frequent (82 percent) while the remainder are crimes against property. Among the factors causing crime among women are passion, as they attempt to escape dishonor and seek revenge, and, on a minor scale, drunkenness, disorderly conduct, and those due to economic motives.

I do not pretend to have exhausted the topic nor to have covered it in all its latitude. These lines are a simple sketch of the penal system of Ecuador.

COLOMBIA'S NEW PENAL SYSTEM

Penal reform in Colombia since 1936 has been stimulated by two main objectives: the prevention of recidivism and the increase and improvement of measures of social defense. Plans promulgated by the Director of Prisons at that time, Dr. Francisco Bruno, envisaged a scientific attack on the offender with the following objectives:

The prevention of crime and the scientific treatment of criminals
The segregation of the various types of delinquents
The social readaptation of those released from prison

The first main objective was to be accomplished by the following program: the control and regulation of immigration and the repression of habitual migrants or those temperamentally antisocial; the education and protection of neglected, deficient and handicapped children; and the social treatment of vagrants and beggars.

The second objective was to be realized by: the establishment and wider use of reformatories for children and youth organized by means of a system based on medical, educational and correctional treatment with a normal homelike atmosphere; establishment of jails and penitentiaries large enough and well enough equipped to permit classification and segregation of their inmates as well as to provide scientific and hygienic services, schools and workshops; penal colonies designed to prepare their inmates for a life of stability and service in the agricultural regions of the country; judges and physicians familiar with anthropology and psychiatry; directors and other personnel of prisons trained in education, criminal anthropology, penal legislation and, in addition, sympathetic of humane principles of penal treatment; social agencies for released prisoners and children; and by a financial budget adequate enough to realize these reforms within a reasonable time.

The penitentiaries of Colombia are divided into three categories. The Central Penitentiary at Bogotá is the only one in the first category. It was built many years ago and is well designed. It was patterned after the Eastern Penitentiary at Philadelphia with radiating wings. In the second category are the penitentiaries of Ibagué, Pamplona and Tunja; in the third are those at Cartagena, Manizales, Medellín, Pasto and Popayán. A new model prison was planned for La Picota. There are, in addition, two farm penal colonies at Acacias and Araracuara with another projected in the region of Caqueté.

Each judicial district is provided with its own jail (*cárceles*). Reformatories for the treatment of children and females complete the list of institutions provided for measures of security.

PENAL CODE. The penal code of 1936 replaced that of 1890. It classifies all infractions of penal law into felonies and misdemeanors (*delitos y contravenciones*). In general, the supervision of misdemeanants is in charge of the police.

PUNISHMENTS. Punishments for adults over eighteen years of age are long term imprisonment, short term imprisonment, arrest, simple confinement and fines. The following disciplinary measures may be used when it is established that the offender is not guilty of a serious offense:

Prohibition of residing in a determined place

A conspicuous or special publication of the sentence

Prohibition of public rights or functions

Prohibition or suspension of the arts or of a profession

The loss of all pensions or wages of retirement of a civil character

The guarantee of good conduct

Banishment (*relegación*) to penal agricultural colonies

Loss or suspension of the rights of citizenship (*patria potestad*)

Deportation of foreigners

Long or short term imprisonment or jail sentences or arrests are fulfilled in each case under separate confinement during the night with industrial or agricultural work during the day.

MEASURES OF SECURITY

(a) For delinquents who suffer from mental disorders or from chronic alcoholism or from drug addiction or from grave physical handicaps:

Detention in a special institution or agricultural colony

Probation (*libertad vigilada*) by entrusting them to he care of their families or of placing them in a health sanitorium or hospital under the inspection of the Council of Patronage and for a time not less than two years.

Mandatory labor in factories or on public works

Prohibition of being present in certain public places

(b) For delinquents under eighteen years of age:

Probation which consists of entrusting them to their own families or to another worthy family or to an educational institution, factory or private establishment or the prohibition of being present in public places where they will be morally endangered. Detention in work school or reformatory

CONDITIONAL RELEASE. This is granted to short term prisoners if they have completed two-thirds of their sentence; to long term prisoners who have completed three-fourths of their sentence, providing that in each case the prisoner can convince the judge that he has conducted himself well in prison and that he will be no longer a detriment to society.

After the Public Ministry and the Disciplinary Council have given their report as to the conduct of the prisoner to be released, the granting as well as the revocation of the release are in the hands of the judicial authorities.

PROBATION. (*Condena Condicional*). When a long term sentence does not exceed three years or a short term sentence does not exceed two years, the judge can suspend the execution of the sentence for a test period (*período de prueba*) of from two to five years if the following circumstances concur:

(a) That the probationer shall not commit another offense
(b) That his previous conduct shall have always been good, and
(c) That his personality shall convince the judge that he will take advantage of the privilege, not be be dangerous to society, nor revert to crime.

JUVENILE DELINQUENTS. Children up to fourteen years of age who are not morally deficient and can give a good guarantee may be placed on probation if they commit an offense. They are entrusted to their own families under the court's supervision until they become eighteen.

However, if the minor is morally deficient he is cut off from his family and placed on probation for not less than two years or until he reaches his eighteenth birthday.

If the circumstances of the minor make it impossible for him to be placed on probation he is interned for the same period in a work school.

The minor of eighteen years of age who commits a crime can be placed on probation provided the offense does not call for long term imprisonment and legal arrangements can be made. However, if such arrangements cannot be made, he is placed in a work school for not less than two years and until he effects reformation, providing this does not exceed his twenty-fifth birthday.

JUDICIAL PARDON. Without knowing the reason or motives for the measure, the Colombian Penal Code gives authority to the judge to grant a law violator a judicial pardon at his discretion. This pardon consists in rescinding the penalty applicable to the offense. The same circumstances exist as those applying to the granting of probation.

The principal institutions for minors are: The Refuge for Abandoned Children in Bogotá, Children's Reformatory of Bogotá, The Reformatory of Fagua, and other departmental reformatories.

PENITENTIARY MANAGEMENT. The prison and penitentiary code which governs all prisons provides penal and agricultural colonies, jails for judicial districts and women's institutions. Some of these are equipped with small spinning and weaving shops, iron works, foundries, and carpenter, mechanical and tailoring shops. In all institutions, work is obligatory.

URUGUAY'S PRISON SYSTEM

The penal system of Uruguay is administered by the Ministry of Public Instruction and Social Prevention, the schools under one division and the prisons under another. The Supreme Court also exercises supervision over the prisons. There are three Federal prisons and an Educational Colony of Work. In addition, there is to be established, within the Educational Colony of Work, a section for the Criminal Insane. In the various Departments of Uruguay there are some small jails for temporary confinement, but any person who receives a prison sentence is brought to Montevideo for incarceration in one of the above prisons, all of which are located in or near the city. These establishments are known as Prison No. 1, Prison No. 2, the Establishment for the Correction and Detention of Women, and the Educational Colony of Work.

All accused persons are kept in Prison No. 1 until sentence is passed, and meanwhile they are examined by the Observation Pavilion, which determines medically and clinically the degree of physical and mental health of each individual. Once sentence is passed, the prisoners are kept in Prison No. 2, generally until the completion of their sentence.

All women are confined separately in the Establishment for the Correction and Detention of Women. The Educational Colony of Work is still in a somewhat experimental stage, and is designed to aid in the recovery of prisoners for whom labor, particularly of an agricultural nature in healthful surroundings, is believed to be helpful.

PANAMA'S PRISION ADMINISTRATION

PENAL CODE. The Penal Code of 1922 provides for crimes and misdemeanors. The former are under the jurisdiction of the judicial authorities whereas the latter are under the administrative authorities. The penal law is applied to the entire national territory except those immune by International Law.

PUNISHMENTS. For serious offenses: imprisonment, arrest, confinement, fines and the prohibition of the exercise of certain rights or public functions. For less serious offenses: prohibitions of the exercise of certain rights or public functions, supervision by the authorities, and confiscation of certain goods.

There is a distinction between "reclusión" and "prisión"; both apply to imprisonment but the former means confinement in the penitentiary of Coiba while the latter means incarceration in a provincial or circuit jail. Arrest applies to jails and station houses of the district police.

In agreement with Decree No. 467 of 1942, a new classification of prisons is being realized in Panama. This Decree was the result of the recommendations of Mr. Howard Gill, of the Federal Bureau of Prisons of the United States who was in Panama as a technical advisor and made a survey of the penitentiary system of the country,

As a result, a Department of Correction was created, directed by a Commissioner; an Institute of Vigilance and Protection of the Child, headed by a Commissioner General, its purpose being the treatment of all cases of delinquent, abandoned, dependent and mentally retarded children; and a Psychiatric Clinic.

The Department of Correction has the responsibility of allocating all classes of prisoners into the different penal establishments. It attempts to distinguish between the jail population and those sentenced to prison. Heretofore the police have had charge of all prisoners.

Recently there has been constructed an agricultural penal colony, one of several planned by the Panamanian Government. This is in combination with an experimental farm and an agricultural school located at Divisa.

The penal colony of Coiba is in the process of reorganization and the *Cárcel Modelo* (model jail) is being used entirely for the lodging of prisoners, although not long since it was occupied in part by the personnel of the National Police Body. The personnel to have charge of the Model Jail has not yet been named but plans are being prepared by the Department of Correction in whose charge is the training of all prisoners.

The Institute of Vigilance and Protection of the Child, with its social workers, makes social investigations relative to each minor who constitutes a problem. It also is charged with providing the necessary relief in cooperation with official and private agencies. In spite of the fact that there are no juvenile courts nor codes for minors, a special procedure has been agreed upon whereby minors of 16 years or under are withdrawn from ordinary jurisdiction and placed under the supervision of the Institute.

The Department of Correction and the Institute of Vigilance and Protection of the Child are being organized by a Commission which visited the United States in 1942 to study American procedures.

CONDITIONAL RELEASE. In Panama conditional release is an administrative function, attributed to the Department of Correction in accordance with the following procedure: Delinquents sentenced to *reclusión* or prison, who have completed three-fourths of the former, or two-thirds of the latter, and have observed good conduct showing repentance and reformation, may be placed on conditional release for the remainder of their sentence.

Conditional release is denied those who have been members of a criminal gang (*asociación de malhechores*) or who have been committed for robbery, extortion, or larceny, or to those who have been previously convicted or those on whom a sentence of more than three years has been imposed.

PROBATION. (*Condena Condicional*) When the punishment imposed does not exceed four months in prison, arrest, or confinement, or more than fifty *balboas* fine, the court can suspend the execution of the sentence providing the condemned person has never before incurred punishment and it is demonstrated that he has always observed good conduct. If such is the case the authority is limited to giving him a warning in public and notifying him of the suspension of the sentence. He must then place a bond or obligate himself personally that in case he violates any other law within two years he will pay a fine.

For adults there is no real probation, except that as described above. However, for minors, the Institute of the Child is practicing with considerable success a kind of "probation" without any intervention of the courts. This is similar to what is known in the United States as social treatment.

Those who require institutional treatment are interned in a reformatory, hospital or asylum, according to their needs.

RECENT EXPERIMENTS IN MEXICO'S PRISONS

Probably the most interesting and novel idea to be introduced in modern penology is to be found in the prisons of Mexico. Much has been written in the journals and popular magazines of this country relative to the so-called "conjugal" visits which are permitted the immured prisoner for a few hours weekly. While such visits present only one small phase of the progressive penal philosophy that is being attempted in Mexico, it is undoubtedly the most spectacular, judged by our standards. Sex in prison is one of our most serious problems, one that is practically untouched and, in fact, almost unmentioned. In Mexican prisons, not only married men, but unmarried as well, are allowed to have a female visitor and enter into normal sexual relations unmolested by both officials and other prisoners alike. Special sections are reserved for these visits and, in the case of the unmarried, the visiting señoritas are serenaded by friends of the prisoner receiving the visit.[1]

Mexico's prison system operates under a progressive measure which was put into effect in 1937. It is far reaching in its various objectives and, judged by its results, meets the many problems not only found in all prisons throughout the world, but some that are peculiar to the mores of countries lying south of the border of the United States. As Sr. Teodoro A. González Miranda says regarding the law: "We feel, naturally, that this penitentiary system (the Penitentiary of the Federal District in Mexico City), which we have planned to meet our problems and our situation, may be ineffective in other lands. This new ordinance contains all the necessary points for the rehabilitation of each individual through systems of normal work. . . The practice of this principle, we hope, will produce an important reformation of our penitentiary laws and the transformation of the inmates necessarily confined."[2]

There is no doubt that the all inclusive work program is Mexico's outstanding achievement. Every man is gainfully employed and receives adequate wages. The authorities have brought insight and vision to the solution of this problem, which is considered in all parts of the world as of outstanding necessity if a penal program is to function successfully. We append here the main features of the work program manifesto as presented by Señor Miranda:

1. All prisoners must work in the industrial shop except those whose subsequent status has not been ascertained by the examiners.

2. For their work the inmates will receive a salary wage which will not be less than that fixed as the minimum wage for the Federal District, namely $2.00 Pesos Mexican currency.

3. The assignment of all work is to be made in accordance with the vocation of the recluse and treatment prescribed, taking into consid-

(1) See *Life Magazine*, October 27, 1941, for an account of this practice as reported by Professor Norman Hayner of the University of Washington.

(2) From the *Prison Journal*, October, 1937, pp. 371 f; a reprint of a speech delivered by Sr. Miranda at Oakland, California, August, 1937. See also, Jose Almarez, "Mexico's Prisons in the Light of the New Penal Code," *Annals*, September, 1931, pp. 221-224. Reference is also made to *Derecho Penal Mexicano*, by Raul Carranca y Trujillo, 1941.

eration his age, health, physical constitution, and previous occupation.
4. Obligation of the inmates to pay for their food and clothing with
the product of their earnings, distributing the remainder in the following manner:
  (a) Forty per cent to be applied toward the reparation of the damage
      done by the offender for which he was incarcerated.
  (b) Thirty per cent for the family of the recluse, when same is
      needed.
  (c) Thirty per cent for the formation of a reserve fund. Another
      important factor found in the prison labor program is that 50 per
      cent of the profits of the various industries is applied to the re-
      pair and improvements of the same, whereas the remaining 50
      per cent is used to form a social insurance fund which provides
      for accidents and illness of the prison workers.

There are several interesting features emphasized in this program
of work, but probably the most revolutionary is that which compels the
offender to repay, to some degree, the damage he has wrought by his crime.
While remunerative compensation cannot undo the harm that is done
by criminals, there is no doubt that it is a gesture that should meet with
no opposition where it is suggested. We see in our system a complete
negation of the claims of the person offended. The offender goes to prison
and his victim is expected to gain his modicum of satisfaction through a
form of mild sadism. Another feature is that which calls for at least a
minimum wage as found in free society in the particular district. This is
unusual and probably would meet with tremendous opposition in the
United States.

It is significant that in the work program, prisoners are permitted
to organize a sort of trade union for the purpose of bettering their "physical, moral, cultural, economic, social and penitentiary conditions," provided
this does not infringe upon the rules and regulations set up by the administration. This organization is known as the Union of Criminal Workers
and carries no little weight with the authorities. Individual prisoners may
present their grievances to the executive committee of the Union after
which the administration is presented with the convict's case. One case
presented to the committee, probably not typical, was that of a convict
who was sentenced to the Isle of Marías (Mexico's penal colony in the
Pacific). He pled with the committee to be permitted to take his family
with him.[3]

Mexico looks upon its new penal code as an attempt to provide
means for the "social readaptation" of delinquents. Offenders are classified according to their criminal tendencies, their personnal conditions, the
causes or motives of their crimes as ascertained at their trials, the kinds
of crimes committed and their potential danger to society. Psychiatrists
and social workers of the Social welfare Bureau make a study of "the
somatic characteristics and functions of each 'biological unit' formerly
called delinquent."[4] There is considerable evidence that Mexico follows
the new "Constitutional School" of Italian criminologists, particularly
that phase deliniated by Sr. Nicholas Pende, which, according to Sr.

(3) See *Pic*, March 4, 1941, p. 42, "El Prision Grande."
(4) Miranda, *loc. cit.*, p. 371.

Miranda himself, "treats with the study of constitutions, temperaments, and characters of this mysterious and formidable functional synthesis called life.[5]

To quote Miranda further we find that the recluse undergoes a radical transformation from the "oppressed and expiatory tradition of our old jails and reformatories toward a higher and more dynamic plane of positive and rational judicial culture where criminal anthropology and sociology not only fix their attention 'upon effective mental processes, but on the physiological and psycho-physiological functions of mankind in relation to the dangerous surroundings before and after the commission of crime.'"[6]

Classification seems to be carried on within the institution rather than between prisons. Each type of convict is segregated into various tiers. So called "biological unstudied units" are arranged in different cellblocks until their cases have been thoroughly diagnosed. Youthful delinquents are kept segregated as are also first offenders.

While we have little information concerning the district prisons of Mexico, we do have interesting descriptions of the famous Penitentiary of the Federal District, located in Mexico City, as well as the penal colonies in the Pacific. The former is a huge structure erected in 1900 on the Pennsylvania plan. The corridors between the cells, however, are open to the sky. The form of the prison is that of a star with seven corridors running off from the center, each block containing two tiers of cells. Everywhere there are flowers growing in the many gardens. Unusual is the feature of two swimming pools together with many small cubicles for bathing purposes. In addition, there is a tennis court and a court for the playing of the Mexican game, fronton. Volley ball and boxing are also played by the inmates.[7]

One interesting feature of this amazing prison is the commercial or business avenue. This consists of posters and lithographs in all colors calling attention to the various merchandise sold in the cells by the prisoners. It is a veritable retail shopping mart. Practically any commodity necessary for every day existence is for sale. Thus, to quote from an article in a popular magazine,[8] there is to be seen,"La Vencedora" Hat Shop, "La Elegancia" Tailoring Shop, and "El Puerto de Acapulco" Fine Groceries. "Some prisoners continue their old professions, including the dentist who still advertises 'painless extractions'; 'Melva—hair dresser'; and Señor Alatris, proprietor of the shoe shop "El Brodequi Perfecto—Shoes Repaired and Made to Measure.' There is even a printer who makes visiting cards, a miniaturist who does work in marble and silver, and a seller of dogs. A lawyer offers his secretarial services to illiterates who wish to write to their families; he also directs petitions and appeals for fellow-prisoners to the authorities and the Supreme Court. On the door of this important personage is the following curt warning: 'Time Is Money—Don't Waste My Time.' "

(5) *ibid.*, p. 375. For a statement regarding Pende's Work in Italy, see page 67.
(6) *ibid.*, p. 374.
(7) Rachel Hopper Powell, "Visit to La Penitenciaria del D. F. Mexico City," *News Bulletin*, Osborne Association, New York, December, 1931.
(8) See *Pic*, March 4, 1941.

Another unusual sight to be found in the women's section of this great prison is the presence of children who normally live with their mothers while serving sentence. According to the officials, they do not seem ready to remove children from mothers since it is believed that their presence keeps the women on a higher plan by maintaining, in a sense, a domestic scene. We present a description of the women's quarters submitted by one observer:

> It seemed almost a domestic scene: a mother leading a little child by the hand in the open air space like a long yard, betwen the rows of cells; plants growing here and there, to meet the Mexican love of them; the doors of the rooms open (for the cells are large enough and furnished fully enough to be called rooms). . . . A teacher for the children has been coming every day, but the provision of the children has been inadequate, and I was told. . . that a building outside of the institution is under construction where they will be from 7 a. m. until bedtime at night. There they will have their meals, their schooling, their baths, their games; and they will be taken about the city and in every way given as normal a life as possible.[9]

However, indications point to the fact that Mexico is very backward in her treatment of the youthful offender. The conditions in her establishments for children are deplorable, if we may judge from an article in one of our pictorial weeklies.[10] In an article entitled "The Most Shocking Child Pictures Ever Published," we find that Mexico is beset with thousands of marauding children, many of them known as "boy bandits," who loot, derail trains, and wander over the country committing all types of depredations. These children are the neglected youngsters of that country where infinite poverty abounds. They are rounded up by the police and thrown into the most abominable "dormitory reformatories," where they are subjected to the most meagre diet, appalling overcrowding and tragic idleness. Bad as our children's institutions are in the United States, they are models of sobriety and decency compared to those of Mexico. According to *Pic,* the Mexican government released these pictures without any compunctions, probably to demonstrate the type of problem with which it is confronted in these days of upheaval.

There is also a penal colony in Mexico known as Les Tres Marías. It is comprised of three small islands located about 75 miles off the mainland in the Pacific Ocean. Specifically, their names are María Madre, María Magdalena and María Cleofas. In early days they were merely hideouts for pirates. However, in 1905 Mexico sent a few of her most incorrigible criminals there. But it was in 1925 that it became an integral part of the prison system. While the more dangerous and longer sentenced criminals are sent there, the objective is the same as that of the District Penitentiary—social rehabilitation.

The islands are beautiful but lonely. Men may, if they wish, take their families with them to the islands but not many of them take advantage of this. The state will even pay transportation costs if they wish them to. There are no cells in the colony. Prisoners live in barracks and small huts. Work is the guiding principle of the colony, the wages for same may accrue to the prisoner's benefit or for the support of his family. Violation of the colony's regulations means a sort of "exile" to a forbidding "hump in the ocean" nearby which is named San Juanico. Supplied

(9) Rachel Hopper Powell, *loc. cit.,* p. 2.
(10) See *Pic,* October 14, 1941.

with only a few matches, water, corn and beans, the prisoner may be sent there for a week or two. It is a disagreeable place as it is quite small and the flies (*jején*) are unbearable. Seldom does a man spend more than two weeks there.

Escapes from Les Tres Marías are rare indeed. The great distance from the mainland together with the shark infested ocean makes such an attempt almost doomed to failure. Single men may send to the mainland for a women companion; the town of Mazatlan, the closest to the colonies, has many women available for the purpose. However, such a person may cater only to the one man who sends for her. It is contended by the authorities that prostitution does not and cannot occur in the colony.

As stated above, life on the islands is lonely and monotonous although the men are treated well, fed and housed adequately. But most of the inmates prefer to return to the District Penitentiary where life is much more interesting and even exciting. It is no wonder that the prisoners of the Penitentiary fear being transferred to Les Tres Marías.

We have seen that the Mexican prison system is at least unique. It has wrestled with many conventional problems found in prisons all over the world and has had courage enough to experiment boldly with radically new ideas. It may be argued that such solutions dare not be attempted in the United States because of the sharp contrast between the temperament of North Americans and those of Spanish extraction. That may well be true, but we cannot help feeling a degree of admiration for the sane and objective attitude maintained by those who are rapidly placing Mexico's penal system on a realistic and progressive basis. However, as we showed above, it has a long way to go in its treatment of children before it can rank among the really progressive states in matters dealing with penology.

THE NEW CUBAN PENITENTIARY SYSTEM

A revolutionary step was taken in Cuban penology when, on October 10, 1938, a new penal and penitentiary system was inaugurated. Prior to that date, the legislation and regulations controlling Cuba's prisons were those which had been enacted by the old Spanish colonial system.[1]

The new philosophy is based on the principle of individual treatment of the offender, to which end a system of compulsory study and labor has been adopted for all convicts. The administration of this new system, far-reaching in its effects, is vested in a newly created body known as the Superior Council of Defense. It is composed of: (1) university professors who are authorities in Penal Law, Legal Medicine, Pedagogy, Psychiatry, Anthropology; (2) representatives of the Department of Justice; and, (9) various representatives of private and public organizations. The chairman of this Superior Council is Dr. Guillermo Portela Moeller, Dean of the School of Law of the University of Havana. He is largely responsible for the improvements in Cuban penology.

The Council is made up of two sections: (1) technical, which has charge of such matters as parole, transfer of inmates, granting of reduced sentences, and the supervision of penal treatment; (2) administrative,

(1) See Israel Castellanos, M. D., "The Evolution of Criminology in Cuba," *Journal of Criminal Law and Criminology*, May-June, 1933, pp. 218-229.

which deals with budgetary matters, construction of new prisons, prison industries, and inspection.

The Cuban law calls for the establishment of certain types of preventive institutions, which include agricultural colonies, work shops, hospitals, asylums, all destined to the application of detention measures set forth by the Council. In addition, repressive institutions are provided for the execution of the sanctions imposed by the court. At the present time there is only one preventive establishment. But included in the repressive institutions are to be found: six prisons, each located in the capital of the provinces; thirteen jails, scattered throughout the island; two national penitentiaries, one on the Isle of Pines, for men, and another at Guanabaccoa, for women. The Guines prison, in the province of Havana, has a capacity of two thousand inmates, and the national penitentiary on the Isle of Pines, four thousand. A new prison is to be erected on the Isle of Pines, on the order of the Panopticon style of prison architecture, with special quarters for inmates on good behavior.

The new law calls for individual treatment, without any form of violence. "Learning and labor" is the new slogan. All institutions are congregate, so far as work is concerned, with individual cells provided for each inmate. The old punishment cells, so familiar in the past, and known as "bartolinas." are a thing of the past. A system of marking of prisoners will be carried out as follows:

1. Observation and preparation of the inmate for other grades, lasting generally from two to four months. Inmate is confined in isolation cell for this period, and visits from relatives allowed at the rate of one monthly.

2. Period of isolation and restricted privileges including the prohibition of communication with other prisoners.

3. Characterized by intensification of academic and vocational training and free communication and less laborious work.

4. Period of parole.[2]

Labor in the new prison system is compulsory. The inmate receives a wage, part of which must go to indemnity resulting from his criminal act. Part of the remainder is applied to the prisoner's maintenance, and the balance is held for him upon release. The usual prison trades are engaged in: shoemaking, tailoring, woodworking, and manufacture of soap. On the Isle of Pines there may be found a printing establishment, bookbinding, marble shop, a brick mosaic industry, and the farm.

Discipline is in the hands of the local advisory board, one of which is in each institution. No form of violence is permitted and corporal punishment has been abolished. The system relies chiefly upon the denial of privileges for punishment. Conditional parole is granted by the same advisory board, although actual authority is vested in the Supreme Council. A Board for the Protection of the Released has been set up and investigators employed to serve as parole and probation officers. All must be college graduates. The new penal code also provides for the suspended sentence.

(2) The material for this digest is taken from *The Prison World*, March-April, 1941, and supplied by Dr. Frederico de Cordova, Jr.

Cuba's prison population at present is approximately four thousand although the annual average is slightly less than that number. This is estimated at about one per thousand of the population. About 45 per cent of the convictions are for offenses against property; 32 per cent on charges against life and personal integrity; and 7 per cent against good behavior. About 40 per cent of the criminals are white, the remainder are Negroes and mulattoes.

A recent work of significance in the field of criminal law is *Principios de Derecho Criminal* by Sr. Emilio Menéndez (Havana, 1942). The work is described as a contribution to the study of the Social Defense Code. It includes chapters on the philosophy of the criminal law, the theory of crime, of responsibility and punishment. However little is included on rehabilitation, parole or probation.*

PUERTO RICO AND ITS NEW PENAL SYSTEM

A new penitentiary was erected in Puerto Rico in 1933. It occupies 112 acres in the city of Rio Piedras. About eighty acres are used for farming. The institution has 332 cells and 12 ward dormitories.

In line with modern thought, the institution was conceived as an establishment "for the physical and mental regeneration of delinquents rather than as a place for their punishment, and it is also considered as a place in which sound moral habits may be inculcated, and where educational, industrial and agricultural instruction may be furnished to those who need it."[1]

This new prison was projected with two thoughts in mind, according to the Supervisor of Prisons for Puerto Rico, Sr. Martin Ergui: (1) the reform and regeneration of the delinquent; and (2) the administration of the institution within an economic system which will guarantee it own support.

Rudiments of traditional classification of the inmates are carried out. This calls for the separation of the following groups: the youngest, the reformables, the unreformables, and those convicted of crimes against morals, persons and property. All who can work are assigned to the industrial shops or to farming and horticulture. Reformable prisoners or those who maintain good conduct are granted certain privileges and are also given wages for their labor. Of this compensation, a certain part may be used to help support the dependents of the prisoners, a part for their current needs, and the remainder placed in an account to be surrendered to them upon release. As stated above, one of the main purposes of the prison administration is to make the labor of the inmates pay, so far as is possible, for the maintenance of the institution. A system similar to the American state-use concept is employed. Furniture, clothing, hats, shoes, etc., required by state offices, asylums, hospitals and other institutions supported by the government, are furnished in this manner.

The model Penitentiary attempts to put in force the "honor system" found in some American prisons. That is, those inmates who are apparently "reformed" are granted privileges which may go so far as to permit them

---

* *The American Sociologist*, July, 1943.

(1)   Martin Ergui, "Puerto Rican Penitentiary," *Journal of Criminal Law and Criminology*, vol. 24, March-April, 1934, pp. 1118-1120.

to leave the institution to attend to urgent personal matters in the vicinity of the prison; also to attend to certain tasks assigned them by the administration.

In regards to farming, certain inmates who are adaptable to that type of work, are given instruction in the cultivation of legumes, vegetables and fruits. It is stated by Sr. Ergui that about half of the prisoners coming to the prison do not know any trade.

It would seem, from this description, that Puerto Rico is attempting to develop a penal program patterned after those where modern methods are stressed; that the prison is there primarily for reformation and treatment, rather than punishment.

CHAPTER XI

CURRENT PENAL PHILOSOPHY AND TREATMENT IN THE UNITED STATES

TYPES OF CRIMES

The average citizen of the United States is so accustomed to the decentralization of our governmental institutions that he may well overlook the fact that our methods of dealing with the criminal may be very confusing to citizens of other countries. An attempt will therefore be made in this chapter to describe our systems of penal treatment so that persons living in other countries will be able to compare them with their own.

In the United States, offenses against society have a twofold classification: felonies and misdemeanors. The former are the serious offenses and are punishable by death (in most states) or imprisonment in a state prison or state reformatory.[1] The latter are, in theory, the less serious offenses and are usually punishable by fines or short terms of imprisonment in a county jail or workhouse. What offenses are considered felonies or misdemeanors are determined by the penal codes of the various states. There is no uniformity in this since a felony in one state may be a misdemeanor in another. The penalty may also vary from state to state. More confusing, however, is the fact that a misdemeanor may carry a more severe penalty in a state than a felony in the same state. In short, there is no consistency or logic in the penal codes of the various states. Students of the problem are in agreement that much reform is needed in this important field.

In addition to the offenses which fall within the jurisdiction of the state, which naturally include all traditional and quaint crimes, there are specific offenses which have been made crimes against the Federal government and are handled through the Federal courts. Such offenses are made Federal by acts of Congress from time to time and they, too, are divided into felonies and misdemeanors. The penalty attached to the offense determines its status. Those calling for a fine or prison sentence of less than a year and a day are misdemeanors; all others are felonies.

In the early days only such crimes as treason, piracy, sedition, counterfeiting, robbery of the mails and a few others were considered Federal offenses. With the complexity of modern life there has been a marked expansion of Federal jurisdiction into other fields. In 1910 the Mann Act was passed making it a Federal offense to transport a female across state boundaries for immoral purposes; in 1914 the Harrison Narcotic Act was passed which dealt with the sale of drugs. With the increase in the theft of automobiles following their general use after 1920, the National Motor Vehicle Theft Act was passed in 1925. This made it a Federal

(1) Capital punishment is observed in 41 states; 7 do not have it. The methods used are: electrocution, 22; hanging, 11; lethal gas, 8. In one state, Utah, the victim has the option of hanging or shooting. An average of 150 persons are executed annually. The Federal government resorts to capital punishment (hanging) for treason only, and has invoked it only a few times in the history of the country.

offense to drive a stolen car over a state line. In 1932 the Extortion Act was passed making it a Federal offense to send a threatening letter through the mails.

Following a wave of kidnapings in 1932 Congress passed an act which makes this particular crime a Federal offense. In fact, this date marks the development of an alertness by the Federal lawmakers to control the more dangerous types of criminal who, with the aid of the automobile and sub-machine gun, roved the entire country terrorizing society by committing many forms of violent crime. It also focused attention on the fact that in some cases the local forces of law enforcement were unable to cope with dangerous criminals, due in many instances to inadequate personnel or equipment and in all too frequent cases to graft or to collusion between politicians and criminals.

Congress passed these laws through the powers inherent in the Federal Constitution to regulate interstate commerce, to tax and to control the mails. To show the ratio between Federal crimes and crimes against the state we may note that in 1942, 13,725 Federal offenders were received from the Federal courts by the Federal prisons and reformatories; in the states there were 46,700 offenders received from the courts of the forty-eight states by the state penitentiaries and reformatories. These figures do not show the extent of crimes committed but merely the number found guilty and sentenced to penal institutions.

During the past decade criminologists have begun to focus their attention upon another type of crime which, heretofore, has been carried on with impunity. We refer to the so-called "white-collar" crime. Perhaps the best definition of this type of crime is that formulated by Professor E. H. Sutherland, noted criminologist: "A white-collar crime . . . is a violation of the criminal law by a person of the upper socio-economic class class in the course of his occupational activities. The upper socio-economic class is defined not only by its wealth but also by its respectability and prestige in the general society."[2]

Such crimes run the gamut of largescale frauds by which financial wizards extract people's savings for spurious investments to shady deals and operations by some lawyers, doctors and others posing as respectable professional men. The collusion between criminal gangs and lawyer-criminals and with unethical medical practitioners, together with so-called "ambulance chasers" among lawyers and abortionists among doctors are good examples of the latter type of white-collar criminal.

The epitome of white-collar criminality is the stock salesman who represents his ware as a particularly safe investment. Millions of dollars are lost to the public annually through such crooks. Then there is the widely prevalent practice of adulterating food or of misrepresenting the contents of packaged goods sold on the market. The public is almost helpless against fraudulent claims of manufacturers since the laws operating to safeguard the consuming public are inoccuous in their wording and difficult of enforcement. In this category may be found certain canned food, cosmetics, patent medicines and the like which cause deaths, sickness, blasted hopes and misery, the extent of which is difficult of measurement.

(2) In "Crime and Business,__ The Annals of the American Academy of the Political and Social Science, September, 1941, pp. 112-118.

White-collar crime flourishes in war time also. The most obvious form is profiteering in the production of goods. Not satisfied with liberal profits, some manufacturers, a few of which have established national reputations in the past, have sold defective and shoddy goods to the army and navy, in some cases actually endangering the lives of the armed forces.

We must emphasize the fact that none of these practices are particularly new as they have been in operation from the beginnings of the development of the country. There have always been crooks and unethical men in business and the professions. But, in the past, our society has not only failed to denounce their activities but has even tended to condone them as smart business practice. In recent years, however, we have begun to focus attention on this type of crime which is far more devastating to society than the traditional and quaint crimes such as robbery, pocket-picking, kidnaping, and even murder. For in such offenses only a few individuals are endangered or victimized whereas white-collar crime is usually an attack upon the whole of society. Aside from the monetary and physical damage done, this type of activity is a threat to our moral code. This is so since few such criminals are ever brought to court, not to mention to prison for their chicanery, and hence the belief circulates that they can participate in shady deals with impunity. Thus an ever-widening group begins to participate in the same sort of criminal activity since their chance of ever being punished is remote. The general mass of the people develop a cynicism and a defeatist attitude toward honesty and integrity which never resulted from the traditional criminal activity which we have been emphasizing in the past.

Unfortunately we have so far been unable to crystallize social disapproval against white-collar crime except in the most glaring instances and even in these few cases the public has been forced to be content with the too frequent acquittals or nominal penalties that have resulted. Until we can focus much greater attention on this streamlined crime we shall continue to talk about the same old traditional crime that has served as a topic of conversation in the past.

THE EXTENT OF CRIME IN THE UNITED STATES

This is a big country and of necessity everything is done on a big scale. However, there is a tendency to exaggerate this bigness. The United States has been accused of being a very lawless country. If this is so, it is probably due to several facts. It is a new country, its citizens are composed of all the races and nationalities of the earth with their own cultural concepts and customs with an inevitably large amount of maladjustment. Then, too, many so-called crimes are merely the violation of certain traditional moral concepts which have been translated into crimes such as petty gambling, prostitution, sexual irregularities, drunkenness, disturbing the peace, and the like. All of these offenses in the aggregate take on a serious complexion but individually many are quite trivial. The enforcement of the laws and city ordinances governing such offenses depends on the good judgment of the police and local prosecuting attorneys. Then, too, there is a differential in arrests and convictions, the strong arm of the law being weighted heavily against the poor and the friendless and, in some sections of the country, against the foreign born and persons of races other than white.

When one examines the statistics of crimes known to the police in one year he is surprised to note that by far the bulk of the offenses are petty rather than serious. Less than three per cent of all offenses, year by year, can be considered serious. Of the less serious offenses approximately three-fourths are violations of traffic and motor laws. Gambling, drunkenness, disorderly conduct and prostitution make up the bulk of the remainder. Of the serious offenses, larceny outranks all other felonies. Auto theft looms large followed by burglary. The homicide rate, which includes all forms of manslaughter and murder, is much higher than it should be, but this figure is misleading. From the manner in which the crime of murder is defined by law it is doubtful that more than 4,000 are actually perpetrated in the entire country annually. The figure that gains wide circulation is the homicide rate which includes nonnegligent manslaughter along with premeditated murder.

As we have already stated, most misdemeanants are sent to county jails. There are over 3,000 of these institutions in the forty-eight states. Most of the offenders incarcerated in these jails serve relatively short terms, from a few days to a year or less. In some of the states long term prisoners are sometimes sent to jail but, in general, they are sent to the state prisons. State prisons, to which adults are sent, are called penitentiaries. Those to which young offenders (not juveniles) are sent are known as reformatories. Women's institutions are usually referred to as reformatories although some states have women's prisons also for long term female felons. Juvenile institutions are usually referred to as reform schools although there is an attempt to abolish the term and refer to such places as correctional institutions or institutions for delinquent children.

PENAL INSTITUTIONS

The institutional picture in the United States must be very confusing to the foreigner. Each state has at least one penitentiary for adult males and some of the larger ones have two; one or more reformatories for young adults from sixteen to twenty-three, or thereabouts; a reformatory for females and sometimes a prison; usually separate institutions for delinquent boys and girls; and often other specialized institutions for defective delinquents and the criminal insane. New York state maintains eighteen state-supported institutions for her various types of criminals and delinquents; New Jersey has eight; California has seven and Pennsylvania, seven. Altogether, counting all types of institutions to care for those who have committed offenses other than misdemeanors, who are housed in county jails, houses of correction and work farms, local in character, there are over two hundred state institutions. This figure does not include hundreds of privately supported schools and homes to which delinquent children may be sent by the juvenile courts. In the adult state prisons and reformatories for the year 1943 there were roughly 125,000 prisoners. The figure is probably somewhat lower today.

In addition to the state institutions and the county jails, the Federal government maintains a large number of institutions to house its prisoners. Most of these have been erected since 1925. These institutions are scattered throughout the country with the various specialized types geographically localized. There are thirty-two Federal units housing approximately 17,000 prisoners at present. A few of these units have been turned over to the army and navy for the duration.

When one attempts to describe the conditions of the prisons or the treatment of the prisoners he is at once faced by a dilemma. The worst possible conditions may be found all too frequently and the best examples of modern penology are likewise available, sometimes both types within the same state. Perhaps the words of a British visitor will explain this paradox. Miss Margery Fry visited the United States in 1942. Writing in the *Spectator,* a British publication, she says:

> In writing of the United States it seems equally difficult to exaggerate and to generalize. In almost everything, from the primitive to the sophisticated, from poverty to wealth, from the "toughest" to the most sensitive, the extremes are so unbelievably distanced, the mean so hard to ascertain. This is most bafflingly true of those social institutions which depend upon the administrations, Federal, State and local, whose triple network covers the country. Not only do they vary widely from State to State, but within the States there are often startling divergencies. In the matter of penal administration this is particularly true. Everywhere four sets of authorities are responsible for different kinds of places for the housing of prisoners; everywhere two sets of laws are working, the State law and the Federal law, each with its own courts, police, probation officers, etc., and, to a certain extent, prisoners.[3]

Miss Fry describes conditions in some American jails. What she writes about their abominable conditions is true of most of the 3,000 local establishments of the country. The fact that not more than twenty per cent of them are considered fit as to security, sanitation, food, housing and medical service for the detention of Federal prisoners is ample proof that they are deplorable. Yet there are many good jails. But the jail is an anachronism in these days of modern penology and should be abolished in favor of special detention quarters for those awaiting trial and regional farms for misdemeanants, the latter being placed under state control rather than local management as the jails now are. Britain has pointed the way in this progressive reform.

Most of the penitentiaries of the country are a survival of early nineteenth century achitecture. They are the Bastille-type of prison with thick high walls, venerable inside cellblocks, little sunlight and scanty space for outside recreation. Many institutions, however, have been built during the past twenty years that feature outside cellblock construction, roomy cells with modern plumbing, ample yards for recreation, modern kitchens and dining rooms. Miss Fry describes a kitchen in a modern prison:

> Marvelous kitchens, shining with chromium plate, equipped with every kind of machinery, huge dining halls, where the food is served in cafeteria style.

And the hospitals attracted her attention:

> This attempt [to send the prisoner out into the world a fitter man than he came in] is continued in the prison hospitals, some of which are marvelously equipped, and staffed by bands of specialists who are prepared to carry on research as well as to give treatment. In one Federal prison, housing some 1,300 men, there is a staff of three full time physicians, two nurses, a psychologist, and two dentists, as well as attendants. Quite elaborate dental treatment, including the provision of plates, is frequent. Special attention is given to such conditions as obesity, which may need careful dieting.[4]

(3) August 6, 1943, pp. 122-123. Miss Fry's more complete description of the institutions in the United States appearing in the 1943 *Howard Journal,* pp. 162-170, "Notes from an American Diary," evaluated our penal systems fairly and accurately.
(4) *idem.*

The Federal system has experimented with new types of prison architecture but still clings, in most instances, to the cellblock type of construction, disguised though it is by ingenious corridors and selfenclosed sections. The cubicle cell with partitioning, together with small dormitory units have also been installed but these have not proved satisfactory, especially if it is recognized that the inmate should be afforded privacy.

A few states have broken with the past and developed cottage type institutions for adults and there is some feeling that this departure from tradition will eventually prove to be the construction of the future. One feature of good administration, whether in a cellblock or cottage institution, is the sound thesis that two men should never be housed in the same cell. However, this is the rule in most prisons of the country.

There is a strong difference of opinion in the United States regarding a wall for an institution. There are some who think that a wall should be placed around children's institutions, minimum-security units and, in fact, all types of penal establishments. As it is today, the best efforts of the guards or custodial officers, as they are now being called, is directed toward custody rather than training. It is argued that if custody or security of a prison can be guaranteed by a wall, the life within can approach that of a normal community.

Others, however, take the position that the wall itself is an abnormal characteristic of free life and should be abolished in the case of all penal establishments except for those housing dangerous criminals. They state that a wall nullifies any attempt made to develop a sense of responsibility among the inmates. A compromise has been made in resolving this dilemma by erecting fences around many of the recently created prisons with guard towers scattered around the reservation.

It is true that prison administrators are concerned with treatment rather than punishment although the general public and to a large extent, the judges, are still obsessed with the idea of making the criminal pay by punishing him. And there can be no mistake, the prisoner does pay by being denied of his liberty. The best prison and the most honest and realistic treatment are little compensation for the loss of liberty that makes a prison of the institution.

The routine in the best American prison is monotonous and deadening. In many of the more backward institutions it is little better than that of the old nineteenth century régime. The lockstep and the silence rule have been abolished in most prisons but the inmate finds plenty of regimentation. There are innumerable rules, for instance, many of which are sheer nonsense. The old inmate-guard complex is present in practically every prison. In fact, the guard is somewhat of a prisoner himself in the autocratic system that dominates the prison.

Idleness has long been a curse in the prisons of the country. This is no fault of the administration, however, but due rather to vicious restrictive legislation passed by the various states and the Federal government which forbids prison made goods from being sold on the open market in competition with free labor. At the moment the prisons are busy with war contracts but there is little promise that there will be much production after the war.

Most of the prisons manufacture goods on the state-use basis—for institutions and agencies within the state. The Federal prisons manufacture mail bags, army and navy products and products used by the various Federal agencies. Prisoners' wages are quite meagre in normal times and still are in the state prisons. However, in the Federal prisons it is possible now for inmates to make higher wages in war work. State laws forbid this in the state prisons.

Agriculture is carried on in many of the state and Federal prisons and reformatories. Every state has at least one institution that includes a farm of some sort. Many have their own milk herds, piggeries and poultry and a few can their own products. De-hydrating is being introduced in some farm-prisons. In many of the southern state prisons farming is carried on in an extensive manner since the growing season is longer than in the northern states. Road camps are also a feature of southern prisons. The old chaingang that degraded southern penology for so many years is slowly disappearing although there are still remnants of it in some of the states.

Trade training is still a feature of boys' reform schools and young adult reformatories. However, it is gradually being realized that less emphasis should be placed on skilled trade training and more on vocational guidance integrated through the prison school. It is conceded that testing for potential abilities, training in good work habits and preparation for social and economic adjustment are more fundamental than the old type reformatory trade training.

The modern prison school, and there are many of them now, goes far beyond the mere teaching of illiterates and the furnishing of academic education for those who have not previously had that opportunity. They are closely integrated with the factories and are accomplishing a great deal of good in preparing the skilled and semiskilled worker with classroom work. Then, too, correspondence courses are provided for those capable of profiting from them. In the better prison schools, the personnel is composed of civilian teachers but the use of inmates is widespread. There are still many backward schools in which only prison inmate teachers are employed and in which the equipment is very crude and inadequate.

Perhaps the most encouraging phase of penal treatment in many of the prisons in the United States is the classification clinic which has had a tangible and fruitful development since the early nineteen-twenties. The clinic has for its purpose the individualization of treatment rather than the old form of mass treatment which characterizes the older prison discipline. Mass treatment is still the rule, however, but there is a decided trend toward individualization.

Where the newer philosophy of classification is in operation a centralized system of penal establishments has been developed. Usually there are units based on maximum, medium and minimum security to house various types of prisoners. Those considered bad risks are placed in maximum security prisons. Good risks are sent to open institutions where farming is usually carried on. One of the purposes of the classification clinic is to ascertain where each inmate is to be sent.

The clinic is composed of trained personnel which has gradually entered the prison. The psychologist, the educational director, the director of industries, the psychiatrist, the social worker and the chaplain each play their special role in examining and diagnosing the inmate. The clinic is usually presided over by the warden or his deputy.

The ideal classification clinic is called upon to perform the following functions: first, to place the inmate in the penal unit where he belongs; second, to work out a treatment program for him including industrial, educational, social, medical and religious; third, plan for his eventual release from prison in terms of his program; fourth, reopen the prisoner's case at regular intervals; fifth, take an active part in the discipline of the institution; and sixth, recognize the prisoner's interests as of vital importance so that the safety of society may be preserved.

CONDITIONAL RELEASE—PAROLE

Aside from being released from a penal institution through the expiration of a sentence, the inmate may leave the prison by means of what is known in the United States as parole. The laws regulating parole vary widely with the states but in general it may be applied for by the inmate at the expiration of his minimum sentence. In the states where this exists, the courts are required by law to set both a minimum and a maximum limit when pronouncing sentence. This form of sentence is the so-called limited indeterminate sentence.

In some states, however, only the oldstyle definite sentence is used. This is also true of the Federal system. In most of these states a prisoner is permitted to be considered for parole consideration at any time after his incarceration. In some, however, a fixed portion of the offender's sentence must be served.

The machinery of parole falls into three categories. First, preparation; second, selection of those to be granted parole; and third, supervision of the man finally granted parole. The status of parole is none too high in the United States although there are a few states in which it functions on a high professional level. It is no longer looked upon as a favor granted the prisoner but as a right that society should be accorded as an integral part of the rehabilitation process.

Theoretically, good parole suggests that the penal institution should be given great responsibility in preparing for and recommending parole. Yet in most states the granting of parole is in the hands of a designated body outside the prison, usually known as a parole board. However, in some states, this power is still in the hands of the governor of the state which is not considered good practice.

The practice of vesting the granting of parole in the hands of a part time board is not recommended by most penologists. Too frequently such a board is composed of political appointees or one which assumes parole work only as a side issue apart from their regular duties which often lie far afield from parole.

The best general practice found in a few of the states is a full time parole board composed of individuals of distinction, freed from political patronage, well paid and possessing tenure. In such states, the institutions are called upon to share in the responsibility of recommending those inmates who are prepared for release under supervision.

The states that have developed strong classification procedure in their prisons do a reasonably good job in preparing for parole. Theoretically the inmate begins his preparation for parole the day he enters the prison. A plan is worked out for him which points toward his release to a free society. Thus preparation is vitally important.

After his release, that is, after he has been granted parole, he is then supervised through the remainder of his initial court sentence, that is, until he has finished his maximum. This supervision is in the hands of paid personnel. In some cases these parole officers are trained and approach their responsibility with dignity and professional insight. However, in most states the parole officers are untrained, poorly paid, lack definite tenure and are politically appointed. Because of these conditions supervision of parolees tends to become merely a routine matter with little sympathetic insight or practical realism. Parole violations are notoriously high in states where the system is not well developed or where it is financially starved. No one who understands the ramifications of good penology, however, is opposed to parole in principle. Most of the complaints against it deal with the manner in which it operates. In those states where a full time parole board functions, in which the penal establishments have a real responsibility for preparing inmates for parole, and in which supervision is on a high level, parole violations are extremely low.

The older concept of "good time" which, in the past, has been used not only to maintain good discipline in prison, but also to select inmates for parole, is rapidly gaining disrepute in the United States in spite of its persistence in most of the states. Good behavior is easily simulated by shrewd convicts and is hence not a good criterion of readiness for release. The practice of withholding "good time" or of curtailing it is too often held over the prisoner as a threat and for this reason also is not good penal practice. Under a good parole system this practice of giving a prisoner time off his sentence for good behavior could well be abolished. However, until the states now maintaining a shoddy parole system actually install a flexible and well-administered system and develop an efficient penal philosophy with classification procedure, "good time" laws should be retained.

The complete record of the prisoner while serving his sentence, together with his prospects upon release, such as an adjustment to normal society, are far more important in granting parole than sentiment, political influence, length of sentence served or so-called good behavior while in prison.

Parole has a long way to go before it will be considered satisfactory in the United States but the more modern concepts regarding it are being grasped and expanded by more and more jurisdictions. Certainly supervision by trained personnel is an advance over the older methods of relying on voluntary organizations or politically appointed and untrained officers.

COMMUTATION OF SENTENCE AND PARDON

The practice of commuting the sentence of a prisoner is frankly one of substituting a lesser punishment for a greater one. Its use is widespread in the various states. This is resorted to, primarily, to mitigate the practice of judges meting out excessively long sentences, a habit which is certainly not condoned by most progressive penologists and many judges themselves. For years it has been asserted in progressive circles that long sentences make reformation extremely difficult. It is also claimed that many prison inmates are ready for release long before they have served their minimum sentence when, in most cases, they are eligible for parole.

Commutation, then, is a device for hastening the time when parole may be considered for the inmate. It is also used to change a death penalty to life imprisonment or less. The various states have set up machinery to take care of petitions of prisoners asking for such a reduction of the original sentence for parole purposes. In some instances a commutation may result in the immediate termination of a sentence although this is less frequent than merely mitigating the sentence by reducing the long minimum to a shorter one.

Commutation is usually vested in a central board composed of personnel not connected with institutions although in many states provision is made by which the prison administrations may recommend commutation, based on the petitioner's exemplary record. In most states the Governor has power to commute, subject to statutory or constitutional limitations. In thirty-six states the commuting power is specifically included in the pardoning power conferred by their constitutions. It is held, however, if the power is not expressly conferred it is included in the general power to pardon.

Commutation does not wipe away guilt nor does it restore civil rights which have been lost because of a prison sentence. Its purpose, as stated above, is merely to mitigate a sentence imposed by the court. The practice has been much abused in this country since political pressure can be asserted on the governor or board having the power. It has been frequently stated that until a wider use of the unlimited indeterminate sentence is adopted, it represents the only means of undoing the harm inherent in an excessively long sentence.

The power to pardon has its roots in antiquity and is generally associated with a miscarriage of justice. It is usually thought of as a prerogative of an executive, such as a king, and in the United States, a president or governor of a state. In reality, however, it is a power belonging to a people or to society exercised through the elected executive.

The power to pardon in the various states has gradually passed from the governor alone, to a board of pardons acting in an advisory capacity with the governor. In only a few states today does the governor have unrestricted power to pardon.[5]

Full and unconditional pardons are rare today. Clemency is usually thought of as a conditional pardon and in some states it is synonomous with parole. A high percentage of the pardons granted today serve the purpose only of restoring the civil rights lost by a conviction of a crime. The abrogation of these rights varies with the states and includes the right to vote or hold office, to serve on a jury or to testify in a court trial, make contracts or to marry, to serve in the armed forces, etc.

There is little machinery in the United States to compensate or indemnify a man wrongfully accused of a crime. Since it is assumed that the

(5)   For details regarding the power to pardon, the reader is advisd to consult the *Attorney General's Survey of Release Procedures,* vol. III, "Pardon," Department of Justice, Washington, 1939.

State can do no wrong, the law has been quite indifferent to those who can prove they have been wrongfully accused of a crime. Only a few states have made provision to bring about relief to such persons. Special legislation is usually necessary to provide for compensating the person mistakenly accused and convicted of a crime. European countries have gone much further in this regard.[6] It is in such cases that the governor's pardon can wipe the slate clean so that, at least, the victim's reputation and moral integrity are no longer questioned by society. It is more difficult, however, to compensate him financially.

PROBATION AND THE SUSPENDED SENTENCE

Probation, in the United States, presupposes supervision and good general practice calls for trained personnel. It is also emphasized that it should be granted, not as a form of leniency to the offender, but as an integral part of the rehabilitative process.

Because of certain venerable precedents, such as benefit of clergy, judicial reprieve, right of sanctuary, and other similar safeguards thrown about the offender, it has been assumed that courts have had the right to suspend a sentence indefinitely. It was decided that such was not the case. This paved the way for statutes expressly authorizing the suspension of sentence so long as the offender manifested good behavior. In time, this new device took on added meaning when the courts placed certain restrictions on this quasi-freedom granted the culprit. Later, this trial period, under some sort of supervision became known as probation.

The first probation law passed in the United States dates from 1878 when Massachusetts made it possible for the city of Boston to appoint a probation officer. Later, in 1891 a second law required the criminal courts of the state to appoint officers for the extension of the service. By 1900, however, only six states had legally recognized probation.

The establishment of the Juvenile Court, following Chicago's and Denver's lead in 1899 gave impetus to the probation philosophy. Today forty-two states have some sort of legislation dealing with probation for children and adults.

There is no little confusion regarding the terms suspended sentence and probation as they are used interchangeably. But, a suspended sentence is not regarded as probation. Judges are restricted by statute relative to the suspended sentence as well as probation. In some states, the imposition of the sentence is suspended whereas, in others, the suspension of the execution of the sentence is practiced. In still others, both types are in use.

Probation is a form of suspended sentence but it always implies supervision during the trial period. Methods of supervision vary and because of this, there is much poor probation. Each jurisdiction practices its own type of probationary methods. In general, those offenses which are repugnant to society are excluded from probation such as crimes of violence, crimes against morals, crimes involving the use of deadly weapons, mercenary crimes, crimes against the government and crimes carrying a certain penalty.

There is a wide disparity in the use of probation by the judges in the United States. Socially minded jurists usually are more liberal in its use

(6) For details see Edwin M. Borchard, *Convicting the Innocent*, Yale University Press, 1932.

but they also provide for professionally trained supervisors. In most jurisdictions its use is generally associated with leniency rather than with social protection. Studies made in the use of probation show that judges invoke it more frequently when the defendant is immature, has dependents, or shows no previous delinquent record.

In a few progressive jurisdictions the judges depend to a wide extent on presentence clinics for investigations and rely heavily on their recommendations. Such investigations are made by trained personnel composed of social workers, psychologists and psychiatrists. If probation is granted, its success depends upon sympathetic supervision by trained staffs who are adequately paid and not overworked by too heavy a case load.

Probation in the United States is both good and bad. In some jurisdictions it is very bad and operated in a slipshod manner. Gradually, however, it is being accepted by more and more judges both for juveniles and adults so that it may be stated that it will become the one real device that will keep more and more persons out of prison and effect a much higher percentage of re-adjustment than the prison ever realized. Probation is the one bright hope of future penology. As Sanford Bates, former Director of the Federal Bureau of Prisons, has stated:

> I am persuaded to the belief that the probation service in America will not always be contented with the role of advisory service to our courts; that the day is not far distant when probation will be independently organized and administered with the same dignity, initiative, and independence that our hospital systems now enjoy. . . . Probation will retain its rightful place in the correctional scheme when it becomes wholly responsible for the treatment, care, control, and restoration of the wrong-doer from the moment his guilt is decided by the court.[7]

CARE AND TREATMENT OF JUVENILE OFFENDERS

Early treatment of delinquents. The most distressing problem confronting our colonial ancestors, insofar as the treatment of the delinquency of children was concerned, was the practice of placing those convicted in the jails and prisons of the day. It seems strange that children were obliged to wait thirty years after the initial penal reforms were initiated following 1790 before special institutions were created for their reception and treatment.

There are few available statistics of those early days that would show just what offenses were committed by children. We do know, however, that many were nothing worse than runaway apprentices who got tired of working for their masters. Hundreds of children were picked up by the police of the day—they were known as watchmen—and thrown into a common jail along with adults.

The first institutions for children were known as Houses of Refuge. Such institutions were developed in New York in 1825, in Boston in 1826 and in Philadelphia in 1828. The inspiration for these schools came from Germany and Switzerland where work and education were combined to train dependent and delinquent children to become good citizens. John Griscom, a Quaker from New York, had visited a number of these schools and returned to the United States fired with enthusiasm to do something constructive for neglected and incorrigible children.

(7) "The Next Hundred Years," *Yearbook*, official publication of the National Probation Association, Inc., 1790 Broadway, New York City, 1941, p. 84.

The program, treatment and training in the early Houses of Refuge differed widely. Most of those erected during the nineteenth century were little better than prisons, some surrounded by high walls. In all of them was to be found a stern oldfashioned form of discipline. The New York and Boston schools, however, did attempt to experiment with new forms of educational treatment, especially by inaugurating a type of honor system.

Children were sent to these institutions by the court on an indeterminate basis. This represents the first attempt to make the sentence indefinite since the child was obliged to stay in the school until he had completed a specified type of training after which he was apprenticed out in the free community to remain under the supervision of the school until he had reached his majority.

The older type House of Refuge gradually evolved into the cottage institution, the impetus for this development coming from the splendid system created at Mettray in France under the judge Demetz. Today we find every state in the Union with one or more such cottage institutions to house juvenile delinquents, some of which are quite attractive from an architectural standpoint but few of them going far beyond a stern disciplinary régime of treatment.

The development of the juvenile court. Perhaps the most revolutionary departure from tradition in the field of penal treatment was the establishment of the juvenile court in Chicago and Denver in 1899. One of the earliest pioneers in this field, the first to call delinquents *wards* rather than *enemies* of the state, was Judge Ben Lindsey who, at the time, was a judge in Denver. In his book, *Revolt of Modern Youth,* he set down his social philosophy regarding children and while it did not appear until many years after the establishment of the juvenile court, it gave tremendous impetus to a more humane and rational treatment of the child.

While the United States is proud of its part in developing the juvenile court with its progressive philosophy regarding the treatment of delinquents, we should not lose sight of the fact that this unique court was first established in South Australia as early as 1890, nine years earlier than the one in Chicago.

The chief characteristics of the juvenile court are known to all who deal with children. It includes separate hearings for the children's cases apart from the criminal court; informal procedure; regular probation service; detention separate from adults; privacy from the public; and provision for physical and mental examinations. It is true that one or more of these is ignored in many juvenile courts but is is asserted that where these are not scrupulously adhered to the court falls short of achieving a good brand of treatment.

Socially minded juvenile judges insist upon a trained staff of experts to assist them in the disposition of their cases. These include social workers, psychiatrists, psychologists, trained probation officers, capable "referees" who handle the initial hearings, and sympathetic personnel dealing with children while in detention quarters.

An honest attempt is made by the judge *to keep children out of correctional institutions*—known to the public as reform schools. It is becoming more widely accepted that fewer children should be sent to institutions. Rather, they should be treated in the community, in their own homes, if possible, on probation under the supervision of a capable officer. The use of foster homes is also resorted to in cases where the child is homeless or comes from an inadequate home.

A very important adjunct to the juvenile court is the child guidance clinic. These are, in general, supported privately and have for their purpose the diagnosis and, in some cases, the treatment of juvenile behavior manifestations. While they employ every scientific device known to the field of treatment, the psychiatric approach dominates. This technique regards the maladjusted child as a rejected personality due usually to deep-seated emotional disturbances. If these can be cleared up the child will make an adequate adjustment. Many of his escapades against the law are merely symptomatic of serious problems confronting him which he cannot solve or even understand. The psychiatrist can be of immense help in isolating the causes of the child's difficulty and perhaps clear them up by holding conferences with the parents, teachers and others who have contact with the child.

While the psychiatric form of therapy is quite valuable, the child guidance clinic cannot ignore the psychological and sociological contributions to child delinquency. Hence, a well staffed clinic will include trained personnel from these fields. Close cooperation with school and church as well as with the home is maintained. The progressive juvenile court works harmoniously with such clinics since it recognizes they have a real contribution to make in combatting juvenile delinquuency.

The first such clinic was founded in Chicago in 1909 with the well known authority on juvenile delinquency, Dr. William Healy, in charge. Later, when the Judge Baker Guidance Center was established in Boston, in 1917, Dr. Healy took charge there. Most of the larger cities of the country have several clinics, many of them connected with universities. Unfortunately, however, there are few of them in the smaller communities and almost none in the rural areas. Traveling clinics have been established in some sections of the country which visit the rural areas periodically and examine children who seem to need such treatment.

An evaluation of children's institutions. Opinion is divided in the United States regarding the conventional types of institutional treatment for the delinquent child. Naturally, those working in this field are enthusiastic about their results. The public is also satisfied with them although rarely is the average citizen in a position to judge since he cannot be informed as to their shortcomings. The reform school, for that is what it is called in spite of more modern names attached to it, represents a vested interest just as the adult penitentiary or reformatory.

Many judges are frankly critical of the juvenile institution and some almost never send a boy or girl to one of them. Other judges make a wide use of the institution and send their charges to it on the slightest excuse.

But a critical, objective evaluation of institutional treatment for children must agree at the outset that an experience in one of them carries a stigma. It is a truism that in many cases they serve as a training ground for more adept and serious offenses in crime. The boys and the girls are denied wholesome experiences with the opposite sex and thus tend to resort to homosexual behavior. This serious charge can be substantiated by studies that have been made of these institutions.

While the girls' institutions are more pleasant, some of them resembling college campuses, and provision is usually made for individual rooms for the girls, the boys' schools are as a rule repressive and in some, the management is downright cruel. Dormitories abound in most boys' institutions, a condition that all agree is deplorable. The inadequate salaries paid to most employees make it difficult to secure trained persons with a degree of sympathetic insight toward the child and his problems.

Even in the best institutions most of the attention of the officers is focused on the practice of absconding—running away. This is usually considered a heinous offense and calls for dire punishment such as a flogging or detention under strict surveillance for long periods of time. Most girls are sent to institutions for sexual irregularities and many boys for nothing more serious than persistent truancy. If sex is a problem it will never be solved by locking girls up in a segregated institution; if truancy is a problem, it will not be solved by sending a boy to a reform school. Truancy is usually symptomatic of something more serious than mere staying away from school. It calls for analysis and understanding which can be supplied adequately by a psychiatrist in a child guidance clinic.

Doubtless there are boys and girls who need an institutional experience but it should be resorted to only as a last resort. In spite of the claims of these institutions it is conceded that the child's delinquency should be evaluated in terms of his potentialities for re-adjustment within a more normal environment, if at all possible. The studies that have been made by the Osborne Association of New York within the past few years are convincing proof that in time this older form of treatment for children's delinquencies will disappear as ineffectual.[8]

Adolescent Courts for the older boy and girl. In recent years specialized courts for the older boy and girl have been set up in some of the larger cities of the country. The problem of responsibility for crime on the part of the non-adult has puzzled the courts of all ages and of all countries. The English common-law placed the age at seven as the point below which a child needed protection of the court and was not responsible for committing a crime. This age was extended to sixteen with the establishment of the juvenile court. Today, the term "child" is defined by the statutes of the various states. It fluctuates from sixteen to eighteen but in a few it is twenty-one.

This trend made it imperative that some new method be evolved to cope with the peculiar problem of delinquency among older boys and girls. The Adolescent Court was the result. In Chicago, as early as 1914, the Municipal Court set aside a division known as the Boys' Court to handle cases involving older boys between the ages of seventeen and twenty-one. This court received jurisdiction over misdemeanors and quasi-criminal offenses committed by boys of this age group. In 1915 the Philadelphia Municipal Court set up a similar court known as the Men's Misdemeanant Division which dealt with minor offenses of adult men and women and idle disorderly youth between the ages of sixteen and twenty-one.

But a real Adolescent Court was finally created in Brooklyn in 1935. It was established under a New York state law known as the Wayward

(8) See their reports: vol. I, 1938; II, 1940; III, 1940; IV, 1943.

Minors Act. This court proceeds as follows: When an older boy is arrested for an offense he is first interviewed by a probation officer connected with the court. In order to comply with the law he is asked if he wishes to waive examination and a trial by jury and have his hearing immediately in the Adolescent Court. If he agrees he presents his story before the judge with the police officer who made the arrest testifying as to the crime. The judge confers with the district attorney and between them the case is disposed of. Similar courts have been established in two other boroughs in New York, namely in Manhattan and in Queens.

There can be no doubt that this departure from tradition is commendable but there is still much confusion over procedure which must be cleared up by legislative action. It is a step in the right direction but it merely represents development in a philosophy that made possible the more hopeful concept created by the American Law Institute in 1940 known as the Youth Correction Authority.

The *Youth Correction Authority*. Perhaps the most violent break with tradition since the establishment of the juvenile court, occurred when the American Law Institute studied and recommended a more progressive type of treatment for older boys and girls known as the Youth Correction Authority.

The American Law Institute is composed of many outstanding lawyers and professors of criminology and criminal law. According to Dr. William Healy, who was a member of the committee to draw up the proposal, its provisions are:

1. That an independent agency of the state government be created with statewide jurisdiction, the function of which shall be to provide and administer corrective and preventive treatment for persons committed to it.

2. That whenever in any criminal proceeding in a court of that state, other than a juvenile court, a person between the ages of sixteen and twenty-one has been adjudged guilty of a violation of a law, unless he is merely fined or sentence is suspended or he has committed a capital offense, he shall be forthwith committed to the Youth Correction Authority.

Under this proposed Authority there will be provided training and treatment services in the hands of specially trained professional experts such as educators, institutional people, psychologists, psychiatrists and social workers. The Authority itself will be composed of three members drawn from the fields of education, probation, the legal profession, penal administration and from psychiatry. They will be appointed through civil service.

The individual offender coming before the Authority will be thoroughly studied by the staff and his case disposed of in terms of scientific treatment. New types of institutions will be created such as camps and hostels for the most hopeful cases. Others may be sent to existing penal institutions and many will be granted probation.

Little has been accomplished thus far to actually create the Youth Correction Authority. Its philosophy has been warmly debated in penal circles during the past three years and some authorities are opposed to it. The state of California has adopted it and New York State is considering it. A few states have studied its possibilities but have gone no further. It may be true to state that it is one of the casualties of the current war since this is not a very propitious time to consider such a radical measure. However, there is reason to believe that it represents the future technique and philosophy in dealing wth the perplexing problem of delinquency among the older boys and girls. There is no doubt that it is a direct challenge to the archaic principles upon which practice is based and will usher in a realistic plan of individualized treatment as opposed to the mass treatment found today.[9]

PRISONERS' AID SOCIETIES

Much of the aftercare of discharged prisoners from penal institutions has been done by private philanthropic organizations. Aside from the supervision of parole officers over those paroled from prison, this is still the case. The state has done nothing to assist the ex-prisoner in making an adjustment to normal life except to give him a handclasp, perhaps, when he leaves the prison and clothe him with a new cheap suit and a few dollars—usually five or ten dollars—to pay his railroad fare back home.

It is thoroughly recognized that those leaving prison are bewildered as well as seriously handicapped. They have a serious time picking up the threads of life that were so abruptly snapped when they were arrested and convicted of crime. The re-adjustment is a terrifying process in most cases and, at best, a difficult task.

The oldest prison aid society is the *Pennsylvania Prison Society,* formerly known as the *Philadelphia Society for Alleviating the Miseries of Public Prisons,* established in Philadelphia in 1787. It was this venerable organization that receives the credit for establishing the Pennsylvania System of separate confinement which, save for Pennsylvania, was repudiated in the United States and accepted so warmly abroad. It also was responsible for cleaning up the old Walnut Street Jail in Philadelphia in 1790 and making of it the first *penitentiary* in the country, if not the world.[10]

This organization made much of prison visiting. Its members visited the prisoners in the Eastern State Penitentiary at Philadelphia and attempted to bring about their reformation. Later in its career it became a prisoners' aid society in the aftercare of the ex-prisoner.

Other early organizations especially concerned with prisons and prisoners were the Boston Prison Discipline Society, founded in 1825 and controlled by Rev. Louis Dwight, arch-foe of the Pennsylvania System, who advocated the competitive Auburn System known as the silent system; three New Jersey organizations established between 1833 and 1849 but all shortlived; the Prisoners' Friend Association of Boston, founded in 1845; and the Prison Association of New York, founded in 1846 by Isaac Hopper and still influencing penal reform, under the able leadership of E. R. Cass who is also secretary of the *American Prison Association.* This latter organization is unique since it enjoys official recognition in New York state. It is called upon, by law, to make an annual report to the legislature on the status of the penal establishments of the state and hence

(9)   Cf. Thorsten Sellin, *The Criminality of Youth,* The American Law Institute, Philadelphia, 1940.

(10)   For details concerning this organization, see Teeters, *They Were In Prison,* Winston, 1937.

wields a healthy influence in suggesting reforms. It is this society of which Enoch C. Wines was secretary for so long a time. He was one of the greatest and most astute penologists produced in the United States and deserves a much belated recognition.

Much of the work of aftercare of prisoners has been in the hands of such organizations as those mentioned above, scattered throughout the country in the leading cities. However, the Salvation Army, the Volunteers of America, and other religious and philanthropic groups have also done considerable work in this field.

Much of this type of work took the form of providing "shelters" or "homes for ex-prisoners. Some of them took the names of "Houses of Industry" or "Homes for Discharged Prisoners" or "Hope Halls;" others took more maudlin names, such as "Doors of Blessing" or "Parting of the Ways." They attempted to serve as a link between the prison and the community where some sort of handicraft work was supplied and encouragement extended.

The prisoners' aid societies of the past have been mostly concerned with finding jobs for ex-prisoners and giving them handouts in food and clothing, as well as shelter. Few have gone beyond such a program even today. But it is becoming more apparent that these organizations are not equipped with the specialized personnel needed to counsel the ex-prisoner, assist him in his adjustment and certainly not to find him meaningful long term employment. This latter service calls for a skilled knowledge of working conditions, the economic situation at the moment, the labor market, etc. Prison aid societies have done much good work in the past but they have undoubtedly done much harm in making the ex-prisoner dependent on them too long or too often.

If such a program cannot be condemned it certainly cannot be accepted with much enthusiasm. The "handout" system, whether it be material aid or a stopgap job, has no place in modern penal treatment. Such a program belongs to the horse-and-buggy age of penology.

The care of the ex-prisoner rightfully belongs to the state which obviously shirks this responsibility except in case of parolees. Even here some type of aftercare from private agencies is necessary. With the development of better paroling facilities, such as careful selection and correspondingly careful supervision, few prisoners will need much help from private agencies except through their parole plan.

Within the past twenty years, however, a new emphasis has been placed upon the problem of assisting prisoners released from penal institutions. A few prison aid organizations have definitely broken with the past and eliminated promiscuous financial aid from their programs, except in a few dire cases.

The new approach envisages the stimulation of the released prisoner to help himself. It is the thesis of this therapy that selfreliance must come from within in terms of one's own potentialities. What he needs most is expert guidance. Such guidance can come only from trained persons— trained in the social worker's technique and philosophy.

SOCIAL CASEWORK AND PENAL TREATMENT

What is recognized as social casework was hinted at in the above section. It is a relationship between persons one of whom needs help and the other in a position to give it. There must be mutual trust and self-respect. In penal institutions there are many men and women who are frustrated and all of them must, from time to time, ask for advice concerning personal matters.

The *Pennsylvania Prison Society* has for the past twenty years been experimenting with this philosophy. All of its personnel are graduates of accredited schools of social work so that they bring to their tasks the techniques of social therapy. The secretary of this organization is Albert G. Fraser who introduced this new philosophy when he became identified with the organization in 1923.

The philosophy of treatment upon which this society operates transcends the level of bare necessities of life. It is expressed in terms of emotions, feelings, understanding, relationship and trust. To be successful, it must be acceptable and, to a degree, satisfying to the client. This newer concept pushes the old concept of temporary material aid into the background and emphasizes the relationship between the client and the staff worker.

This personal relationship can exist within the prison also. Many problems beset the immured prisoner, many of which he can resolve himself if he were wisely guided. The social worker is able to be of service to the prisoner on such a level.[11] Such a worker does not possess a monopoly of this insight. It exists wherever there is sympathetic understanding together with some knowledge of human behavior. It is more likely to occur though where trained persons compose the prison personnel.

Social work can be of real service then, not only to the released prisoner, but also to the man still in prison. In many of the more progressive institutions there is a social worker on the staff of the classification clinic. In fact, social work has gone further within the prison than outside in the field of aftercare.

The new philosophy suggested above has had difficulty in being accepted even among prison aid societies. Here and there may be found an organization that goes beyond the financial "handout" practice but such a change in emphasis has come slowly. Many of these organizations have no program at all, that is, judged by any dignified professional standards. The next decade or two should see much improvement in this important field, especially when more men and women, interested in the penal field, are being graduated from schools of social work.

VOLUNTARY AND PUBLIC DEFENDERS

For a long time it has been noted that thousands of defendants in court have been too poor to employ legal counsel. Out of this realization has spread, to a limited degree however, the movement to bring some relief to this unfortunate class of people.

(11) British, as well as American readers will be interested in a recent article by W. David Wills, in the 1943 *Howard Journal*, "The Place of Discipline in the Treatment of Delinquency." The point of view expressed there sounds familiar to those who employ case work methods in and out of prison.

The institution of the Public Defender dates back to Spain of the fifteenth century when such an official was attached to the Cortes of Toledo in 1480. Argentina adopted such a service in 1886 and eventually it spread to several other countries.

In the United States it his assumed two forms, following 1914. The first is known as the Public Defender who is a trained lawyer paid from public funds. Several of the larger cities of the country have adopted this method of assisting those who are unable to pay for a counsel. The second type is the the Voluntary Defender. Funds for the support of this functionary and his staff are supplied through private channels. Both systems have their ardent supporters and several cities have adopted one form or the other.

The philosophy underlying both systems is that justice should not be denied anyone confronted with a legal crisis and that the prevailing notion that there are two kinds of justice, one for the rich and the other for the poor, must be eliminated. As a rule social casework investigation is provided in conjunction with the service.

POLICE SYSTEMS

The detection of crime and the apprehension of criminals are extremely important if a country sincerely wishes to be freed of the menace of criminals. For efficiency in this field the first prerequisite is a well trained and honest police system.

Four serious charges have been hurled at the police systems in the United States and all are substantially true in spite of the heroic work that has been accomplished by courageous and realistic administrators throughout the country. These charges are: control of the police by politicians; lack of training and inadequate pay; faulty organization through decentralization; and their persistent use of the "third degree" which is the use of physical force and other forms of pressure to extract confessions from suspected offenders.

Here and there, throughout the country, police systems have been placed on a high level of professional efficiency so that politics have been reasonably well removed from their operation. But so long as the theory of local autonomy of governmental functioning persists it will be very difficult to divorce the police from local political control.

In recent years several large cities and some smaller communities have overhauled their police administrations and placed their personnel on a high professional basis with civil service appointment, adequate pay with possibilities of promotion, a pension system with retirement and equipment at least as efficient as that used by criminal gangs. Police science has developed to a very satisfying degree with a widespread use of criminalistics with crime detection laboratories employing all the contributions that the various sciences have to offer.

Each political subdivision has its own enforcement officers and because of this there is much jealousy between them, thus leading to much inefficiency. This is especially true with rural and village police. Then, too, in the United States, practically every state has its own constabulary which has jurisdiction throughout the entire state and they often find it difficult to work with local police officers. To complicate matters even more, the Federal government has its own officers together with the efficient Federal Bureau of Investigation. Local autonomy is jealously guarded in the United States and in all too many cases it seems preferable that a crime remain unsolved than a high degree of cooperation be maintained between the various systems. The only solution to this deplorable condition is the centralization of police functioning under state control but it is highly doubtful if this will ever be attained.

The charge of the use of physical force and protracted questioning against suspects is one that will not down in this country in spite of frequent denials that such tactics are used. When the police are obliged to work under pressure from the public, through its newspapers, there is likely to occur a sensational case of "third degree" methods. The practice is too prevalent to ignore although there are doubtless many police systems that never employ it. But a practice which is even more prevalent and which approaches the "third degree" is the denial of arrested person of his constitutional rights, especially if he is poor and friendless and does not know his rights. And even good police administrators insist that protracted questioning is justifiable in getting evidence.

With the spread of scientific devices and knowledge in the detection of crime and apprehension of criminals there will be less use made of the older methods of browbeating suspected persons and denying them their fundamental rights. Many police systems are pointing the way and in time the police function in the various states will be placed on a higher level than it now is. In justice to the police it should be stated that the public demands more than it is willing to pay for and also that it reflects a philosophy incompatible with good control and intelligent understanding of the criminal.

CRIME PREVENTION

Perhaps in no country in the world have so many volumes been written on crime prevention, so many speeches made on the subject, and so many organizations and agencies created to deal with this problem. Even now a new crop of books is being written and agencies developed to cope with crime and delinquency during war time.

Statistics are produced to prove that each succeeding year there is more delinquency among children and more crime among adults. The newspapers print sensational stories that are quite convincing and police officers and other public officials make speeches decrying the wide extent of antisocial behavior.

Delinquency and crime represent behavior which is socially disapproved. Much of it is due to current social maladjustment and no little of it may be directly charged to war. It represents one of the costs of war and should be recognized as such. The problem of coping with delinquency is as acute now as it was during the great depression or during any period of great social and economic upheaval. It is not the purpose here to discuss the extent of delinquency or to evaluate the various remedies suggested. Rather we merely wish to point out the approaches that are made in attempting to combat the perennial evil.

Aside from the sporadic attempted solutions that are announced periodically through the press, such as invoking curfews for minors, prohibiting them to attend moving picture houses at night unless accompanied by their parents and other methods obviously as futile, crime prevention in the United States may be listed under the following headings: (1) more and better recreational facilities such as playgrounds, supervized dance-halls, clubs for adolescents, character-building agencies, and the like, most of which are promoted by public agencies and private social centers; (2) community coordinating councils which are composed of several groups of interested citizens of a community having for their purpose a community-wide attack on delinquency; (3) special projects under the supervision of churches, schools, police departments or civic clubs; (4) specific plans based upon social research by various university or municipal groups which are approached from an experimental point of view such as the Chicago Area Project, under the direction of Dr. Clifford Shaw and his associates.

One is impressed, if not amazed, at the wide variety of such projects. Many of them are promoted by enthusiastic groups of people who feel they have something worthwhile to contribute and convinced their particular project is the answer to the problem. A great deal of money is spent in carrying on these multifarious programs, much of it doubtless well spent.

Space forbids a description and analysis of these various projects but, in general, they are all dedicated to the task of re-enforcing the family, neighborhood and community against the forces of neglect, indifference, greed and ignorance which strike deep in modern social and economic life.

The best informed students of delinquency in the United States, as well as many in other countries, are convinced that the causes of delinquency are *multiple* rather than specific. Most delinquent children are emotionally insecure and need individualized treatment, preferably psychiatric. There is certainly no harm in providing wholesome recreation; in fact it is essential that every child be provided a decent place to play under proper supervision, if possible. In addition, parental education is of tremendous importance. Little has been accomplished in this highly important field thus far and this presents a real challenge for the future. Then, too, those conditions that make for widespread poverty should be eliminated in the social and economic order so that every child will be able to start from birth without handicaps that make for frustration and emotional instability. A new social and economic order is a *must* in postwar planning.

A social philosophy that encompasses adequate prenatal care for prospective mothers, careful medical and dental care for children, proper schooling based upon the child's potentialities, decent housing, counseling in the schools, and the right to a job with adequate pay will go far in eliminating delinquency and crime. The patchup attempts that have been made to date will accomplish very little in cutting down the crime rate that causes so much alarm throughout the world.

WAR PRODUCTION AND THE PRISON

The global nature of the war has altered our thoughts and modes of living in numerous ways. Unity of spirit, elevation of morale, a determined will to victory, great output in war industry, community cooperation in rationing—all come to mind as positive results. But few persons realize that the war has also produced many of these same results in our prisons and reformatories. It literally took a war to blast our prisons out of the stagnation and sterile apathy that has characterized them for a century.

Patriotism is not limited to the free citizen. The inmates of this country have been equally fervent in love of country. Unable to pour out their blood on the battlefronts, they have given it to the Red Cross plasma banks on a much higher proportion to that of free citizens not in the armed service.

In 1943 a bomber drive was put on in the prisons of the country and the almost penniless inmates contributed nearly a million dollars, enough to build three super-bombers. Few free communities of comparable size of the inmate population, with far greater resources, have done better.

Prison production of war commodities has reached amazing records. This all-out production has been a veritable "industrial revolution." This phenomenon was the result of liberalizing rulings and executive orders by the Federal government which swept away, temporarily at least, the stultifying restrictions against prison labor that have accumulated over the past decades. Between August, 1942, and November, 1943, the state prisons produced industrial products for war purposes valued at almost ten million dollars. Agricultural products were also increased by over five million dollars. This amazing increase is in addition to the conspicuous showing of the Federal prisons which have not been shackled heretofore by restrictive legislation and consequently maintained a head start on production. These prisons produced some eighteen million dollars in war material with the year ending July 30, 1943.

The impressive work accomplished during these war days by the state prisons was stimulated by the dynamic leadership of Hon. Maury Maverick, Director of the Government Division and Major William H. Burke, Chief of the Prison Industries Branch, of the War Production Board. and carried through by the excellent spirit of the various wardens and the prisoners themselves. New equipment was added, additional farmland requisitioned and more worker inmates added by inaugurating three shifts instead of the traditional curtailed prison work day. This all-out war program has demonstrated that all that is needed to solve the dilemma of prison industry—perhaps the knottiest problem of prison administration—is a well-planned program and proper motivation.

While it may be too much to expect the prisons to be called upon after the war to produce on the same impressive scale, since the present restrictive legislattion is still on the statute books, the impetus thus gained will result in far-reaching effects, some of which bear mentioning.

Public opinion is in a better frame of mind toward prisons and prisoners. The new penology is demonstrating that society cannot continue to keep thousands of men locked up without work. It is slowly being accepted by an ever-widening group of citizens that the day of social revenge on the rockpile or of purely dollar-conscious commercialism is past. One of the factors in social protection is a prosperous prison industry.

Prison administrators themselves are slowly accepting a more rational perspective regarding prisoners. Not content with being mere jailers and no longer paralyzed by inertia, many of them are aggressively exploring the possibilities of enriching their programs with more meaningful educational curricula, with the installation of social casework, permitting more inmates to work outside the prison walls, and by encouraging research on the part of their professional staff.

Those concerned with building programs are now thoroughly convinced that the conventional prison architecture of the past is definitely outmoded. Architects are exploring the possibilities of newer and more wholesome designs which are far removed from the old nineteenth century Bastille-type construction. While security and custody are of prime importance, it is agreed that a prison can be humanely built so that it approaches the normal type of living rather than nullifying every aspect of decency as has been so pronounced in the past.

The war program has also demonstrated that many prison inmates can, under proper supervision, leave the institution day after day and be employed miles away. Thousands of men have worked on farms, in army camps and in work camps doing vitally needed work for the war effort. This can be expanded materially after the war if the will to do so is present.

In conclusion, then, it may be stated that the war has stimulated, in a healthy manner, prisoner and prison administrator alike. Certainly it has not solved all the problems of prison control, but there can be no doubt that its impact has at least touched, in a favorable manner, practically every phase of the institutional program.[1]

(1)   The reader is referred to the brochure issued by the Prison Industries Branch of the War Production Board, "Prisons in Wartime," November, 1943.

CHAPTER XII

LESSONS FOR THE UNITED STATES FROM A WORLD VIEW OF PENOLOGY

A New Day in Penal Treatment

In this birdseye view of penal systems in operation throughout the world one is impressed by the paradox of punishment and enlightened treatment of the offender. Scientific enlightenment does exist but sometimes it is found side by side with reaction of the worst sort. This is just as true in the United States as it is in many other countries.

Certain interesting vestiges of sixteenth to nineteenth century thought regarding criminals are to be found in most of the countries surveyed. A few of them have gradually discarded most of the ideas that existed prior to the beginnings of the penitentiary movement following 1790 and several have explored the possibilities that have been advanced by progressive penologists during the past quarter century.

No country has yet freed itself completely from the retributive philosophy that made our penal treatment so barbaric in the past. Here and there we still find brutality of the worst type. Some countries are coldly objective in the type of treatment employed and appraise the criminal as one who needs repression and restraint if not actual physical punishment. The past century was characterized by physical punishment; the twentieth has fortunately seen the elimination of much of this but to too large an extent has merely substituted forms of mental cruelty. This manifests itself in such refined techniques as badgering prisoners, "pushing" them around, of lecturing them, regimenting them, and in other ways that elicit feelings of inferiority and even selfabasement. The programs of treatment are designed to "help" the prisoner but seldom does one find a plan by which the inmate himself has any choice in accepting or rejecting what has been worked out for him. Much is written these days about the "dignity of the personality" but few will permit such an enlightened philosophy to take root in the prison.

But courageous experimentation may be discerned in many countries, including the United States, which augurs well for the next period in penal treatment. The thesis is gaining strength that the criminal is a human being and that he is a victim of either biological handicaps or social maladjustments, or both, rather than being a perverse creature who wrongs society because he is just devilish by choice. While jurisprudence is still shackled by the Classical theory of responsibility, penologists and many penal administrators take the more progressive view and think of the prison inmate as one who needs opportunities for growth. They see individualized treatment as the answer to the problem.

This treatment may be medical, psychological, or industrial; it may well be a combination of all types. It is interesting to note that medical treatment and some type of education are employed in practically all

countries. In some, the standards may not be high, but there is a recognition everywhere that the bare minimum of halfway decent health
and literacy are necessary. We see also that some type of good work
habits are of value to the incarcerated convict since so many of them never
learned to work with any degree of diligence.

We have come to expect these minima in every prison in every
country. Certainly there is no excuse for any of these fields to be neglected.
We are, then, agreeably surprised and encouraged to see penal administrators going beyond these bare essentials. Yet it is no more than we
have a right to expect since few countries are so isolated by their geog-
raphy or cultural background to know what is being tried or what is
accepted throughout the world in the treatment of the offender. Cultural
differences may decree what specific reform is or is not expedient but
to ignore persistently the fruits of the social sciences is inexcusable on the
part of any country.

It would be presumptuous for penologists of the United States to
assume that there is a monopoly of all that is good in penal treatment
right here at home. True, many ideas and techniques that hold promise
for rehabilitation and re-adjustment of criminals are in operation here
and there throughout the country, many of which can be recommended
to other countries. Many new devices in therapy have originated in some
of the prison systems here. But a fair appraisal of what is actually being
done would suggest that other techniques and concepts operating abroad
might well be adopted, at least for experimental purposes.

It is the purpose of this chapter to set down some of these concepts,
techniques or practices merely for perusal. Some of them are being tried
in some penal systems in the states or by the Federal system. Some may
be rejected as impracticable or even unconstitutional.

The use of prison labor outside the penal establishment. Here is
an interesting and fruitful departure from tradition but one that is also
laden with potential danger. After more than a century's experience with
the evils of contract and leased labor it certainly is not suggested that
any reversion to these systems be advocated. Rather, any plan that permits
an individual prisoner or small group of prisoners to bargain themselves,
through the prison administration, with a free manufacturer or employer
of free labor, might be encouraged. The inmates could leave the prison
during the working day and return at night. Wages would be paid at
the prevailing rate and the prisoner pay the institution for maintenance.

This system is in operation in Canada, Italy and Czechoslovakia, to
mention a few of the countries that have adopted this method in some
instances. During the present war, here in the United States, many instances can be cited in which prison inmates have worked for private employers.
Agriculture lends itself to this practice much more easily than manufacturing but there is no reason why it cannot be tried in plants and
factories. Cotton picking, harvesting potatoes and other crops by prisoners
of state institutions have been tried with success, thus serving as a prec-
edent for further exploration into this field.

Naturally those who are to work outside the prison must be chosen
wisely by classification clinics. Short term prisoners, those who will soon
be eligible for parole, those who have dependents and can assume responsi-

bility, may be granted this privilege. The practice might well serve as a proving-ground for re-adjustment to society. Supervision by the institution would, of course, be necessary, but more and more freedom of operation could gradually be granted. In short, there are favorable possibilities inherent in such a plan.

It never did make sense that a man's labor is degraded when he goes to prison. He is the same man and his work is still as valuable in the institution as it was on the outside. The opposition to prison labor in this country, or elsewhere for that matter, is due primarily to a misunderstanding of the facts. All the products of prison labor, in the heyday of the contract system in this country, amounted in value to less than one-half of one per cent of the total industrial output of the country. So any labor performed by an inmate of a penal institution is not in direct competition with that of a free man. Then, too, a fact frequently overlooked by the free laborer or manufacturer is that an idle man in prison is nonproductive and must be supported altogether by the taxpayer. By seeing that he is productively employed either inside the prison or outside by the day, the cost of his maintenance is just that much reduced. In addition, he can also assist quite materially in supporting his dependents rather than force them to live by charity or public relief.

It is no exaggeration to state that thousands of men and women in prison at the moment could be economic assets if they were permitted to work outside the penal establishment under some plan similar to that mentioned above. A new era in penal treatment must explore such possibilities.

Work Camps. The more extensive development of camps to which prisoners could be sent to reclaim waste land, clear out scrub trees and undergrowth, blaze trails, work on projects which prevent soil erosion, and the like, is highly desirable. There is a host of such projects that falls within the field of maintaining and rebuilding our natural resources that might well be undertaken by the state and Federal prisoners. A number of our states as well as the Federal Bureau of prisons are already engaged in such worthwhile undertakings. The camps now under the jurisdiction of the Federal Bureau are for short term offenders and are maintained for road building in mountainous regions.

Sweden has gone far in developing this type of work activity for some of her prisoners. Many men are permitted to join work camps that operate without any supervision whatsoever. This is also true of Australia and New Zealand.

If this sort of project is to be recommended, however, it is quite important that safeguards be developed to eliminate the stigma so often associated with "convict camps." Humiliating garb should be eliminated as well as the conventional guard with a shotgun over his knees which, even now, is too prevalent in some sections of the South. If camp life is to have any meaning for the prisoner he should be free to accept or reject such work and it should be made attractive enough for him to see in it real possibilities for re-establishment into the free community.

The work camps and farms developed by Switzerland at Witzwil and by Belgium at Merxplas are interesting experiments that may well be studied by not only our state penal administrators but also by those

who have given thought to regional colonies for vagrants and misdemeanants. A novel plan operating in India, which might well be adopted in
the United States, calls for small gardens to be cultivated in connection
with every jail and prison.

Any plan to keep men out of the unhealthy atmosphere of a large
prison should be studiously considered. Penal institutions with their fetid
air, inside cellblocks, lack of open recreation space and monotonous routine
are inimical to reform so that their renovation, if not elimination, is of
significance in ushering in a new day in penal treatment. Work camps
represent such a plan.

The Wider Use of Leaves or Furloughs. The prisons in the United
States might well develop a system of furloughs for many of their prisoners.
Weekend visits home, furloughs at Christmas and on other holidays, visits
home once a month could be granted on the basis of a good work record
or on some other basis determined by the classification clinic. There are
thousands of men and women in prison today who could be depended on
to return to the prison. A few of our institutions grant such leaves even
now but their use should be widely expanded.

Russia has gone in for this sort of thing in a big way. It is a healthy
practice because it keeps up the morale of both the man in prison and
the members of his family. It is far more desirable than the conjugal
visits found in Mexican prisons, at least for our own prisoners, since the
mores of the United States are much too rigid to countenance such a
practice.

Furloughs are particularly healthy because their adoption would eliminate the dubious practice of having the inmate's children come to the
prison for visits. A visit of the prisoner to his home would maintain
not only sexual ties but also be of inestimable value to the children who
also have a claim to their father.

The Abolition of Flogging in Children's Institutions. It seems
strange that in a country presumed to be so enlightened as that of the
United States, the flogging of juveniles is still maintained on such a large
scale. In many respects, children in our reform schools are more liable
to physical punishment than adult prisoners. The recent *Handbooks* published by the Osborne Association of New York referred to in an earlier
connection, testify to the widespread use of physical punishment in most
of our reform schools. France, for example, abolished flogging and the use
of handcuffs for children as long ago as 1899.

The scrupulous segregation of those awaiting trial in our jails. This
presupposes the erection of special houses of detention for those awaiting
trial and unable to furnish bail. The Scandinavian countries are far
ahead of the United States in this respect. It is patently unfair that
this group of unfortunate people, many of whom will later be found innocent of the charges against them, are placed in the same institutions
with vagrants, drug addicts, misdemeanants and other offenders. Every
county in the United States should establish without delay a separate
House of Detention to care for this class of person.

As it is today, the rich and influential person who runs afoul of the
law may secure bail; not so the poor man. He is remanded to jail to await

disposition of his case. Hence, this practice is a form of unfair discrimination against the poor and friendless.

The wider use of female police. Many of our large cities have female police officers but none has as many as needed. Female and juvenile delinquents should be handled by women rather than males. Austria has gone far in this respect.

The development of a more progressive philosophy of treatment for youth between the ages of 16 and 23. The British have accomplished a remarkable feat in establishing and developing the Borstal system, one that is worthy of emulation in this country. Our reformatories are outmoded since they are too large, too regimented and repressive, and too much like the ordinary prison. Few of them measure up to good standards of what they were originally intended to accomplish—that of *reformation.* Smaller units for different types of offenders should be established in the various states. Boys and young men could be sent to a small institution that features a type of program to which the individual is or could be adapted. The Borstal practice of enlisting university men as personnel as well as eliminating the wearing of uniforms by the instructors is worthy of consideration. It is possible that the Youth Correction Authority, discussed earlier, would develop into a similar venture for America. The war is probably responsible for the postponement of this excellent plan. If each state developed such a system it might well measure up to the British Borstal System.*

Preventive detention. This system is in operation in Britain and other countries of Europe, notably Italy. It calls for an extra sentence for habitual and professional criminals after they have served their regular sentence. It is frankly a method of keeping under restraint that class of criminals that persists in living by crime. Australia's penal code permits her courts to place "persistent misdemeanants" in what is termed "reformative detention." This is the same as that employed in Britain, except for minor offenders.

Whether this form of extra treatment could be established in the United States is debatable since the individual is protected by constitutional rights that might make "preventive detention" impracticable. But we must admit that Britain succeeds in restraining her dangerous criminals more effectively than we in the United States. The only hope in this country is the development of a realistic indeterminate sentence which will make possible segregation for a long period of those who are admittedly a menace to society.

Restitution for crime. Many countries, especially those in Latin America, maintain a realistic system whereby the offender must make restitution to his victim, if this is at all possible. Part of the wages of the prisoner is used for this purpose. There is no possibility in this country of a person who has been robbed, for instance, recovering any of his money from the criminal who has victimized him. It cannot be denied that there are possibilities in this realistic practice which should be explored. There is small satisfaction under the existing practice of sending a criminal to prison to atone for his crime if his victim receives no restitution except a sadistic

* Cf. Raphael Lemkin, "The Treatment of Young Offenders in Continental Europe," *Law and Contemporary Problems,* Duke University Press. vol. IX, No. 4, pp. 748-759.

satisfaction of knowing the person who wronged him is languishing in prison.

That this is a knotty problem was demonstrated by the ponderous discussion that took place at the Sixth International Prison Congress held at Brussels in 1900. Thirteen scholarly reports replete with ingenious suggestions were presented, one by the American jurist, Simeon Baldwin of New Haven. There was universal agreement on the desirability of securing indemnity for the injured party, but the methods suggested for realizing the financial increment were in question by the delegates.

The elimination of short term sentences. We have noted in our discussion of Latin American penology that the criminologists and penologists of the countries to the South have gone on record as deploring short term or "privative" sentences and have urged the substitution of fines based on the individual's capacity to pay, by suspension of sentence or the compulsory performance of certain duties for the benefit of the state. They recognize that these nuisance punishments accomplish little if any reformation but rather cause the humiliation and degradation of the offender.

We in the United States could profit much by exploring the possibilities in eliminating such sentences, especially those that must be served in our local jails, some of which are as short as a day or two. It is conceded in penal circles that nothing is accomplished by throwing a man in jail for a few days or weeks except to degrade him further.

We recognize that if a man is an alcoholic or drug addict he needs medical or psychiatric treatment but rarely does he receive either in a jail sentence. Many in this class are chronic repeaters going in and out of jails many times during their career.

The problem of the short sentence calls for the best thought that can be applied to it and the experience of Latin American countries will be watched with interest.

The development of hobbies. Meaningful occupation of one's spare time is something that has to be nurtured. Not only do men in prison need encouragement in developing a wise use of their leisure time, but millions in society can well profit by the development of a hobby. Many men and women now in prison are pursuing some type of constructive hobby but seldom does the administration employ someone to encourage them in their sparetime activity. While we saw little of value in the prisons of modern Spain, in giving credit where it belongs, we must point out that what is being done in sculpturing and painting there is worthy of adoption in our own prisons. Many persons have latent talent in these areas so that some encouragement should be given them by calling on volunteer painters and sculptors from nearby communities to give instruction.*

The use of community volunteers. Great Britain has developed prison visiting on a large scale. Aside from a few states, this country has not realized the significance of enlisting the members of society in assisting penal administrators in their work of reformation. Pennsylvania is the only state

---

* The pioneer work done by Boris Blai of the Tyler Art School of Temple University at Fort Dix near Trenton, N. J. for soldiers is the type of thing we have in mind. Hundreds of soldiers who have never done any sculpturing are enrolled in classes and are achieving notable results. Mr. Blai's thesis is that work of this sort has wonderful therapeutic value.

having an unbroken history of lay prison visiting that compares favorably with that of Britain.

Aside from mere visiting, some other countries have gone even further by actually soliciting volunteer agencies and individuals to assist prison authorities with their problems. Poland, for example, selects citizens to assist in the "moral regeneration of criminals" and to contribute their opinions relative to the "remission of sentence and pardon of prisoners."

In Czechoslovakia over 8,000 private individuals and eighteen organizations are specifically interested in working with the immured prisoner. In addition to this service, it is noted that every prison and county jail in this country has a special fund out of which released prisoners receive assistance.

Obviously, such efforts should be organized and supervised by the state or country. It is significant that the authorities in the countries mentioned above actually recognize the potential value of enlisting its citizens in this type of reformative work. This is in direct contrast to the practice in the United States where there is an almost studious effort made to keep the prisons isolated and apart from the free community.

Officer Training. While a few states, as well as the Federal Bureau of Prisons, carry on officer training, there is doubtless much to be learned from Belgium, Sweden, Germany, Italy, Japan and China, where study courses have been installed, in varying degrees of efficiency and scope. Turkey also expresses more interest in good personnel than in elaborate prison plants.

Mention should be made here of the organization of prison personnel into labor unions as has been done in Britain. In addition, it is interesting to note that they have been recognized by the authorities. Here is a real departure from tradition—one that certainly merits comment at least. And why should not prison guards be organized?

Biological laboratories and clinics. The crimino-biological approach has long been dominant in many European and Latin American countries. This country has given little thought to this phase of criminal analysis since the environmental school has been most emphasized. While this approach may well be justified, the biological, as practiced in Italy and Belgium, for example, should not be entirely ignored.

Scientific classification. Classification procedure has become almost universally acceptable in the United States although even now many states either ignore its major implications or merely follow an elaborate paper program. We doubtless have something to learn from classification of prisoners as practiced in Great Britain, especially in its Borstal System, and from the scientific methods used in this connection in Belgium. It must be recognized that we in the United States possess no monopoly on this highly important phase of new penology.

Criminal responsibility. The question of criminal responsibility has long been a dilemma in many countries, including the United States. Our jurisprudence has consistently followed the Classical theory of responsibility yet science has just as consistently proved that the individual is motivated to act because of his biological and environmental limitations. Italy, we found, has been especially bedeviled by the conflict between Beccarian philosophy, on the one hand, and the positive school of thought, advocated by Lombroso and Ferri, on the other. This quandary may never be resolved.

The country of Chile has at least faced the paradox honestly and practically. The penal code of that country does not attempt to define crime. The confusion between free will and determinism is avoided. While scientific methods are used in analyzing motives, background of the criminal, and the like, he must be penalized for the protection of society. The recognition of this dilemma is at least a step in the right direction.

This realistic philosophy is accompanied by the extensive use of the indeterminate sentence and, equally important, the training of those judges who are called upon to sentence the criminal. Aside from the law, judges must be trained in sociology and psychology. In this respect alone, the United States has much to learn from Chile.

Social consequences of crime. How much we can actually benefit from Russia regarding the treatment of the criminal is debatable since that country has changed so radically during the past decade. We read of great freedom given her prisoners, of furloughs, of families of prisoners living in penal colonies, and other departures from conventional practice. It is doubtful if the mores of this country could adopt any of these ideas. It is repugnant, for example, to think of allowing children of prisoners to grow up in a penal colony.

But Russia's reorientation of the social responsibility of crime is worthy of serious thought. Crime against society as a whole, against the welfare of the state, is only beginning to be appreciated in this country. The old conventional notion of the harm done by those committing the traditional crimes, such as robbery, pocketpicking, assault, and the like being greater than white-collar crime, for instance, is at least being questioned in penal and judicial circles. What is called for in this country is a complete revamping of our archaic criminal codes. This would necessarily mean a reappraisal of all crimes, placing each in its proper category in terms of harm done to society as a whole. Then, and not until then, such offenses as financial chicanery, adulteration of food, the sale of defective products to the consuming public, and a host of other such white-collar criminal activity, would be considered more dangerous than crimes against specific individuals. In this respect, at least, we have something to learn from Russia.

Miscellany. A further scrutiny of penal methods in use in the various countries of the world would find many other isolated important instances of progress, perhaps worthy of examination and adoption by the United States. Sometimes it is only the little personal amenities that carry real meaning for reformation.

Large and commodious prison compounds with plenty of sunlight, fresh air, a profusion of flowers, and attractive low buildings that bear no resemblance to the conventional prison, such as may be found in India and Ceylon, might be recommended for architectural study.

Permission for prisoners to wear their own clothing on Sundays and holidays and to have pets, as in Holland, is worthy of consideration. The installation of theatres within the prison as exists in the Vác prison in Hungary, is commendable. Many of our more modern prisons do have auditoriums but few, if any, actually encourage dramatic or musical festivals. Along the line of recreation it might be proposed that swimming pools be constructed in prisons for the inmates. While such a proposal would be repudiated immediately, it is of interest to learn that two pools were constructed in the large national penitentiary of Mexico City.

Many countries, not mentioned in this concluding chapter, doubtless have penal concepts or administrative procedures that may well call for favorable comment. However, some of these are either already practiced in the United States or may not be appropriate of adoption because of cultural differences. It is certainly not the purpose of this survey to draw invidious comparisons between countries.

Constructive work with juvenile delinquents is almost universal. Colombia, for example, shows considerable tolerance for recidivism among minors. Serious attempts are made to keep children out of institutions in Panama. Hungary is also disturbed about delinquency and attempts special treatment for minors. This is equally true of Ecuador, Argentina, Peru, Chile and other Latin American countries.

Along other lines, we might mention the excellent work being done in the prison schools of Czechoslovakia, or the work of the surveillance judge in Italy. In the former case, we might admit that there are many excellent prison schools in the United States, although a great many are inefficient and most of them are financially starved. In the latter case, it is questionable that this country would gain very much by creating an official position of a surveillance judge vested with dictatorial powers over all prisons of a state. Even in Italy it is doubtful that he is very efficient.*

There can be no doubt that we in the United States have much to learn from other countries. On the other hand, many other countries can learn something from our practices. We do not intend to point out those phases of our penal treatment that could or should be adopted since it might be considered presumptuous. We have set down in our chapter on the penal philosophy of this country various concepts which may be considered by those who care to do so.

Penal philosophy is dynamic. It is constantly in a state of flux. We in the United States have borrowed from other countries in the past and there is no reason why we cannot try out some of the practices being carried on now. We hope, too, that some of our own concepts may well be adopted abroad.

All penal programs are theoretically attempting to cope with the crime problem. The last quarter century has convinced progressive penologists that punishment is no longer effective. Discipline, training, productive work, religious experiences, therapy—all have a place in the modern penal program. The gradual elimination of penal institutions for most of those who are now sent to them must eventually be recognized as of paramount necessity if society is to be protected and made secure.

The conviction is gaining ground in the United States that the prison is no answer to the crime problem. It has been advanced, for example, that it is sheer nonsense to think reformation can be effected in a place originally designed to punish. Prisons have been called "monuments to stupidity" by one outstanding penologist; another prominent penologist has stated that we must "destroy the prison, root and branch." As early

(*) See pages 62-63 for a discussion of the duties of the surveillance judge.

as 1868 the Frenchman, E. Desprez, called for the abandonment of prisons. There is scarcely a penal administrator who has not, at one time in his experience, questioned the advisability of continuing institutional treatment.

The financial investment in prisons is tremendous. The annual outlay in overhead and equipment necessary to maintain institutional treatment is staggering. The cost might conceivably be justified if satisfying social results were realized. Yet it is highly questionable that a term in a penal institution can be helpful to a person who has violated a law. The social stigma, the contamination, the wholesale abnormalities and the badgering an inmate experiences when he is incarcerated in the best of prisons certainly militate against any easy absorption into a normal society upon his release. The so-called New Prison and the New Penology which have permeated penal thought during the past decade or two are merely a patching up attempt to make the institution work. But even these heroic attempts are not enough.

The extensive use of probation is the only hope of the future in cutting down the number of those sent to prison. Any effort, therefore, to develop probation standards and techniques is socially desirable. But this is only a partial solution to the problem. Imprisonment cannot be abolished overnight and even the most optimistic will be obliged to admit that some criminals must be segregated, perhaps for life, or, at least, until their danger to society is definitely passed.

It has been suggested by some progressive penologists that the institution become a *diagnostic depot* where the prisoner would remain only temporarily. Such a concept has interesting possibilities, especially if a realistic indeterminate sentence could be put into operation. The depot thus envisaged would be called upon to collect data regarding the inmates and work out plans for their treatment. The initial part of the treatment might be consummated in the prison but the final objective would be to transfer prisoners to the free community as soon and as rapidly as possible. Those proving their ability to respond to community treatment would be sent out under some carefully worked out plan. Plan "A" might require some to work in the prison during the day and return to their homes at night; plan "B" would be the reverse—work in the community and sleep at the prison; plan "C" would call for community work with only periodic conferences with the prison staff. Other similar plans could be adapted to specific personal needs.

Supervision would, of course, be necessary, but this should prove no difficulty since parole and probation staffs are already equipped to handle those who have run afoul of the law. Those making an early adjustment to community life need not return to the institution. Thus more and more persons would be readjusted at the earliest possible moment without danger of contamination as exists today. The institutionalization that now occurs could be avoided, sexual perversions could be eliminated, the taxpayer saved large sums of money and a realistic system of readaptation be effected.

As we pointed out earlier, the war has made it possible for many men to leave prison to work in the free community. The results have been favorable. Hundreds of prison inmates have been absorbed into the army long before their sentences have expired. The future of penology points in the direction of this new type of penal procedure. Thus, in time, the barbarities of imprisonment may become completely eliminated.

The above recommendations are certainly far from complete. The writer of this volume is aware of its many shortcomings. But it is an attempt to present a world view of penology. The superficial treatment of some countries and, even more serious, the complete neglect of others, is deplored. The only explanation is that the task of collecting information has been arduous since the paucity of material written in English is conspicuous by its very elusiveness. Any work of so wide a scope will find critics. In anticipation of their strictures it might amiably be suggested that they too might write their own world surveys.

As the writer stated on his dedicatory page, not since the days of Enoch Wines, Major Arthur Griffiths and Charles Richmond Henderson have comprehensive data on prison systems been assembled. What is sorely needed is a periodic report on the work being currently accomplished by the various countries of the world on curbing crime and readjusting criminals. A postwar plan of this sort should be developed by he International Penal and Penitentiary Commission. The material collected should be published in every language so as to ensure its assimilation by all who are charged with the organization and maintenance of prison systems. Thus real comparisons could be made and a healthy process of give and take be developed.

COOPERATION BETWEEN COUNTRIES

The interplay of ideas and concepts between students of penology and penal administrators of the various countries of the world has been made possible not only through the various journals, pamphlets and volumes written throughout the past century, but also to the periodic Congresses of the International Penal and Penitentiary Commissions.

These Congresses, composed of distinguished groups of penologists from many countries of the world, have assisted greatly in the spread of new ideas and administrative practices in the field. Their history, however, has been somewhat stormy and interrupted, due in the first place to a conflict of ideas, and in the second to the two great World Wars.

The first International Congress met at Frankfort-on-the-Main in 1846. It was attended by such outstanding penologists and criminologists of the day as Ducpétiaux, Jebb, Mittermaier, Moreau-Christophe, Julius and Suringar. The only American delegate was Rev. Louis Dwight of Boston.

Two subsequent meetings of a similar nature were held in Brussels in 1847 and in Frankfort again in 1857. However, these three meetings had no official relationship with any government and so no steps were taken to effect a permanent organization.

The United States government took the first step to inaugurate a permanent international organization in 1871. Congress passed a resolution which made it possible for Dr. Enoch Wines, secretary of the Prison Association of New York, to visit most of the countries in Europe to fraternize with penologists and administrators, with the aim in view of developing an international organization. Out of this visit the First Congress was subsequently held in London in 1872. Twenty governments were represented. Since then it has met as follows:

Second, Stockholm, 1878   Seventh, Budapest, 1905
Third, Rome 1885   Eighth, Washington, 1910
Fourth, St. Petersburg, 1890   Ninth, London, 1925
Fifth, Paris, 1895   Tenth, Prague, 1930
Sixth, Brussels, 1900   Eleventh, Berlin, 1935

The presidents of these Congresses were: 1872-1878, Dr. Enoch Wines; 1878-1880, M. G. F. Almquist, Sweden; 1880-1885, N. Nartino Beltrani-Scalia, Italy; 1885-1890, M.Gálkine-Wroskoy, Russia; 1890-1895, M. L. Herbette, then M. Ferdinand Duflos, France; 1895-1900, M. de Latour, Belgium; 1900-1905, M. J. Rickl de Bellye, Hungary; 1905-1910, Mr. Samuel J. Barrows, then Mr. Charles R. Henderson, United States; 1910-1926, Sir Evelyn Ruggles-Brise, Great Britain; 1926-1930, M. Emerich Polak, then M. August Miricka, Czechoslovakia; 1930-1935, M. Erwin Bumke, Germany; since 1935, M. Giovanni Novelli, Italy. The secretaries have been: M. Louis Guillaume, Switzerland, from 1875 to 1910; M. Simon van der Aa, Netherlands, from 1910-1938; and M. Ernest Delaquis, Switzerland, since that date.

The *Proceedings* of these various international meetings have been published and there can be no doubt that they have been of inestimable value to those who have been unable to attend the meetings. They reflect, through the years, the evolutionary development of penal thought and ideas of the world.

The current war has made it impossible for meetings but even during this period of international strife the annual symposia are carefully prepared and published. This is being done through the efforts of the General Secretary, Professor Ernest Delaquis of Berne, Switzerland. They are entitled *Recueil de documents en matrière pénitentiaire*. Volume Ten appeared in 1943.

Other organizations of an international nature, although perhaps more restricted to Europe, are *The International Union of Criminal Law*, founded in 1889, and *The International Society of Criminal Anthropology*. *The American Prison Association*, founded in 1870, and *La Société Générale des Prisons de France*, organized in 1877, are two groups of penologists more local in character. Recently a Penal Congress has been holding meetings in Latin America.

The effects of such organizations are far-reaching. They have accomplished much in disseminating progressive ideas and after the present conflict it is hoped that they may continue to function on a world-wide basis.

INDEX OF NAMES*

(*) Because of the peculiar nature of a survey the author has deemed it inexpedient to include a topical index.

217